Canadian Cataloguing in Publication Data
Gibson, Valerie, 1939-
You can't say that!

Includes columns reprinted from Vancouver Magazine.
ISBN 0-9695187-7-3

1. Vancouver (B.C.) -- Social life and customs. 2. Gossip
columns -- British Columbia -- Vancouver. I. Title,
FC 3847.394.G52 1994   971.1.1'3304   C94-910924X
F1089.5.V22G52 1994

Chapter 1: THE YEAR 1981

Chapter 2: THE YEAR 1982

Chapter 3: THE YEAR 1983

Chapter 4: THE YEAR 1984

Chapter 5: THE YEAR 1985

THE GLOVES ARE OFF
From mansion-warming to moon-walking with Michael.

SEASON'S DOINGS IN PARIS AND LONDON
Euro-trashing at the top.

POLITICS AND POLITESSE
The right dinner, talk and people.

OF DISHES AND RAGS
Hearts throbbed for Michael York, and society mobbed for Jesse Jackson.

Chapter 6: THE YEAR 1986

Chapter 7: THE YEAR 1987

Chapter 8: THE YEAR 1988

Chapter 9: THE YEAR 1989

Chapter 10: THE YEAR 1990

Chapter 11: THE YEAR 1991

Chapter 12: THE YEAR 1992

Chapter 13: THE YEAR 1993

THE WAY OF ALL FLASH
A tell-all Florida update, from the old-money power plays of Palm Beach to the low-key loafers of Key West.

THE SOUND OF MONEY
The third annual Lover's Ball opened up the treasure chests for the VSO's benefit.

WINNER'S DINNER
On the road to 24 Sussex Drive, our Kim stirs a Campbell soup of Vancouver bankers, barristers, and brass hats.

MOGULS ON THE MOUNTAIN
The VSO rolls into Whistler for a hot flamenco fund-raiser.

THE VALERIES AND THE GLORY
The Valeries. A review of months past. Parties, people, clothes, parties. The important stuff.

*F*irst of all, let me tell you right up front that it hasn't all been sipping champagne and eating truffles. The last decade or so in the city's life for you, *mes amis*, may have meant a spectacularly fluctuating skyline, enough political ping-ponging to make your head spin, sufficient insider trading to make Forbes sit up and take notice, a spectacular rise in monster houses, and diminutive designer boutiques, and a tumultuous tossing of what we always considered some of the city's most secure fortune cookies.

For me, at three to four black-tie to-dos a night, it has meant enough flutes of bubbly to keep me afloat into the next millenium, ample caviar to make a Romanoff sit up and take notice, and more than enough meatballs on toothpicks to keep MacBlo going another fifty years. Along the way I tried to snaffle an artful eyeful of life at the peak as the town tested its own temperature at some of its smarter parties.

Can I help it if a couple of deflationary darts impaled the few while the many were being embraced? If I've learned anything it's that the whole social ritual is a little goldmine of nuggets to be sqirrelled away for cheeky measured droppings at a later date. And from the Dom-laden parties of the early 80's to the heavy Perrier/Evian H2O's of the 90's, as Vancouver and I eventually made our peace with each other, a racy readout on the whole raucous scene just sort of evolved...Like me.

Flin Flon born (I got out of there at the age of nine months—absolutely *no* night life, trust me) raised on Sentinel Hill in West Van, I did the cheerleader thing at West Van High, the requisite swing at U.B.C., marriage, the three perfect kids, all those 50's things.

Then it was off to Boston for two brim-full years while hubby did Harvard (an incredible cross-section of the current U.S. elite in business and politics was coincidentally passing through at the same time. I mean *Eleanor Roosevelt*, for heaven's sake came to speak to the Harvard Business Wives one night!)

A year in jolly old (it really isn't you know) England followed, while himself did the London School of Economics and I did London. And what a London it was. Carnaby Street, Chelsea, the Profumo Affair—all that good stuff. London was at its international ultimate and I could hardly drink it in fast enough. Appetites for not staying down on the farm definitely whetted, we headed off to Ottawa for the decade to die for. Trudeau was at his political apex, hubby his executive assistant, and Camelot North was about to swing fult tilt. And sooner or later, the whole world filed by to give the international media's *nouveau* darling the once over.

If you were lucky enough, you could find yourself beside the Queen's secretary at a Government House dinner one night, (he used *my* finger bowl, and I have *never* worried about using the right fork since) the next night, you might be rubbing cashmere shoulders (hers) with Barbra Streisand around the baby grand at 24 Sussex. Heady days indeed.

Cocktails with Kosygin one week, a state dinner with Marshall Tito the next. And on side trips to Washington as wife of, you might not actually meet Lyndon Johnson, but you got a wonderful insider's tour of the White House, and that *was* Hubert Humphrey on the tarmack when you tagged along on a government plane that parked right beside his.

Everyone who appears to be anyone in Canada today seemed to be getting their tootsies damp as they passed through the nation's capital on their way to wherever. Chretien had just arrived from Shawinigan—he wasn't even sure "which side to part his hair on" (he asked a friend of mine which was best) and you think he fractures his Henglish now.

Enduring icons-of-a-sort like Leonard Cohen who was just starting to whine about Suzanne by the river, poet Irving Layton who was still chasing young girls, Ian and Sylvia who were still together—they sang at dinner at the Prime Minister's one night—and folkie Bruce Cockburn were all on the scene. And it was fairly normal to find the likes of saloniste Mordecai Richler had drunk all your scotch again as he sat in your living room 'til midnight telling you what was really wrong with Canada. Again.

Scores of now-in-place corporate heads, a remarkable number of *haute* honchos in the arts, communications, acquisitions, and current provincial premiers who were backbenchers back then, were also—because of the serendipity of right place-right time—friends and acquaintances.

And in just one day in a House of Commons elevator, if you were really fortunate you could run into, at different times John Diefenbaker, Tommy Douglas and Mike Pearson, and if you were in a name-droppy mode, and who wasn't in those days, you could mention over lunch in the Parliamentary restaurant that you had met with Tommy D. that morning. So what if the conversation was only his asking, "Excuse me, Miss, could you help me with my coat?" Who needed to know?

A marriage ended, and a move back to Vancouver called for a fresh look at the city by the sea. And it didn't take a multi-carated twinkling to realize that while there may have been a legitimate lingering of heir-conditioned Old Establishment loot, with the accompanying clout still filtering down to the few, my goodness there was a growing cache of flashy new money makers! They were making it, or flipping it, or inventing it or importing it. In any case, flashing it for all and sundry to see. At charity balls, and lavish costume extravaganzas, and sumptuous dinner parties. And if all of us couldn't get there, how about those of us who did, telling the others all about it.

Objectively, of course.

This was hardly ever a one-Porsche town, but big-buck control had always been in relatively few fingers, and now it was beginning to "seep through and spread around a little" as one former basker-in-Mammon's light mumbled to me over smart martinis one night. What had started as a semi-personal odyssey—what had happened to Vancouver in the intervening ten years that I had been gone and where it was now—quickly snowballed into a semi-serious look-see at latter day life in Lotusland.

After doing a speedy on-camera tell-all whisk-through the revolving door that was the Vancouver show on what is now UTV (right off the stress scale—ask the myriads who worked there) I headed into the relative calm of a monthly magazine column—a loose-knit mesh of what's hot, what's not, who's who and why are they doing that and where. And it spread like quicksilver to include all those celebs one trips over at those world class watering holes and fantasy resorts one gets to when a column is a passport to the stars and semi-stars that people *People*. So a headline-grabbing gang of globe-trotters started side-by-siding with our local luminaries.

Those who travelled loved hearing about where they had been, or really must go next, (because, they noted, their friends certainly did) and those who didn't, seemed to enjoy the trip anyway. Telling about the 80's eased into being a tribute to the city's highrollers in their heyday. A wide eyed glimpse at the weighties in the eighties.

Trying to pin the players down now (the real rollers keep their cards so close to their vests nowadays, that you'd have to crawl into their pockets to find out even remotely how they play their often foreign-based game) is almost a no-win win.

In the early 1980's private luncheons in private clubs (the Vancouver, the Terminal City) lounging in high-backed chairs and sipping J&B on the rocks may have been the norm, but cigars are rare today, cigarettes extinct (or at least those who puff are pariahs). Squash, tennis and the weight room have done in the three martini lunge.

There are no diamond pinky rings (even on Vancouver Port/casino courter Steve Wynn), no Cadillacs, more likely a mountain or cabin-friendly Range Rover. Facials are *de rigeur* as are manicures for men and haircuts-with-scalp-massage. No-name sports gear is unheard of. When charity boards are joined, it's for the access to those not otherwise socially gotten to. Good art is in, and recognized or advised upon, and condos in Whistler, Maui, and Palm Springs are foregone delusions. Some of the wives have changed, some of the players have died, fallen from grace, or suffered ego-bruising bankruptcy.

As we all know, fortune doesn't change men, it unmasks them, and although there were a lot of don't-touch with-a-barge-pole stories over the years, my theory was always that gentle gossip is like a toothless vampire, and you shouldn't be hoping you make or keep friends with it. As to "How can you keep biting the well-manicured hands that feed the column?" I've always felt I pulled back just before lancing the jugular—no sense decimating when the dearest little deflating does the trick. The snobility are so sensitive.

Cruising this gilded turf is tricky work. The current lines between high society, cafe society and tinsel society (and this town is Hollywood North whether we are inconvenienced or not) have definitely blurred. You've got these little bits of golden wheat you have to separate from tons of chaffe.

And you have to be a very savvy sifter to not get buried. Deliver me from would-be limelight loungers who say things like "Don't you dare repeat this" or launch into the most mundane _non mots_ that drone on forever before ending with, "now that's off the record", while a giant neon "Who cares?" sign is blinking in your brain.

Being hoodwinked by a source who has an axe to grind and sets you up or tells an in-their-own-favour incomplete tidbit only happens once. After that, you know that if you didn't see it with your own laser blues, you take it all with a half kilo of salt or better yet, skip the whole thing. Besides, "never complain, never explain" goes two ways and you learn to stash away more than just bad bubbly and unidentifiable hors d'oeurves next time someone tries it.

Upper class hostesses, I find somewhat schizophrenic. They want their parties to be snapped and chatted about as long as every obstacle possible is put in the path of anyone doing it. Then of course, they are the first to ask later for a complete set of prints and a hundred copies of the article to send abroad. There were those who, through the seasons sent pictures from afar. Mustique, or Gstaad, or Vienna. Clippings of their doings from local papers and mags or actual pictures of themselves or their adorable offspring on location in Tuscany, Timbuktu or the Med, on the beach with rock stars or resident royalty, and then lamented to friends that there was no escaping you.

A throw-away gag in a social caption could actually cost the future cooperation of an entire clan, and since (formerly) everyone was related to the same nine families in this town—you just had to travel, travel, travel (upscale of course) til the ill wind blew over. Or become, ever so briefly, a professional chameleon.

"Inside is the place to be", a friend contends, and "background", fascinates and repels, entertains and binds us. Being privy to the scoop, not to put too fine a spin on it, helps us understand what's going on. Gossip is actually an antidote to boredom—it keeps all of us from talking about ourselves. It makes it possible for a newcomer to test the waters, probe the boundary lines of what's acceptable and unacceptable behaviour. What's right and what's wrong, what's stepping over the line, and what might slide by.

Keith Spicer might never have known that leisure suits in 1982 were truly *passe* in Vancouver no matter what he could get away with back east, had I not pointed that very thing out to him. It made me feel positively anthropological when I discovered that more than one of these off-the-cuff observations were being taken seriously by the tribe and had actually altered their behaviour. A fellow scribe took to labelling me "the Margaret Mead of Pelican Bay."

And why pick on well-knowns? It's safe. They've already done better than the rest of us. People think that celebrities or those in the news have in some way gotten away with something. They've escaped from the pack, the daily grind, their lives seem so golden, so blessed with fame and money and power. They have a hammerlock on happiness and a platinum pipeline to prosperity, and the rest of us don't mind watching, if not exactly their decline and fall, at least their minor trippings.

The more you rub elbows with the world's eyebrow-raisers, the more you realize they all have insecurities, and they all celebrity-watch too. (Andy Warhol told me one night at the Ace Gallery that Jackie Kennedy used to ask him about what Elizabeth Taylor was really like.) Up-close peeks at some of the world's high and flighty only confirmed that everyone has flaws. Friends would ask just what Indira Ghandi was like in person or Maggie Thatcher, or the Queen Mum. Faux Pas give pause.

People got riled over the years when I wrote about lifestyles. It really got them where they lived and breathed. "What a lot of pedantic snobbery you managed to reveal in your last piece on Vancouver's most distinguished dinner parties", one poison-penned, "If I want my guests to bring their own boooze, and I decide to serve them in my kitchen, then I will, and you can't tell me I don't know how to entertain."

You know, I've had 24-carat gold hammered paper-thin, and drizzled over ice cream as a dessert at the Indian Embassy in Ottawa, and been to luau parties in the East, in houses overflowing with live orchids and palm trees in the middle of a March snow storm. I've just had to hope some of the satire came through. It's never really gone to my head. I've always hoped it went into my column. I could just gosh-golly my way through so many blowouts before I thought they were silly too.

Soirees, night-after-night may sound glamorous and exciting and like one long mad whirl. But in the morning, that typewriter would be waiting for me. Everyone else who was at the party was probably sleeping in. And I was trying to recall just how riotous it was, and tell it as much like it was as I could get away with. Kiss and told can be a very slippery slide.

So, could you possibly think of me as a "diarist" who, right time-right place, happened to catch the city at its zenith for this brand of flash? My mother—she of the "if you can't say anything nice, don't say anything at all" would be so pleased. And since the secret of boring is to tell everything, let me assure you that I didn't, there is so much more.

I'd better go. I hate being upstaged by reality. It's highly over rated anyway.

Valerie

THE YEAR 1981

VIVA HAS A BIRTHDAY
Vancouver didn't have Studio 54, but it had Viva.

DROP'EM
Name dropping isn't a gentle art, but it works.

HIGH AND LOW JINKS ON MAUI
Hitting Luauland once a year keeps up that topical tan.

FROM FROG GARDEN TO WHISTLER
Sometimes the best salons are right in your own backyard.

THE YEAR 1981

*T*his was the year that their Royal Haitches Chuck and Di got hitched and Dallas-at-the-palace started slipping from the small screen into the tabloids, after of course, a very short honeymoon. Our weekly dose of Dynasty was a must-see, and the era of really conspicuous consumption started a tenacious ten-year grip that would be just about a stranglehold by the time we came to our dollars and senses and realized this madness as unrealistic as it was, had to end.

More than 30 major Canadian head offices had located in Vancouver by 1981, and the Acquisitors, as Peter Newman so ably labeled them were in full show-off-flight mode.

The old society dictum that one's name should appear in print only when they are hatched, matched or dispatched (born, married or buried) fell by the wimpy wayside, and the boys and their ever-more-flamboyant toys began a meet-em or beat-em high stakes monopoly game that was right out of Southfork!

And such a hoot it was to watch. Bud Kanke's nightclub, Viva, was the hip, happening party that seemed to satisfy our primal urge to run with the pack. Peter Brown, and J. Bob Carter had their own tables, and evenings were judged by the number of empty champagne bottles that had been racked up by evening's end. "It was a ten-Dom night" (at, in those days, $100-plus-tip-a-bottle) was a good night's work well done.

Limos and private jets were more than often a part of the family jewels. And the out-of-town hi-jinks, always, somehow filtering back to Vancouver were as outrageous as the Gordon Gekko "Greed is good" trash that we were being fed off the big screen.

Ron and Nancy were in the White House, Pierre was at 24 Sussex, Mike Harcourt was in City Hall and Bill Bennett was aiming for immortality with the building of B.C. Place.

VIVA HAS A BIRTHDAY

Barbie Darling,

You'll never guess whose birthday you missed last week, just because you *insisted* on taking that stuffy old job with your father's London firm. I mean, leaving the entire *country* just because of one little incident was really a bit much don't you think?

The apartment looks as good as it did before the fire. Jonathan is *really* sorry he told you that the syndicate is going to try to collect the $10,000 for the white powder you threw on the fire to try to put it out. It really *was* baking soda, dear. You know Jonathan—that's just his idea of a little joke.

I know you were totally hysterical at the time, and I do think he could have waited until you had something more than the fireman's coat on when he told you.

If I may suggest one teeny thing though, the next time you try to make peaches flambé at three in the morning, after a bottle-and-a-half of Mandarin Napoleon, don't wear the sheer pink with the maribou feathers. We could have had *Barbie* Flambé old bean.

But where was I? Oh yes, the birthday party. Well, it was Viva's, our favorite D'n'D (dance and drink, have you forgotten?) where that spacey lady in front of the mirror said, "They did this place backwards. They should have made a tiny, little lounge and a great, big powderroom. After all, this is where the action is." Well, the old girl has weathered rather well, and after a whole year, it's still the late night singles spot.

David's still on the door - as cute as he was at Mulvaney's but he looks somehow happier, you know? Anyway, as I checked the red fox at the door, naturally I ran an eye over the other coats being racked up. Trust me, there is a *great* deal of money in Vancouver! A glass of bubbly from the tray, and into the main dining room.

First person I ran into was Paul Manning - a little trimmer than he was in the fall, or was it the jacket? If you were wondering why he didn't pop over from Paris when he was there last month to see you in old London town, it's because we had an election here. Volrich has been traded for Harcourt, and so Paul's stadium plans have altered ever so slightly, n'est-ce pas?

Ralph and Brenda were there. She was wearing her red pleated. Said her company is going really well, and I never even asked Old Ralphie how he was doing. We all know how gold stocks did last year, don't we?

Trevor was there. Remember what a butterball he was in high school? But what a hunk now! He looks like a young Anthony Newley.

Joanne Leach was in a very swish pink-striped Zonda Nellis knit. She *loved* Rome. Got a great story out of the bomb, and missed the earthquake. She was talking to Martha Sturdy. Martha's jewelry is *so* fab. She's a walking ad for her own designs. Jet black sweater and knickers, and those beautifully placed baubles everywhere. She's made *Harper's Bazaar* next month, for heaven's sake.

Had the longest chat with Jack Lee about absolutely everything, and then as I turned to talk to someone else, I heard him ask who I was. Really!

Denny Boyd was in great shape - told me it took him only 45 minutes to write what I thought was one of his best pieces the other day. Bud Kanke was his usual once-an-accountant self. How a man whose idea this sleek haven of sophistication was, can appear to be so square...

The fashion show on the main staircase (remember that satin parrot you knocked off the railing? Well, it's back on) was half again as long as it should have been, but the men's stuff was great.

I did overhear one classic piece of advice from a Lavender silk jumpsuit (looked like one of Zo's) to that $350 backless black we saw at Holt's in October: "Don't sit down whatever you do. Look like you are just dying to dance. Don't look like we're together. Look mobile." Boy, doesn't that say it all?

And from a blond in a white cashmere dress: "I was dancing with a doctor, I thought I was doing just fine. He spots the redhead across the crowded floor. He excused himself and *left* me. Doctors! They're so, so clinical!"

Remember that woman we see so often at Giardino's, who has always just left another party? Well, she weaved her way up to Umberto, and gushed, "Roberto, how are you?" Umberto cringed just a shade, didn't correct her, and continued talking to the man beside him.

It was the usual mellow groping on the dance floor, but I did hear a new line from that fellow with the beard who no one ever wants to dance with. He said to his partner, "Hold me so I feel like a real person." Hard to resist, what?

As we were leaving the birthday bash, a terribly swish brunette swept out the door. "Mark," she said to the doorman, "would you get the Mercedes?"

"It's Richard," he said, "and the Rolls is ahead of you."

No, it's not Studio 54 in the old days, but it's still Vancouver's best.

Ta Ta, Darling,

Valerie

DROP'EM

Barbie Darling,

"As I said to the Queen the other day, I do not believe in name-dropping." That little put-down (or put-on, as the case may be) was uttered recently by British society photographer, Cecil Beaton, and as one who has personally been within veritable *inches* of both Her Majesty *and* Sir Cecil, I can tell you that everyone does it - nick a few notable names themselves, that is.

I know, I know; I read Ann Landers, too. "Intelligent people talk about ideas, average people talk about things, small people talk about other people." Well, we must all be just part of the little folk. As Foth (sorry, Allan Fotheringham) was saying just the other day about the success of Richard (Gwyn's) new book on Pierre, "We are a land of cautious voyeurs."

Have you ever thought, for instance, about how many things the average person trips over that are absolutely none of his business but that, dropped ever so casually at just the right moment, allow him to participate ever so authoritatively in an inner circle of informed, plugged-in people? Like:

"Coming out of the Fassbinder (Wertmüller, Bertolucci, Bergman) film the other night, I ran into Carole and Art..." An optional ending would be, "Pia and Harvey." In either case, it is a double name-dropper whammy: you go to obscure foreign films, and you are on a first name basis with such local celebrities as the former mayor and his TV personality wife or the talk show host and her wealthy, young journalist husband.

If you watch TV or read even *some* of the myriad of magazines or newspapers on the racks, you are bound to recognize a lot more faces than you did, say, 10 years ago. And since, in our shrinking Global Village those faces are traveling more, the possibility of your bumping into a fair share of them without even looking is correspondingly higher.

Let me demonstrate. We'll call these people Acclaim by Accident or Right Place-Right Time celebs.

While wandering around Habitat Forum four years ago, I was accosted by a small, bespectacled man with a white crew cut who was looking for the men's washroom. A nowhere incident, right? Because of TV, newspapers, etc., though, I recognized him as one of the world's leading engineer-philosopher-ecologists, a celebrated idea man, geometrician, educator, architect, designer, humanist, futurist and developer of the geodesic dome. In short: R. Buckminster Fuller. What I know about any or all of the above is less than negligible. But I was able to tell him how honored we were to have him in our city, and the way to the nearest washroom. He had to be pleased with at least one response, maybe even both. I now read, if not any more about his theories, at least more about what the old (now, dear!) is up to. But you will never hear me say, "As Bucky Fuller said to me..." How would I end it? With, "Could you please tell me where the men's washroom is?" Or "Thank you?"

My previous knowledge of Timothy Leary was that he went to jail on drug charges related to his "Tune in, turn on, drop out" advocacy. But since I saw the former Harvard psychologist coming out of the ice-cream parlor on Marine Drive in West Van., I also know how he dresses (casually, sweater and cords), how he walks (rather distractedly) and what kind of ice cream he buys (peach or orange). And, of course, that the man is not too jaded to enjoy the same kind of innocuous Sunday afternoon treat as do people on less exotic trips than he is used to.

I know that when Shirley MacLaine, however spiffy and glamorous she may appear on TV or in the movies, walks down Georgia Street, window-shopping, she wears a brown fur coat that has seen better days, and scuffed, down-at-the-heel brown boots.

As I say, none of these things are any of my business, and I wasn't looking for them. What do I care that the Dalai Lama, the man six million Tibetans call the Ocean of Wisdom, wears his saffron robes (ironed) in public, carries a matching pouch bag, and has very mortal-type meals (what else do they serve?) at the Grosvenor Hotel's new dining room?

Andy (*No Time for Sergeants*) Griffith was paying his bill at a Gastown café, just as I was leaving, and I heard him ask how far it was to the South Granville antique stores. I was going right by there, and offered a lift, and now know that he collects antique watches and has a Cartier worth $50,000, that actress-wife Solica is his second, that he considers the Elia Kazan-directed *A Face in the Crowd* his best picture, and that the cornmush style ("I preciate it") is the real him.

More? Well, Ella Fitzgerald wears a wig and glasses, and her speaking voice is nothing like her singing voice. (Can I help it if she gets out of a limo right in front of me?) Harry Belafonte is taller than he looks on stage, wears jeans, black leather and shaded glasses better than anyone, at 52 still causes hearts to stop as he crosses a lobby, and has the most perfect thighs. Adrienne Clarkson of _Fifth Estate_ is prettier and more chic than she appears on TV, says she often speaks to strangers "on planes and places like that" (we were on an escalator), and gets many of her ideas from feedback. She had been "dropped" on me the previous week, as in:

"We just came back from China, and as Adrienne said on the plane..." Another two-star drop.

Hollywood is different, of course. There you are bound to find, as I have, Dean Paul Martin (Dean's absolutely gorgeous son) parking right next to you in a Rodeo Drive lot, or Barbara Stanwyck (slim, tiny and still striking) buying a rain jacket right in front of you at Kerr's Sporting Goods store, or nine movie and TV stars nibbling fettucine at an adjacent table at La Scala (two Gabors with golfball-sized diamonds, a very old but well-preserved Walter Pidgeon, and Loretta Swit, M.A.S.H.'s old Hot Lips herself in crumpled wine cords).

Under these circumstances it is very difficult not to note the odd name-face (Mae West in white velvet was not dressing to stay hidden), but on a travel assignment to Guatemala you hardly expect to come up from a dive into the pool and find yourself staring at Ron Ely, TV's Tarzan and new Miss America pageant emcee. Or that on a trip to London, you will meet, in your own living room, Charles Lindbergh's look-alike son, Scott (the best friend of a friend), Edward Albee, the brooding _Who's Afraid of Virginia Woolf?_ playwright, actor John Colicos whose fine Shakespearean training comes through for Midas Muffler and on _Battlestar Galactica_, or Albert Finney (_Saturday Night and Sunday Morning_, National Theater as Hamlet, Macbeth, etc.) who was walking to the Gloucester Road station at the same time that I was, and talked about _Martin Luther_, the play he was then doing in London.

Some years ago, on my first trip to Waikiki, who should stroll by, carrying a surfboard just like any other tourist, but David Niven. I watched a small exchange in which his crinkly blue eyes cautioned the large lady hoving towards him that yes-it-is-but-please-let's-not-tell-the-others-and-spoil-my-fun.

Jim Coutts, the prime minister's principal secretary used to say - still does, I guess - within seconds of re-encountering you, "Well what's the gossip?" So refreshingly up-front, it was at once a challenge and a responsibility. It also reminds me that many people can be called "familiar strangers." You never really saw them yourself, but someone who did said something about them so vividly that you began to feel you had.

Like the executive assistant who spent an afternoon with John Lennon and Yoko Ono before they were to meet with Trudeau. Until then a very heavy smoker, he gave up cigarettes that day because he said that Lennon and Ono had seemed so peaceful and serene compared to his anxious puffing and pacing that he felt he really should get control of his life. Sure, and what were they on at the time?

Also second hand, but described in graphic detail by one who spent four hours with her at a Washington dinner party, I find out absolutely effortlessly that Elizabeth Taylor does indeed have the most marvelous violet eyes. Not only that, she has at least one spare chin, pudgy fingers, an incredible prow-of-a-ship bustline, is even shorter than she appears, and still has that amazing whatever that has men playing musical chairs to get anywhere near her. Also observed, her husband John Warner seems to view these scramblings with the detached benevolence of a proud father.

I know exactly how poet-songwriter Leonard Cohen lives while he is at his home off the coast of Greece on the island of Hydra, and I am certainly going to talk to him about it when we finally meet. All those young girls! Really!

I have always felt James Garner to be more than a passing name. Trying to buy a painting two years ago on 41st Avenue, I learned that it had been purchased the previous day by none other than. Now, I cannot look at that hunk on The Rockford Files without wondering how he is enjoying "our" picture.

Wandering into a Boston antique store, I found a beautiful oval stand-up dress-maker's mirror in the basement, covered with dust and needing resilvering. The proprietor accepted a mere $15 for it, and minutes later I was gone, only to hear his anxious voice on the phone the next day. "Another party" was now offering $275, and would I please bring it back? I told him that I loved it, couldn't give it up, and thanks but no thanks. Mrs. (Clare Boothe) Luce, wife of Time-Life publisher Henry, would be very disappointed, he said. In deference to her, I never miss an issue.

Back to first person name-drops, though, and mostly to Ottawa where I spent 10 years at an interesting level and found it next to impossible to unplait the braid that was power, politics and people.

One night it would be Barbara Streisand, who had the most beautiful pearlescent skin I have ever seen, incredibly long, square-shaped nails and the presence and charisma of a true star. Very sweet and totally unassuming, she was deeply into color psychology at the time. The next night it would be Sir Martin Charteris, the Queen's secretary, who used *my* finger bowl. If the Queen's staff makes mistakes like that, do the rest of us *ever* again have to worry about the right fork?

After a party at the House of Commons, Greek singer Nana Mouskouri, looking small and shy, sang Amazing Grace, without accompaniment, from the speaker's chair. It was a very quiet one o'clock in the morning, and I believe that no-one in our small group of 10 or so will ever forget it.

At a Government House reception one afternoon, I was behind a very demure and unmarried Margaret Sinclair in the receiving line when Prince Charles leaned down, took her hand and said, "You must be an actress, you are so beautiful." She actually blushed. The next time they were to meet, she would be the prime minister's wife and the circumstances quite different.

There would be other princes, such as former Finance Minister Nawaf bin Abdul Aziz, brother of King Khalid of Saudi Arabia, who has exquisite black eyes and likes ladies - _really_ likes ladies - and strawberries (firsthand information) and who, according to a Vancouver source, paid the cabbie who brought him in from the airport a $600 tip and the maitre d' at Annabel's $1,000 while the Hyatt desk clerk turned down a thou. There would be princesses, too. I watched Princess Margaret dance with Lord Snowdon one night, her cobalt blue eyes following his _every_ move - no easy feat when you are a short princess peering over your partner's shoulder. And there would be actors: Peter Sellers, a good dancer, but _very_ nearsighted; Michael Caine, who smelled like wet towels; and Omar Sharif, brittle black-olive eyes and a perpetual five o'clock shadow. British interviewer David Frost sticks in my mind as both bored and nervous, and I came to marvel how incredibly adeptly Patrick Watson managed his wooden leg.

Andy Warhol put the whole business of name-dropping in perspective. Positively bubbly the night I met him, he told me that Jackie Kennedy was a wonderful warm mother, and that she had asked him what Elizabeth Taylor was really like. Feel better, now? Everybody does it!

Now, did I ever tell you about the time I had dinner with Donald Sutherland at the Denman Inn, and he _insisted_ that I come downstairs and see his new baby that he had helped deliver the day before? No? Well, how about Joe Namath at Viva...

HIGH AND LOW JINKS ON MAUI

Barbie Darling,

We missed you on our annual excursion to Alohaland (you _and_ your mother's condo and housekeeper), but we all managed to locate elsewhere, so not to worry. Thought you should know, though, the old darling's changed the locks. Tacky, hmmmm! After all, we did have the piano retuned after they hauled it out of the pool last year.

But honestly, the piano just sort of... slipped. We were going to push it back into the house when George finished his Noel Coward medley, anyway. And, frankly, I don't know why she was so upset about the crack in the bottom of the pool. That map of the islands in blue Delft tile was so passé.

The blue Pacific is just not the same without our Barbie, but we gave it the old college one-two, even though lining up at 8:00 for a 9:30 a.m. takeoff was not my idea of an auspicious beginning. Once aboard, though, we settled into our own mini-section, and George came to the rescue with six chilled bottles of Dom - we toasted you twice - and a very smooth French brandy he had decanted into a twist-top Perrier bottle.

At the Maui airport, we managed to snaffle our usual limo driver, who seemed genuinely surprised we weren't staying at your mother's this year (he knew nothing about the piano, so at least she's not a gossip), and trundled off to that new white adobe-and-beam job on the Wailea golf course. The owners, friends of Jonathon, are holding out for a million-five, and while they're waiting for it to sell, they said we could have it for the month. That Jonathon can talk anyone into anything! But we all resolved to give very careful (tapes-only) parties this year.

We settled in, freshened up, and then piled into a Word of Mouth rental car. Monica just loved the name; better than Rent-a-Wreck, what? The Datsun 810 Maxima talked to us all the time - "Please turn off the lights," etc. - in a computer voice that sounds like Tattoo in *Fantasy Island*: "De plane, boss. De plane..."

First night, it was off to the Wailea Steak House. We were travel-weary, and it was so close, after all. Ron and Barbara Howard were there - just bought a place of their own in Kaanapali, and I thought architects were coasting this year. With the ski chalet in Whistler, they are going to be *very* busy, n'est ce pas?

The salad bar was great as usual, the steaks perrr-fect. But down to basics, darling: not a dress over $300 in the room; one Bill Blass blazer on a very warm, very uptight bronzed god; a last-year's Mary McFaddyen print; and a Halston copy of Faye Dunaway's tie-wrap from the Academy Awards four years ago. Nobody else was wearing long.

We stayed pretty close to home for the next week or so and worked on our tans. But remember that great masseuse from the '77 trip? Well, Dimitri (could that be his real name?) came twice for the day. We all chipped in, and he left every aching muscle in the group intact.

Wailea was really *the* place to be staying this year. Migawd, there's some loose change around! Alexander and Baldwin and Northwestern Mutual sure knew what they were doing when they bought those 1,450 acres in '69.

Remember when Wailea was just the scrub forest you passed through on the dusty road to get to Makena beach? Now it's half-million-dollar condos and million-dollar homes, golf courses, tennis courts and world-class hotels. There's an $84 million project called L'Abri in the works (should be finished for our next sortie to the islands) that is selling for more than $400 a square foot! And the whole area is _full_ of Canadians, dear heart. They don't call Maui Little Canada for nothing.

Off for chi chis with that groovy young developer from First City, and, unfortunately, his smashing wife (she's using that très chic little designer from Nerland's to redo her already exquisite condo in jungle print and grasscloth), then over to Raffles that night for a little mahi mahi. The fish was fine, but there was so much staff around, you never saw the same waiter twice as they tripped over each other to get to your table. Afterwards, they brought a smoking cauldron of dry ice to the table, topped with a small metal dish filled with pink-and-green after-dinner mints. Showbiz! It's not the original Raffles, Babs, but they _do_ try.

Went upstairs to the Aloha Suite (at $500 a day you _should_ feel welcome) for an after-dinner drink with those tedious friends of your sister. Remember, they were at the Intercontinental last year? Well, he's lightening up on the Grecian Formula, and her new lift, nip and tuck looks terrific. They served unchilled Bollinger Brut, but we asked them to join us for dinner at the new Hyatt the following week anyway.

Now _there_, Pet, is a hotel! Opened last November, and the very innest of inns. You are going to love, love, love it. Chris Hemmeter, the boy wonder who gave us the Hemmeter Center in Waikiki, spent a cool million-an-acre for 20 acres just off Kaanapali to build this 460 million Disneyland for grown-ups right on the beach. And guess what? All those flush folk from Beverly Hills and points east sit around the pool on their big, beige cots, with their matching hotel towels, paying $100-on-up a day to avoid all that messy sand. True, it is an entire acre in size, it does have a two-story waterslide to delight foolish old men watching foxy young things come bouncing down into the water (it's for kids, too), and not only can you order a Maui Sunset without ever leaving your lounge cot, you can swim to a subterranean grotto bar and order up without anyone knowing whether you are in any condition to or not.

Forget Claridge's and the cucumber sandwiches served up at three in the morning by that balding, crusty fellow (unlike the sandwiches) who assured us that nothing was too much trouble for the young ladies. Forget the Grande in Rome with the elevators like art galleries and Swiss chocolate squares under the pillow of your freshly turned-down bed. The Hyatt Regency Maui is _more_. It is sheer fun.

Chapter 1 _____

It is cascading waterfalls and swinging bridges, sparkling streams lit from beneath at night, swan-filled lagoons and oriental gardens. Excluding the guests, there are peacocks everywhere, roaming freely, plus penguins and swimming ducks (George *insisted* on ordering duck au Brouilly just to upset everyone; we were eating in the Swan Court at the time).

Lots of glass-and-brass stores, of course. Mark Christopher is there, and Elephant Walk and Crystal Impressions (gives Boda a run for its funds). Great clothes and sparklies: Brendan Shane, Top Rigger, Altogether Hawaii, Elegant Exposure (everyone in the place was trying for that!), Gold Point, Jewels of the Sea (pearls are never passé) and the Gallery (artwork that was definitely *not* on black velvet!). In all those stores, not one matching Hawaiian his-and-hers shirt and dress to be found. There was one gem of a shop though. Called Postmark Hawaii, it got rid of all your shopping for the folks back home in one fell chocolate-covered macadamia nut and Maui Wowie potato chip swoop.

But the artwork that fills the open-air lobby, and surrounds what they say is the world's largest transplanted banyan tree (they built the hotel around it) is worth a week's stay on its own: Ming Dynasty sculptures backed by John Young abstracts; Tai Ping handwoven carpets; centuries-old silkscreens and oriental statues that Arthur would kill for.

The exotic birds weren't all in feathers. Some were roaming the lobby, and more were down in Spats Disco, a fashion show to behold, indeed, the music Annabelles, London, '79.

Two of our group decided they just couldn't bear to leave, and tried to check into the Presidential Suite. It was $850 a night, and - wouldn't you know it? - full.

We all stayed up far too late because *someone* - we still haven't determined who - had booked a deep-sea charter for six the next morning. Barbie, it is still dark at six in the morning, even in Hawaii, and none of us felt too sporty as we trudged grumpily aboard *Sport Diver* to watch 13 cases of Olympia beer being loaded and absolutely no food at all. Oh well, who was hungry?

The first mate (I'm being generous) looked like a renegade from *The Texas Chainsaw Massacre*. He had wrinkled bib-front denim overalls over nothing, a brown-and-white, polka-dot shirt open over that, a pink-and-green flowered engineer's cap, and the largest set of keys chained to his pocket I have ever seen. The captain, though, was a dreamy, muscle-bound little number with incredible eyes (explanation later), who went by the name of Tad Lucky.

Anyway, just as we were getting ready to cast off, the rest of the charter (nobody warned us) came bouncing down the gangway: five interchangeable, blond and perfect stewardesses in mix-and-match pastel spandex bathing suits and shorts, with flawless hair and make-up. Remember, this was six in the morning.

It is still painful for me to talk about this, but I don't ever want you to go through it. The waves were, oh, seven feet high, and the bait, by the smell of it, was neither fresh nor frozen. The stewardesses stayed bubbly, cheerful and well the whole day. Tad's far-out eyes - he was the man guiding us through all this, mind you - turned out to be the result of some very exotic cigarettes - "Not before breakfast, thanks" - that were passed around. I personally lost four pounds, plus my desire ever again for finger capon in beer butter and hot guava sauce (a specialty of the hotel the night before) and most of my tan. We caught one very large, ugly fish, saw several pods of leaping humpback whales and stayed at the beach from then on.

The rest of the trip was not uneventful, but I'll fill you in later. Ta Ta, Darling, and Aloha,

Valerie.

FROM FROG GARDEN TO WHISTLER

Barbie Darling,

Arthur's party for Ned—the prez of Universal International Pictures—and Kitty Tannen was the usual Erickson elegance. I mean, the man *never* misses. You know: one of those simmering summer nights Vancouver sees once, maybe twice, a season. Push aside the high wooden gate, and there they are, chatting in discreet clusters, moonlight glancing off eternally tanned shoulders into chilled glasses that are never less than half full. A little Oriental stroke of botanical bliss, this backyard. Contoured mounds of earth, small candlelit forests, wild grasses and a shallow, frog-filled pond. Highly disciplined, like everything around Arthur, they (the *frogs*, dear one) chorused on cue whenever the Japanese zither player, who was discreetly ensconced in the tule weeds, paused to allow the reed player to take over.

Scrumptious nibblies (there should be epicurean Oscars), *un cocktail* or two, introductions over, and we drift inside. Beige suede walls provide such a perfect backdrop for one's *ensemble*, don't you agree, Babs? One feels like such a star. Strapless silk jumpsuits cinched with anything metallic, seemed the order of the night, and several were topped with hand-painted kimonos. And these were not the kind of women to check with each other to see who would be wearing what.

Janet Ketcham was her effervescent self, and off to Stratford or Niagara-

on-the-Lake or somewhere theatrical. Daryl Duke had just jet-lagged in from
L.A. (it seemed like half the party had), and since he was still carrying his
luggage was asked if he thought perhaps it was going to be a pajama party.
Fresh from *Hard Feelings*, his latest flick, he was striking off to Spain for the
San Sebastian Film Festival, and hoping to do a Dudley Moore film after that.
His songbird spouse, Eve Smith, was just finishing a long and successful
nightclub run in New York. Norman Keevil Sr. was positively effusive about
the smashing new office Arthur had designed for him in Toronto—called it a
real showplace—not that Teck Corporation's Vancouver office is exactly a hole
in the wall!

Sheila and Peter Bentley were warm and chatty. One day I really *must* find
out what's new at Canadian Forest Products or Cornat-Veratile or Johnson
Terminals, or even just *how* dehydrated Burrard Dry Dock really is, before I
talk with Peter, who is ever-patient with me.

Pia and Harvey, and Leon and our handsome Argentinian friend, all send
hugs (Maggie still says he makes the best Bellinis *ever*). And that yummy on-
the-rise young hunk of an architect whose wife is terminally beautiful—
remember him?—asked why the perfect linen jacket across the room had no
creases at all in it when *he* couldn't get out of the house without looking as
though he had slept in his. I was pleased to tell him that it had been steamed
for an hour after unpacking, and that its impossible owner (I had on very good
authority) would die before he would sit down in it.

Laurier was absent (sailing in the Gulf islands), but Trish and Jolly were
there. They are always so...so...*them*! I missed Laurier. I never think of him
with that accent that I don't remember him describing "baroque" as "someone
who is out of Monet."

I was going to say there was no real, drop-dead chic there, but the guest
of honor forces me to tell the truth, Kitty Tannen was stunning in red silk—a
lot of it. She's very tall, has beautiful wild hair, and was wearing great Joan
Crawford shoes and the right clash of carefully chosen baubles over the kind
of confident cleavage one *never* has to check. *And*, my dear, she is half way
through an architecture degree. There ought to be an Overachievers
Anonymous!

Speaking of anonymous, three quick overheard comments:

"I'm tearing off to Hongkong again, my sweet, but I can be reached at the
Regent, as usual. In fact, the last time I was there, didn't I see *you?*"

"As my great-aunt used to say...Well, come to think of it, she wasn't *that*
great..."

"What's after Conspicuous Consumption, anyway? Blatant Moderation?"

Oh, yes, two new words learned there. *Noctambules* means "night people," who only talk after three in the afternoon, and who really hit their stride from midnight on. We know a few of those, old bean, what? *Fofoca* is "gossip" in Brazil, although "Fill me in on the latest *fofoca*," still sounds like that Italian ice cream dish that our friend David always orders at Al Porto.

And dear Arthur? He was leaving for Kuwait, China, New York or London (I think he's afraid moss will set in if he stays anywhere longer than 48 hours), so do keep your eyes open for him.

Off to Bridges—Vancouver's new blockbuster beanery—the following week. It's the bright yellow, metal exwarehouse nestled down on Granville Island, and somewhat *cher*, but *everyone* goes, anyway. It has a main floor pub, a wine bistro and a top-notch grey-pink-and-beige (David Vance, who else?) 1930's, silk-flowers-and-subtle-brass restaurant upstairs. The *washrooms*, for heaven's sake, are great. People return to their tables raving about antique basins set into a massive, old sideboard, and flowers everywhere. Definitely *not* your average loo, right? Well, as I was gathering up the contents of my Hermes handbag from the counter, I noticed a small piece of folded paper and opened it up, thinking it might be a suitors phone number (hope springs eternal). Printed very neatly were the words: "Please, God, don't let him be gay." Even *fervent* graffiti on these lovely walls wouldn't do!

The place was wall-to-wall designers and models: Martha Sturdy in her own precious metals; Zonda Nellis in her own wonderful weavings; Denise Taylor, whose face is everywhere lately, and whose new apricot-colored tresses make her look like a Botticelli painting; and Maggie Robertson who, alas, is just looking better and inexplicably *better*. Gabriel was playing Great Gatsby in an all-white suite and shoes, and took it quite well when I mentioned that *someone* had gone over the lines when *they* had polished his shoes. He shrugged that one just couldn't get decent help nowadays, and asked me to hold his wine glass while he hurried off to do someone more important.

Whooshed up to Whistler Mountain the other weekend for three mad days and nights of out-of-town fun. Umberto's new restaurant opening (Il Caminetto) just *happened* to coincide with his $300-a-plate celebrity dinner (more later) and Whistler's first and soon-to-be-annual Fall Festival.

A nice mix of celebs and plebs—10,000 of them, in fact—cheek-by-jowled themselves into the new town square which had been turned into a Bavarian beer garden by day and the setting for spectacular fireworks by night. With hot air balloons drifting overhead, helicopters whirring, chairlifts hoisting hundreds up and down the mountain face, and all those great tanned bods mixing and mingling, it looked like a promo for a "soon to be released motion picture." Oh that reminds me, Barbie, Charlton (*Heston*, who else) is shooting *Motherlode* here this month.

Tom Jones wandered by with a casual entourage of ten: three *de rigueur* beauties, two bouncers, and the rest a mixed bag. He was casual perfection in plaid shirt, sprayed-on jeans (Barbie, the hips are slimmer than thee or me will ever see again, and the man weighs 135 tops, soaking wet), and enough good gold that, if he were a shop, I'd plan an hour's browse easily. The nose is not the same one we saw 10 years ago at the London concert, the teeth are a dental delight, the hair was a lot of work but worth it, and every female within range who got hit with those baby blues, thought so.

Peter Brown, sugar-rimmed brandy snifter in hand, was surveying the scene with a contented proprietary air (well, a 20 percent of Whistler Mountain Ski Corp. air) as he wandered the mid-festival setting in his Greenshields-green Lacoste T-shirt. Good thing he did happen to own a fifth of the mountain: his Dom Perignon tab for the dinner that evening—at $85.50 *un bouteille, mon cher*—was a well rounded $4,000.

Ah, yes, the $300-per dinner. It was the old "too many cooks" story, and while they didn't exactly spoil the broth, they just sort of took the roast lambs off the outdoor spits too soon. But since the chefs were all Vancouver's ranking restaurateurs—Bud Kanke, Joel, Jean Claude, Jean Jacques, Jean Luc, two Michels and a Bruno—and since the cause was a good one—the Whistler Hospital fund—no one resisted their *piece* too much at all.

Lilja Kaiser (Henry's ex) slipped into the dinner in a slinky red tunic and pants (static cling *can* be beaten) covered by a full-length rust suede coat. Not a word, Barbie, if you don't. She entered with a very pleasant young man who looked as though he might own several dinner jackets, but spent most of her time on the dance floor with young Scotty...the broilerman from the Keg, remember?

Caught Martin Zlotnick laughing at Herb Capozzi's jokes, which was nice of him. While most men were playing urban cowboy at Whistler, Herb was playing Sioux City Sioux in a leather chemise, concho belt and Indian jewelry. I still believe Herb is a member of Canada's jet set. I believe everything I read in *Maclean's* magazine; *you* know that.

A nice smattering of tycoons—Jack Poole, Andre Molnar and Henning Brasso—and a few splinters off the old cabinet—Bill (the sideburns *have* to go) Vander Zalm and Mrs. Zalm, Peter and Vickie Hyndeman, Pat Jordan and Don Phillips (who posed himself for flash-popping *paparazzi* with Tom Jones *and* his dinner place card that read "The Hon. Don Phillips," while Nancy Greene Raine just got an autograph!)

The wine flowed freely until the end, when oillionaire Bob Carter requested just a tad more. Learning that the kitchen was closed, and that more wine would be impossible, a concerned citizen reminded Mayor Pat Carleton that J. Bob had just matched pledges of up to $100,000, and perhaps a drop more could be found. It was, and cowboy Bob, in full boots, silver buckle and ultrasuede jacket, happily trundled off to the after party at Il Caminetto.

Umberto has done it again. Already the "in" fettucine bin up there, it is all terra cotta and silk _primatif_ tapestries and art works. His man on the door, Carlos, is studying his _petites listes_ to learn, if not the player's names, at least their faces.

As we were leaving, a limousine rolled up (Whistler was awash in them that weekend) with an invitation to ride. Thanking but no thanking, I remembered that driver your uncle had, who was so incensed about the glass partition between them always being up that finally he pulled up to a phone booth, hopped out and called the old man in the back seat to tell him that he was resigning.

Leaving, I looked back at the Town Center with its clubs and restaurants, its Gourmet Deli with the Maurice Bougault white asparagus at $14 a jar, and its croissants like you used to get on the Rue St. Michel in the 1960s. Then I considered current transatlantic air fares and the grandiose digs, with their saunas and hot tubs, springing up all over the valley like gold mining in reverse, and wondered whether Vancouver's BPs might not just skip St. Moritz for Whistler this year!

Ta Ta, Darling, and _write_, dash it all,

Valerie

THE YEAR 1982

A SEASONAL RUBBING OF SHOULDERS
From book signings for the very rich to fear and clothing.

THE NIGHT THAT ENDS THE WATCH
Skating on thin ice always draws a crowd.

PUERTO VALLARTA'S NIGHT OF THE INNUENDO
High octane partying with O'Toole and tout le gang.

TRUE BLUES AND OTHERS IN THE NIGHT
Touch down in T.O. and lift-off in Lotusland.

THE YEAR 1982

*T*his was the year when strutting your stuff was starting to be not only acceptable, but downright desirable. Vancouverites were dressing themselves up with increasing frequency. The Rolling Stones hit Seattle on their tour, and every Stone-ager worth their salt honky-tonked on down for the show. Maggie Trudeau cranked out a second tell-more-than-necessary tome called 'Consequences'.

Whistler was starting its steep climb to number one ski resort in North America as more boutiques and restaurants, (the ubiquitous Umberto's right at the top) scrambled for those destination-resort dollars. Pier B.C. had its very-ceremonious ribbon-cutting and Jean Claude Ramond's chic new beanery L'Orangerie with the retractable glass roof opened to great fanfare, and they stayed fans, most of them, till it was closed.

Really flashy cars were wheeling around town, and valet parking was so necessary that it became a hot-shot art form. Richards on Richards set up somewhat swanky shop, and the fickle fifty flitted over there for awhile. The Roy Thompson Hall opened with a spectacular send-up in Toronto with enough Vanlanders in attendance to care about a look-see.

And the best out-of-town off-the-scale exotic party I've even been to happened one night that spring in Puerto Vallarta reminding me that on the international scene, we were still somewhat small on the potato scale.

A SEASONAL RUBBING OF SHOULDERS

Barbie Darling,

First, congrats to you and what's-his-name. So glad the offspring has sprung. So has Carol and Art Phillips's. Samantha Phillips is a real winner. Sam Phillips, though, which she will undoubtedly be called, sounds like the Minister of the Interior.

Speaking of spawning litter, Maggie Trudeau has taken the *Consequences*, her *nouveau* novel (versus the untarnished alternative?), and is spoon-feeding breathless Shaughnessy matrons...uh, liberal doses of the old sex-and-drugs combo. Bound for success, unless we all borrow each other's copy like last time, one assumes that it is part of a trilogy being lived out at this very. Stay tuned.

Off to James Barber's for exquisite pumpkin soup. The old flash-in-the-pan also sprinkled several ex-ladyfriends around the table—an in joke realized by almost all the revelers in this particular episode of Variety as the Spice of Life. Besides, you know the impossibility of having square meals at a round table.

Sped southward to Seattle to catch the Rolling Stones' second concert. Squeezed into my tightest jeans, grabbed the suede bomber, and just about passed out trying to keep chin and tummy tucked while looking cool and mildly bored at the same time. Everyone was so impossibly young, of course, but one had to catch the jaded Jagger one more time before he or I hang it all up. At least, old Stones' fan Paul Manning had an excuse for allowing himself to get sluiced through an iron gate with tens of thousands of baby boomers blissed on controlled substances: he was checking accoustics and traffic flow for B.C. Place!

On to Peter Newman's book-launching party at the Mansion. An almost complete collection of The Acquisitors, Western Branch, it wasn't, but a respectable smattering to be sure. The missing magnates—Nelson of Skalbania, Jack Poole, Cal Knudsen and Bruce Howe—were obviously somewhat preoccupied with their well-publicized problems since press time. And as for Chunky Woodward, Sam Belzberg and Edgar Kaiser...well, no one tells them where to go, anyway. But *tout le monde* was most definitely there, and thrilled about it. Eye contact was tricky with everyone looking just past everyone else's shoulders. Not quite the 400, but definitely 125 of Vancouver's sure-footed ladder climbers on your basic black side of the ledger. Favourite scenario? The venerable J.V. exchanging ancient anecdotes with the old Bull of the Woods, Gordon Gibson Sr., both of them laughing with first time delight.

47

Most devastating overheard assassination? Two all-day-getting-turned-out size 8s about an obviously absent friend: "The last time I saw her, she was wearing a size 14 dumpy and a half-pound of industrial strength Oil of Olay!" Non-stop to the Perrier I went, hoping it was no one we knew.

To Viva! for a smashing fashion show—Neto Leather's spring line of absolutely everything in suede, chamois, kid and fur, the kind of lines that are showing in London, Amsterdam, Copenhagen, New York, Houston, L.A. and Frisco. One hundred dollars a pop got the wildly dressed crowd—sprayed-on jumpsuits, metallic minis, fur boas and tuxes (on the *girls*)—a chichi peek at what Saks, I. Magnin and North Beach Leathers already know: that one of the best skin games in North America is played right out of Gastown.

Mere nights later, Viva! celebrated her second-to-none birthday with a bubbly bash that is almost a tradition now: red jacketed valets sweeping your wheels away (the best $2 worth in town), tony white ties and roses greeting you at the door, table groaning under brochette, tournedos and escalope nibblies. It was the kind of madly ribald pomp and fluff the pomp and fluff have come to expect from Bud Kanke's rambunctious two-year-old, although one of the more articulate guests, dusting off his version of a 1940s big band number, found it a "slam dunk affair." Some things never change.

The best scenes, as usual, were on the dance floor and in the powder room, such as: "Not *here*, Patrick!"

"But Monica, you say that *wherever* we are."

"That's right, Patrick. Not *anywhere*."

Or from one of the madly powdering ladies facing the firing squad in the mirror: "So, my bustline isn't what is used to be. But then what is?"

From down the line: "Maybe Nautilus will help. Working with weights sure lifted my boyfriend's pectorals."

Finally: "He's so, so...*underwhelming.*"

"Yes, dear (without missing a beat), but unlike you and me, he knows *exactly* how many zeros there are in a million."

The person everyone seemed most glad to see? No, it wasn't a stock exchange wizard, barrister, lumber baron or oillionaire, but Tony Filetti, the body shop dynamo who had restored 90 percent of the room's Mercedes-Benz, Rolls-Royce and BMW fender benders. A most respected Viva! family man is Tony.

Struggled off with the let's-have-brunch crowd one Sunday morning to Dorian Rae's 4th Ave., digs, where she has made business a pleasure by filling the place chock-a-block with Asian art and antiques. To the strains of a kimono-clad kabuki player, dazed non-morning persons took quiche and puff pastry while gung-ho guests, ranging from Laurier Lapierre to the gallery's

Luke Rombout, held forth on the state of the art in the west. (Luke's terminally beautiful wife Maxine didn't need to say anything, most of the men in the room regarding her as a work of avant-garde anyway.) And the blond, svelte Dorian herself? I've always said, become an expert in a field that is so esoteric no one else knows anything about it, and you've got yourself a winner. But then, you know I never attend gallery openings where the invitation comes with lots of tissue paper, so what do I know?

Glossing over the Tribute to the Lieutenant-Governor dinner at the Hyatt (speeches longer than it took him to earn his well-deserved plaudits, and a whizbang fashion show where a hot young designer named Richard Shon shone), and a spiffy West End Vancouver Playhouse party that became a little more _festivo_ than planned (the guests ended up being bad actors in a _succes de scandale_), I'll sign off with two quick rent-a-mod scenes.

The first, a _soiree_ (afternoon, actually at the trendily revitalized Fairview Slopes address of our favourite national columnist, looked rather like a Freedom of Information exchange with Mad Hatter Tea Party overtones. Jack Webster was hearsaying with Marjorie Nichols, Iona Campagnolo chatting up Keith Spicer and vice versa, ex-judge Nancy Morrison leveling Pia Shandel who was in flapper drag a la _Brideshead Revisited_, Nancy Southam nattering to brother Harvey, and that silver-haired renegade from Cold Mountain, Jim Prior, analyzing them all for his next success seminar.

The second was the year-end close-out at Umberto's new Whistler restaurant. Now in its first blush of somewhat international attention, Whistler is full of macho men and moms in mink, well-bred-and-well-off young offspring in $900 Ungaro-designed space suits, spiffed-up locals succumbing to haircuts and new jeans, plus a flourishing breed of out-town-doesn't-counters. Il Caminetto's cloakroom was awash in unendangered species pelts and a sea of just-bought chic sheepskins, and the best located tables were linked (that particular evening) to accommodate Peter Brown and a company of 20. The Ross Southams and the other Browns were there, plus the Burkes, the Bradshaws, McLarens, several silk shirts and Sperry Topsiders put on with longhandled Edward Chapman shoehorns, a cashmere monogrammed JBC in case of mistaken identity, two baby roasted lambs, an indeterminate number of Doms and some very tipsy chairs. Peter, the inveterate host, never missed a beat, and no one noticed that he was delivering his punchline from the exquisitely tiled floor.

Ta Ta, Darling,
Valerie

49

THE NIGHT THAT ENDS THE WATCH

Barbie Darling,

These being parlous times, the "B.C. Buckles Up" campaign has taken on a whole new meaning. Belt-tightening, or to use Howe Street's own current buzz words, "implementing a curtailment of asset-based expansion," has the likes of Chunky Woodward putting the 54-foot *Peppy San* on the ways for half-a-mil; Jack Poole diving into the real estate pond with his waterfront wonderland at a *very* tepid four million; Jimmy Pattison parking his Caddy for a phone-free Chevy; Murray Pezim angling for a little good luck rub-off by naming his new Vancouver Stock Exchange issue Rabbit Oil and Gas after Peter (penny stock prankster) Brown; and our friend Nelson (soon-to-return-to) Skalbania, no longer the good sportster he was, lying so low in the tule weeds that there is scarcely a ripple.

Despite the Dow-Jones doldrums, a respectable smattering of the city's culturati dutifully trundled off at $100 *pour deux* to the Anna Wyman Dance Theater gala. The Lieutenant-Governor, Mrs. L.-G. and various Canada Councillors popped round for a look-see, nodded seal-like at all that precision torque, rose for a squatting ovation, tucked in their tummies and as lithely as possible got themselves from the Queen E. to the Art Gallery for an after-partake that undid all previous good intentions with tons of toasts and a creme de la crumb 25th Birthday cake (the *company's* dear heart!).

Laurier was there playing World War I ace—no helmet, but a rakish white silk scarf—and introducing a darling boy named Michel whose black leather pants and embroidered red-and-black Mexican jacket were the envy of every overdressed female in the room except Maxine Rombout (husband Luke is Art Gallery director and on the board of govs. for Anna Wyman.) Maxine opted for Norma Kamali's sweatsuit dressing—shell-pink jogging pants, a broad-shouldered top, turquoise flat shoes and headband. All the Kamali designs eventually went down to half price as only Maxine could wear them.

Leon Bibb, Jack Shadbolt and Arthur Erickson all seemed oblivious to a small scenario where in critic Chris Dafoe waxed balletic with critic Max Wyman. See, sometimes Macy's does tell Gimbel's! Arthur allowed that his tan was Miami, ("but only two hours, mind you, you know that sun"), and I believed him; that is the longest Arthur ever spends anywhere. He was off to Ottawa to accept the Order of Canada—I guess it was a slow week—and then to begin designing the new $30 million Canadian Embassy in Washington over much complaining by other architects. Now, boys, be nice.

Peter Hyndman and the Hyndmanettes were there—well, Vickie and two of their little corporate consumers. Oh, and Barbie, Pouilly-Fuisse is O-U-T, _especially_ at Giardino's. More later.

Most of the rent-a-mob crowd rose bright and early one spring morn and trudged, high heels straining (at least Herb Capozzi's and mine), over the cobblestones and gravel to Pier B.C. where Pierre, who was still in town from a little din-din with President Mitterand at the Bayshore the night before, allowed as how snipping a ceremonial ribbon was not too much a strain. The backdrop to the platform was Vancouver's usual brilliant blues, greens and snows, and the whole scene looked disturbingly like an old election poster. The man himself played vintage Trudeau with the gold cutting shears—pretending to cut his finger and stab himself (there was a flicker of hopeful interest, and these remember, were the faithful) before he zigzagged through the banner and the $134 million dollar baby was berthed.

That done, Trudeau and his band of merry men (one senator was definitely less merry than the other) ignored the pier pressure of waiting limos and hoofed it up to Al Porto for the Antipasto to Zabaglione of Italian cuisine. Some non-hoofers, most of whom would eat downstairs away from the salt, climbed into the unused limos for the two-block hop. Peter Brown and Co. popped open the Dom before the wheels even rolled, significant only because as the party progressed into the restaurant, on to the Bayshore and beyond (I think 11 business meetings were missed in all) and Peter became even friskier, it was decided that it was time for the Timex test. Spotting one on an aide's wrist, he whipped it off, dunked it into the Dom, and because it didn't keep ticking and ticking, the chauffeur was dispensed in the limo for a replacement. This was definitely better looking than the first model, but like Peter seemed to go in fits and starts. At least it didn't eat its own crystal, as he has been known to do.

Now, Barbie, a quick aside. I have it on very good authority that Elizabeth Alexandra Mary Windsor, daughter of the late King George VI, who had been resplendent in Royal Blue at the ceremonies in Ottawa, also had on matching stockings, or "very close veins" we used to call them. Well, what do people expect after 20 years in the job? Barbie, tell her about support hose—Queen size of course. Harrod's will have them.

The only other report out of Ottawa was that Natalie Austin (who had called me to ask whether to wear a hat and gloves) beat royal protocol with her usual flair by wearing a scarlet headband that matched her smashing outfit and made her the most sartorially splendid bit of untriteness there. I mean, if you're not going to try for a $7 million weekend spectacle, when are you?

Off to Ron Basford's birthday bash at the Vancouver Hotel, where he was welcomed into the Half Century Club. Fifty years for him, forty dollars for each celebrating guest. The birthday boy looked exactly the same as ten years ago: hair still fairly short, parted in the middle, no hint of gray.

It was really the night of the three-piece suits. Between the visiting cabinet ministers, legal eagles, grateful in-debtors and former staff members, it looked as though everyone who should have been there, was. Some of them wary, mind you (what if those feds were checking the room for possible Liberal candidates to run in the west?). The guest book re-read like a veritable Who Was, and for some reason kept reminding me of that old first law of wing walking: never leave hold of what you've got until you've got hold of something else.

Jean-Claude Ramond's new L'Orangerie flashed upon the scene with two fund-raising fetes and the closest to a claque of celebs that could be managed. It is already the *only* place to lunch. I mean, my dear, where else to show off your Porsche, Vuarnets or Carrera sunglasses? There is a glassed-in terrace with a retractable sun roof that was supposed to have water running over it (to make Vancouverites feel at home?), but there were a few leaks on the trial run, and when they land on one of Andrea Molnar's $900 suede skirts from Milan, or even one's fave silk shirt, well, eet does not make Jean-Claude verry 'appy, you know? *Or* zee custumaires—zoz ladies 'oo lunch!

Anyway, back to the opening night. The inner sanctum (which is really the outer because everyone wants to sit outside) is laid out around a silk orange tree, although the rest of the trees are quite real. For $700,000, you were expecting Minute Maid? There is a bistro for snacks, a deli so you can take more home with you, and so many goodies were arrayed the first night, that only a pair of thyroid cases could have eaten their way through a taste of every thing.

Social moth Paul Manning was doing his Samuel Pepys lounge act in the bar, chronicling all. B.C. Place, as co-owner Peter Bradshaw is so fond of reminding, is only an aperitif away, so Paul feels right at home already,

That boyish wonder David Radler who showed us just what we could do with his weekly newspapers (buy them, dress her) finally admits that he is 40, and the spice of his life doesn't seem to mind being seen with an older man at all.

The "just popped-ins" were there in force: Ken Tolmie fresh (as usual) from the Caribbean; Ron Longstaff who always looks to be on his way to something else; and Viva's Dale Mearns (Cuba was great, Castro was dull and The Red Parrot is New York's hottest new nightclub).

The parking lot was so chic-by-jowled with Rollers, Mercedes-Benzes, BMW's, Caddies and Jaguars that a parking attendant was posted to prevent any fraternization with the odd Volvo, Saab or Rabbit some conservationist might slip in.

Remember that nasty little bottom-pincher, the one with the dark glasses who was supposed to have absquatulated with the company funds? Well, his long-time co-vivant (we were never sure) did have a funny line. Flashing her latest bauble on those pudgy, little fingers, she said, sotto voce with mock disappointment, "Yes, but it's the wrong size, I take a six carat."

Pia's preggers, so do pop into Harrods, Fenwick's or Janet Reger's and tell her what the Royals bought for Di, do.

Ta Ta Darling,

Valerie

PUERTO VALLARTA'S NIGHT OF THE INNUENDO

Barbie Darling,

What was clearly needed was a between-seasons resort. You know: between ski-bronzing in the Alps, basking at the Cannes Film Festival, and those three vital August weeks in Capri (before September on Mykonos, of course). The answer this year seemed to be Puerto Vallarta, where, it would appear, there *is* no off season any more, because the smart

The perfect ex-wife:
Christina Chambonnet de Wulff

hotels and restaurants were hosting the very A-crowd they usually do only in high seasons.

They jetted in from London, Paris and Rome, from Houston, Dallas and Sante Fe, with absolutely no regard at all for the calendar. Birds as exotic and primitive as this slice of Eden itself. They seemed to surprise each other and certainly the towns folk by showing up out of sync in this "fishy little sleeping village" as the local know-it-alls call it.

And the locals do know *all*, believe me. Vallarta, or "PV" if you are a veteran (and one trip will cinch that), earned its spot on the *mapa internacionale* in the early 1960s when Liz, Dick and Ava were headline stealers around the globe as much for their steamy off-screen scenes as for the celluloid gems that director John Huston deemed fit to print in the making of

Night of the Iguana. The 2500 or so somnolent souls—the entire population of Vallarta in those days—watched *La Noche de la Iguana* being made, and became absolute experts at spilling the beans (re-fried no doubt) in answer to reporters' daily, "Who was doing what to whom, Senor?"

The film's success—every big newspaper in the world sent reporters to catch the flying rumors (Richard Burton and Elizabeth Taylor were, after all, married to other people at the time)—resulted in a population explosion. The movie people and the press flew off in a battered DC-3, the tourists and 98,000 permanent residents moved in, and *Ole*, Vallarta was launched. John Huston, who stayed on and lives here permanently now, did for PV what the Empress Eugenie did for Biarritz. North America's fastest-growing seaside resort, the acknowledged Acapulco of a generation ago, chock-full of *ambiente* with its casas, casitas and condos clinging to the jungle hillsides, it is known and loved by a small, chic collection of worldly play-abouts and an international coterie of movie stars, writers, producers and artists. You doubt?

Peter O'Toole

With great warnings—"Not *now*, it's the rainy season, no one will be there, *mi amor*"—I headed south to land in PV at the height of a local sound and light show, a violent electrical storm that lit up the beaches as bright as day. But that was the first and last rain I saw (fooled the experts again), and the sky was completely cloudless by the time I reached home.

"Home" was an incredible fortress on a bluff called Ocho Cascadas. The figment of two very fertile imaginations, in this case architect-owner Edward Giddings and his interior designer wife Pat, the act of cliff-hanging has been honed to a fine art as eight airy terraces and pools spill over each other in a tumble of water and flowers that make this spectacular fantasy house absolutely world-class. The two-tier penthouse has a 50-foot, free-form swimming pool, Jacuzzi and underwater bar, plus a maid, houseboy and a jolly cook named Martha whose concoctions are legend. Yours all yours for a minimum of $800 per paradisiacal night; and if that seems as steep as the hillside it is perched on, there is enough room there for you to split pesos with 11 or 12 close friends.

Don't let anyone tell you that the elite still meet at the El Oceano Hotel bar; that is definitely *pasado, Amigo*. Headquarters in town is the small, chic, art gallery of a fabulous ex-stringer for *Time* magazine and UPI named Jan Lavender (watch for her in the next issue of *Who's Who of the World*). Filled with fine sculpture and paintings, Galeria Uno acts as a conduit for anybody who is anybody to touch base with every other body. They pick up their fly-by-night mail, leave messages for other jetters who haven't yet set, and find out who has toddled off and who is due to.

"Peter's in town. *O'Toole*, of course." (How foolish of me; Sellers and "the Great" are dead.) "He's staying at my other flat. And Sygma's in town tomorrow. The photo people! They shoot for *Paris Match* and *French Vogue* and *everyone*. Here to shoot album covers and PR pix of Sylvie Vartan the French chanteuse, remember? Used to be married to Johnny Hallyday, Mr. and Mrs. Perfect of the '70s? They've moved into the Gunzberg mansion for the week. The party's tomorrow night. And of course, Edna O'Brien's here doing a screenplay for Huston" (my mind scrambled—Edna O'Brien, *The Girl With Green Eyes*, several short stories in the New Yorker, an Irish playwright, right?).

"James Coburn was in Carlos O'Brian's bar last night; he's totally silver-haired now, and he wears horn-rims." (I was going to interject that our Maggie Trudeau had dated Jack Nicholson even though he went back to John Huston's daughter, Anjelica. It was the only local trivia that came to mind, but it seemed so, so...Canadian.)

"Olivia Newton-John was at the Ocho Cascadas last week. She didn't surface much—just like Raquel Welch when she stayed at Silver's. And Brenda Vaccaro! Well! Women who don't know how they look when they're leaving...they should just back out gracefully."

The "dishers," the "dishees," and the "dished" swirl about the unconcerned head of Ms. Lavender while she goes on with the business of connecting her Kalungas and her Daniel Brennans and her Luis Serranos and her Manual Lepes (a primitive artist whose vivid, vibrant works are owned by Harry Belafonte, Jean-Paul Belmondo, Vicki Carr and *todo el mundo*) with her fascinated, far-flung customers, some of whom still think of this little hot *tamale* of intrigue as a mere artist's colony.

A quick Carta Blanca beer at Las Palomas, a fine bar and restaurant operated by old-time Puerto Vallartan gentry and the place at which to touch base with anyone you might have missed; then a snappy peek at Gringo Gulch, the elite hillside ghetto where the wild Welshman and Elizabeth Taylor Hilton Wilding Todd Fisher Burton Warner among other well heeled foreigners maintain *haciendas*; finally a taco or two at a beachside eatery, and bed.

_____

Party night. Off to dinner at the incredible hillside villa of a very comfortable LA businessman. The sunset performed on cue (pink-and-blue marbleized sky, blue sea swallowing orange sun), and so, most assuredly, did the guests. Michael Childers, world-famous celebrity shutterbug, was "just in from a visit with Zeffirelli in Positano." I saw the pair of eyes next to Childers glaze over when he dropped that. I could see the mental scrambling to catch up. ("Let's see: Zeffirelli. That would be Franco, the director. Didn't he just do *Endless Love* with Brooke Shields? Positano? Italy, near Capri. The El San Pietro is the place for lunch, isn't it?") A satisfied smile returned. Safe again within the inner circle.

The French chanteuse was there. Beautiful. Blond. Spoke as though she were reading phon-e-ti-cally from cue cards.

Edna O'Brien floated about in something strangely mismatched and filmy, like a deranged Blanche Dubois, asking questions (Do you know who I am, Dear?), then evaporating before an answer. "Her luggage was stolen," someone offered, as though this would explain both the outfit *and* Edna.

There was a sort of man-about-everyone whose name I didn't catch but who asked me. "Remember Beirut in the good old days, my dear? Now...just rubble." And a very bronzed older woman, Christina de something, who assured me, "There is no abject poverty here, you don't have to feel guilty about enjoying yourself. The waiters in PV are like conquistadors; they clear $1500 a month. The manager at O'Brian's makes $50,000 a year, and at Casa Blanca there are waiters who are millionaires. They only work to meet the girls."

Heading for a refill, I overheard snatches of, "It's easier to get a house with a swimming pool here than a phone. If you want a phone, go to Acapulco." Or, "Well, I was in Aca in the '60s when it was going around; now the action is here, and you don't need a letter of introduction, either".

As I passed another clutch, "He's very protean; he does *everything*, my dear." And, "Oh, I know, he's a great guy, but he's so *pinche*. You know: cheap."

Or from a stunning redhead with a heavy French accent, "Is 'ouse is the best restaurant in LA, but 'ee's bored. I just 'ave to think where 'ee would be, and I can find 'im—the Alp, Pah-rees, Scottsdale. I just theenk what time of the year, and I can fine 'im!" The woman she was talking to continued her own musings aloud: "I've been the perfect ex-wife—not a great wife, but...And as for *children*! They're the only thing that date you, they only grow the first year, then you don't remember how old they are."

A handsome male model intoned to the makeup artist on his right, "Of *course* I'm tanned all over. Isn't everyone?" Before "everyone" could respond, a small, very pretty brunette jumped in with, "Malagena? I hate that song. It's the *Melancholy Baby* of Mexico!"

As I returned to my own small group I caught the tail-end of, "So I asked her why she always kissed every bus boy in the room, and she answered, 'My dear, you never know who the next president of Mexico will be.' "

Peter O'Toole, though, was clearly the star of the show. He *does* know how to make an entrance, and how to hold centre stage. Fashionably flaky in a 1930s vanilla ice cream suit à la Gatsby (a somewhat grungy Gatsby), his very long, double breasted jacket ended somewhere between where his arms dangled and his knees. He was pasty-faced, his limpid, see-through eyes red-rimmed. His long blond hair, graying and slicked back as with Brylcreem, stayed behind his ears. He wore a rose-pink shirt, an ice-green-and-pink striped tie, and white cleatless rugby shoes. For him, that was dressed at least to the eight-and-a-halfs. (I had first met him briefly at the gallery, where he was wearing faded jeans, a denim shirt and a headband.) His gaunt, bone-rack body, almost six-foot-four, looked older than its 50 years, and he smoked continuously, often using a black holder and spilling a lot of ashes around as he talked. And he *talked*. Literately, beautifully, resonantly. His current London play was *Man and Superman*, and just when you suspected him of quoting from it, he smiled broadly, almost demoniacally, a great, yellow-toothed grin. He seemed, in fact, all pale yellow: hair, teeth and skin.

Everything, he said, "drives me mad." It was "bloody" this and "bloody" that. He had a glass in his hand continuously, and stared away frequently as though crystallizing something profound in his mind's eye. Then it would be "Wonderful, darling," or a distracted, "Quite right, my love," as he rearranged small things about you or, as he said, "fixed you up."

He had brought his architect, Noel Macrae, with him from Ireland because he was building a retreat at Lo De Marcos, an hour's drive north of Vallarta, and he tore around the house, leaping over furniture and lifting up to show to Noel things he thought he might like in his new house. Then, to the hostess it was, "Must dash, darling," and in his Irish lilt, "We are off, then, to the City Dump," (the city's best disco).

Before he left, two things were revealed about Peter O'Toole: he has houses in Ireland and London, and a sneaky flat in Soho no one is supposed to know about; and he wears jockey shots.

"The windshield's dirty" someone called back as one of the three Titans of Vallarta and his small band went into the night (Burton and Huston are the others). "Do we have some wine to clean it?"

On my first night in that incredibly exotic suite, there were two toads. Two nights later, it must have been 3 a.m. when I was awakened by something sharp on my thigh, *under* the mosquito netting. I didn't scream, but I did claw at that netting until I got out and got a light on. Grabbing a sandal, I scooped out of the bed the biggest land crab I've ever seen and hurled him out the door. When I looked down at the shoe, two of his claws were still moving.

The day before leaving sunny Vallarta, happy to catch a few last rays, I nestled down sleepily on the patio floor, thinking of just 40 peaceful winks. I put those little plastic sun-guards over my eyes, and was just drifting off when something gently nudged my arm. Before I took the eyeguards off, *I knew.* There, at eye-level, was a very bright green, very alive snake, flicking his forked tongue at me. I do not remember my feet touching the ground as I got up. All I could babble was, "Snake, snake, snake," and point stupidly at where it was no more. Spotting the snake stretched out on a railing, around a corner, someone grabbed a rolled-up pink poster of picturesque Puerto Vallarta and flipped it over the balcony.

Only days later, safely at home, did I think of the consequences to those who may have been enjoying a margarita or two on their patio as a bright green snake flew by.

TRUE BLUES AND OTHERS IN THE NIGHT

Barbie Darling,

It's autumn in New York, white truffle season in Italy, saffron-gathering time in Kashmir...and we here are keeping pace as best we can. The Roy Thompson Hall opened in Toronto, stars flew in from everywhere for the Festival of Festivals, and Vancouver itself is absolutely awash in tony new watering holes and frenzied openings.

Toddled off to T.O. to do a TV show called *Should Trudeau Go?* No comment from the cheap seats over there in Blighty if you don't mind, and we won't ask, "Can you trust a Prime Minister who gets her hair done daily?"

Sat beside bizwhiz Jimmy Pattison flying out, who as a small nod to the economy was not in his private jet. He was, in fact, somewhat chagrinned at being found in the Connoisseur section—says he usually travels Seat Saver. He donned his burgundy cashmere Jerry Ford 57th International golf sweater before take-off, and settled down to work on business the whole trip. He skipped the movie about solving an international monetary crisis—probably too pedestrian for him. When you are sitting on a purported $120 million cash in these tricky times, you don't need to watch how the other big boys are handling it. Jetwardly mobile definitely!

It was a warm Indian summer evening in Toronto, and the Roy Thompson Hall was a'twitter with glitter. Another Arthur Erickson triumph (local boy outdoes himself again), its lattice-glassed exterior gleamed in the sunset and spotlights, like a crystal flower pot that had fallen from atop the C.N. Tower.

Limo after limo disgorged at its doors claques of celebrities, a veritable bastion of old guard elegance; bedecked, bejeweled, bemedalled; Pretty Young Things, political heavyweights, new pretenders and social gadflies. It was *haute* everything all the way, and certainly the Everest of T.O.'s social season. Had the stalactite-like ceiling on the $40 million crystal cave collapsed, so would national hopes at anything other than a Who *Was* in Canada.

There were assorted lords and ladies leaping (Thompson of Fleet notably, his Daddy Roy...well, *you* know) and foreign dignitaries who definitely *counted*. Compte Hubert de Givenchy, *par example*. At a suave and silver six-foot-six, his aristocratic (what else?) profile and impeccable manners cut as much of a swatch as his couturier clothes have for the past 30 years. He was part of Arthur's small but honored group of guests, as was Vancouver's Lois Milsom, in a smashing black 10-year-old Givenchy which of course Hubert recognized, and Pat Buckley, solo (William F. was elsewhere), somewhat amiss in bright blue embossed taffeta. "She usually looks sooo wonderful, I guess we all have our off nights..."

John and Jill Turner were there. His eyes are even bluer, his hair more superbly silver than in the old Ottawa days, and she is even slimmer if possible. *Too* thin if you ask almost anyone. Well, anyone *we* know! Conrad Black was stalking around with wife Shirley on his arm in once-a-secretary red ruffled taffeta.

Harried bartenders poured thousands of glasses of Deinhard Lila Imperial—as you know, Barbie, a *very* unpretentious little German Riesling—and they uncorked a whopping 165 cases of a rather good French champagne during the pre-performance Promenade. A show-offy smorgasbord groaned forth oysters on the half-shell, steak tartare, smoke pheasant, mounds of lobster and smoked salmon.

And for the rafter-ringing performance, all 2812 dove-gray seats were filled with black-tied, well-heeled bottoms, 1,000 of whom had paid up to $500 *un billet, ma chere*. What is surely going to be one of the world's great concert halls beats your Royal Albert and the Sydney Opera House all to bits, dear heart.

Arthur had 175 of his nearest and dearest back to his Toronto house afterwards, and by dawn's early light—well, 5:30—the celebratory clinking of glasses and medals could still be heard.

And what did they say to each other over quenelles? What tantalizing trivia, what civilized chat? Wellll.

Remember the latest Ottawa Sinatra concert? It seems several hundred of the $2,000-a-shot ticket holders were devastated when Old Blue Eyes helicoptered straight out immediately after the concert. *Frank*-ly, they thought their big bucks had bought at least a sip with the Chairman of the Board, who pleaded illness—wife Barbara's; but insiders say he *never* mingles with the mundane at these charity affairs. It's against his religion: confirmed snobbism.

Warren Beatty keeps a list of his, uh, conquests—and at last count was up to 820. That French actress we used to see with Pierre in Montreal? She says he is aiming for a thousand.

Teddy Kennedy is dating Lacey Newhouse, the Houston socialite (slim, long blond hair) that the PM was dating last year. If you remember Maggie T's references to her southern senator, the whole thing is even more bizarre!

And under the category of who-cares-but-it-may-be-a-useful-drop-some-day, Givenchy—migawd, we will all be calling him "Hugh" soon—just opened his very first *Haute Couture* boutique in America (954 Madison). He served Dom, Beluga, the works, but at Manoir du Jonchet (his 16th-century chateau in France, you silly goose), he serves only simple, fresh, home-grown veggies, and the bath towels are in Hugh's absolute fave color—"stone." I told you that you might not care.

Two priceless asides, and then we may safely put Canada's glammed-up evening to bed. From the hallowed Hall earlier in the evening, *sotto voce*: "I have a sneaking suspicion she carries her family tree in her evening bag lest she forget." And, "Look, she has her designer gown on backwards. But then how is she to know—she never owned one before!"

On to Toronto's Festivals of Festivals, the world's largest publicly attended film festival (150,000 at 180 featured flicks).

Robert De Niro popped in from New York, just for one night. He is *very* short, still heavy (left over from *Raging Bull?*). Dark suit, brown shoes (that's a no-no, Bobby), and a close-cropped, almost farm-boy hair cut. He seemed to be *very* hungry. He tore off the leg of a chicken before it was carved.

He was the surprise guest at a party later that night. He surprised everyone. He didn't show up!

John Cassavetes and Gena Rowlands were widely touted, and a full 30 of their films were flashed, including *The Tempest*, their latest. I loved it. It was voted most popular new film, even though it was lifted from one of your boys over there, Barbie...William Something. "Johnny," as she calls him, had a smart cut on his face, and when quizzed (no, *I* didn't ask), looked at Gena and then at the considerable rock on her finger and smiled. There was a short strain while no one said anything. Where do you go from fisticuffs?

Dreamy Jeremy Irons was there (*French Lieutenant's Woman, Brideshead Revisited*). He has no mustache, speaks so beautifully you could listen to the alphabet recited. I missed his new film called *Moonlighting* because I was off at Fento's for a little chichi bite, then went on with some film folk to the Courtyard Cafe, or the Yoo Hoo as it is called locally, with very good reason. Everyone was there, but in blue collar drag with pretensions ("Is the menu in English? I don't read English...")

Flew back to Van. Peter Brown's big silver limo was at the airport when I arrived, but Darling, *not pour moi!*

Richard's on Richards (the 1000 block), a somewhat swanky, San Francisco-type saloon, has burst upon the ready-for-it nightclub scene with a middle-whelming opening nighter. A nice, round $600,000 was poured into the old David Y.H. Lui Theatre by a group of fairly professional restaurant and entertainment types, and there are nightly line-ups for the 325 seats.

Opening night in the trendy taproom provided, if not names to drop, at least a few to litter around a little. No one was a split second over 25, although it was the AD's, the After Disco's, the owners were aiming at. Something about disposable income, I think. Not an ounce of cellulite in sight, but unless gypsy chic is in, those were Fashion Victims basking in the spilled light from the TV cameras.

The guest list showed no signs of having been pared. Champagne (barely) was generously served, as hapless trays of nameless goodies made their perilous way through the herd. There were a number of girls there who, as your Aunt, the Ice Queen, used to say, "look like they scrawl their thank-you notes in green ink on funny cat stationery." Judging from the dance floor action (the sound system, the live acts, the music are first-rate), it is obvious that "It just isn't done" has absolutely *no* meaning any more.

That perfect couple—he's a headache, she's a pill—whose name no one seems to know, were there, but they were standing with quite the most beautiful man I have seen recently (dimples you could lose your keys in, eyes the blue of a 450SL), so of course I stayed near them for an unconscionably long time.

There was a minor celebrity shuffle—the Smothers Brothers, smiling, simple; Paul Anka, minuscule, aging, but the hair transplant's taking; and Mike Reno, the lead singer from Loverboy, who told me that he had just bought a 1970 or maybe 1960—you know me and cars—British racing green Morgan.

It was The Night of the White Jackets! Hugh Pickett in raw silk, promoter Bruce Allen (one of the silent partners, none of whom is named Richard) in an off-white, pink shirt combo, and learned Lothario Basil Pantages in an all-white suit. As I listened to Terry David Mulligan talk on, I was reminded how thoroughly apropos his initials are.

Best lines between ear-blasting dance sets, from a mincing minor star: "Limos and fruit baskets, fruit baskets and limos, everywhere I go they love me!" And from a very cool, very ambitious young beauty: "What do I *do*? What do I *do*? Well, whatever I have to, of course."

On to Umberto's new Cafe Mephisto for, what else lately, a champagne reception. If one were looking for exclusive, this was definitely not it: 1500—that's one thousand, five hundred—of Mr. Menghi's closest and mostest whatever were asked to mix and mingle at Bert's new Beanery, as his faithful employees are calling the Davie Street bistro. Davie Street: that posed a bit of a problem, because the "Love is a many-gendered thing" syndrome has to be contended with before you can get into the driveway. Once in, though, the faithful customers from his various establishments exuded a kind of clubby confidence as they fawned over his cashmere-blazered presence. I mean at least they knew *him*.

Oh, and Barbie, from what I have noticed, hugs are in, but cheek pecks are definitely out. Could have something to do with something that's going around. And no one promises lunch any more. They *know* they will never call. One hugs firmly, seriously, as though you have been through Dunkirk together.

Tout Vancouver definitely was not there. There was a modicum of swanking about, but no serious flashing of finances. Oil swell J. Bob Carter looked curiously distracted (business intruding on his pleasure perhaps?). B.C. Place's Paul Manning—or the Knoxville Kid as he is becoming known from his numerous trips to the World Fair—was bar-leaning in a navy three-piece pinstripe, authoritative shirt, silk tie and pouf. Since that was how he had dressed for a football game earlier in the evening, the theory now is he wears three-piece jammies to bed.

That great watershed of modern etiquette—whether to speak to one's ex or not—got a thorough working-out that night; but remembering that being right means never having to say you're sorry helps the decision-making immeasurably. Besides, unrelieved wholesomeness is *so* tedious.

Ta Ta, Darling,
Valerie

THE YEAR 1983

THE ULTIMATE HOST AND PLUMAGE PEOPLE
It's round-up time on the party circuit.

ANOTHER LEGENDARY NIGHT AT MULVANEY'S
Blowing out the candles at Mulvaney's birthday.

OYSTERS AND THE ROCKER FELLOW
Bons mots on the half-shell at Celia Duthie's chic eatery.

ARS GRATIA POPULUS
Carousing with the Culturati.

THE YEAR 1983

A year of endless social shimmyings. B.C. Place finally opened, and the Grey Cup helped us show it off to the rest of Canada. The $25 million Delta Mountain added even more of a sheen to Whistler's unfolding patina. Jane Fonda came to town to show us just what a 45-year-old perfectly toned body should look like, and those of us who struggled through her two workshops never really got over it.

Umberto, becoming too-tiresomely successful we were starting to think, opened an eighth restaurant, this time in Seattle. The indominatable Nelson Skalbania's flipping fortune was going into a deep dive. Labeled his "neo-Baroque period" by some—he admitted to being "half-way between the edge of disaster and the brink of defeat" which made him a fascinating figure to watch skiing at least.

The Queen came to town and she brought her boat with her and threw a to-die-for-dinner aboard it, with every local luminary who could scrounge an invite in attendance. Bill Bennett forgot his tux, but otherwise it went off splendidly. David Bowie blew into town to rock our socks off and Celia Duthie's New Yorky Binky's Oyster Bar bivalved open.

But the drop-dead bar-none unsurpassed gold-plated block buster that year was the opening of the Art Gallery. I tell you—everybody who was anybody duded-up. Dowagers and delicious debs. Wined and dined and primed. It was right up there as the decade's song and dance supremo.

THE ULTIMATE HOST AND PLUMAGE PEOPLE

Barbie Darling,

Things here have been abuzz with excitement—even our city skyline had a coming-out party. Two thousand invited guests donned blue, white, and yellow hard hats (except Senator Jack Austin's assistant Cindy Grauer, who wore a designer gold one). Bill Bennett turned on the fans—a definite *first* for him—and a blast of political hot air inflated the 10-acre teflon dome on B.C. Place.

Exhausted by all that huffing and puffing, a small group of us headed to Ondine's for omelettes. Jack Webster in bright blue hardhat and matching sweatshirt (over striped braces yet), Iona Campagnolo in smashing scarlet silk shirt and Allan Fotheringham in comfy red cashmere gave the buoyant building top marks. Paul Manning, basking in the glow of a roof well-raised, suggested deflating it so we could do it all again.

Off to Viva! for a Club Med night, but it is difficult getting into an uninhibited tropical mood after you have driven through a rainstorm in the pitch-black night, then wait in herds of six or eight as some minor domo sluices the selected through the door because the coat-room is backed up.

A respectable bunch of Vivants included good-looking and fit junior account executives (in the wrong-sized lapels, with *four* buttons on their cuffs), department store buyers, secretaries and receptionists (ah, the conflict between Gucci and punk still unsolved), and a light sprinkling of aspiring social butterflies.

I passed two girls in that sort of 3/4 perch that people on bar stools affect who still want to check the room out, and I heard "Of course he's a faithful husband—his alimony checks are always on time!"

And, passing the "Parrot Punch" (bits of unidentified floating fruit), "Well, I wouldn't say she's *smart*—she has sort of a *National Enquirer* knowledge of the world..."

And, from two older men at the top of the stairs, "Hang-gliding in a strife-torn banana republic is *not* her *coupe de the*, I just *know* it!"

But Barbie, you'll never guess what! I saw my first "chest rug." His silk shirt was unbuttoned to the waist, and he had a gold chain nestled in the middle of "it." I had never seen one before. The man with the balding pate beside him was staring at it intently too. It was thick and curly—no skin showed through, and it just sort of "ended" at his neck. What's that French

67

word for tacky? "Plouc?"

This was neither Viva! nor Club Med in its palmiest days. Everyone left before there was *any* danger of turning into pumpkins, and it was raining so hard no one noticed the valet-parkers' "Well,-it's-better-than-no-car-at-all" looks.

Pranced off with the out-all-the-time crowd to a Friends of Emily Carr fashion show at the Restaurant at Mark James. Since the tickets ($50 per pair) went for the good cause (art scholarships), and since all those people who are always saying, "Let's have lunch," finally did, everyone was in a great mood. Backed by a brace of *very* well-bred young scions of the times—movers and shakers, or shovers and makers as a friend demurs—the Emily Carr college really knows how to raise those funds. And Barbie Darling, you *know* having a hand in any kind of arts group is still *au fait* in the mores of the rational rich! One needs only check the boards of the Playhouse, the Opera, the Aquarium, my dear.

Commentator Pia Shandel Southam was in a "rather be red than dead" mood—even her *stockings*, dear heart. The models were celebrities, but non-pros, and the onlookers were trend-spotters and trendsetters lunching on juicy tidbits and crab-stuffed croissants au gossip, so the competition for attention was stiff.

A larger than usual male audience checked out the Mark James clothes—definitely the right stuff on the right horses. The Whitecaps' Bob Lenarduzzi romped through modeling, a new kind of game for him, and definitely scored. The less-than-proper matron who whispered, "Now, I'd like to take *that* home," wasn't talking about his German import suit. The B.C. Lions' Ken Hinton had the Christians eating out of his hand, and Steven Grauer's rugged *Raiders of the Lost Ark* garb was the *real* him.

Jewelry designer Martha Sturdy played crackerjack coquette as she camped about under the sunlit skylights, the full-size indoor trees, the bamboo shades and chichi artworks in her dramatic coal-black ensembles from Bizo—all showcased with Martha jewelry, *naturellement*. I don't mind telling you, Barbie, it is so difficult for one to smile and be civil when the show's talented models—Martha, once-a-model Mary Butterfield (polished, elegant, VanDusen gardens volunteer/photographer), or Nan Nichols (sleek and soignee single mother of five)—can still pass a thigh-detector test. They make every other woman in the room feel so, so...*creased*!

Panicking that the wish to know what he is *really* like comes to fewer people each passing year, Allan Fotheringham asked the entire world to his *Malice in Blunderland* book-flogging. Cartoonists Ben Wicks and Roy Peterson compared—what else?—lines. Pesky litigators Peter Butler, Nancy

Morrison, and John Laxton weren't overheard (lawyers are _so_ cautious these days), but one of their clients, spotted near the bar, was certainly wearing his lawsuit well.

With so literate a gathering (I spotted six published authors in the living room alone), there was a lot of checking to see just "what exactly" certain remarks meant. Since host Perry Goldsmith has a stable of Canadian speakers like Peter Newman and Laurier LaPierre, anyone with a certain talent to amuse was getting off a well-timed line faster than it takes to eat a caviar-sprinkled egg.

Waddled off to Whistler (last year's ski suit is always a struggle at the first of the season). Checked into the $25 million Delta Mountain Inn, and although Whistler has always been different slopes for different folks—good thing, with 20,000 on Blackcomb and Whistler on a great day—I think I've found the hutch _this_ bunny would like to snuggle down into after the boards come off.

Especially when I found out you can hire a Bertie the Butler to have hot canapes and chilled bubbly ready for you and a few dozen intimates after an afternoon on those mogels owned by moguls. You really should have him butling in the $800 per sunset-to-sundown Blue Suite. As sleek as some Shaughnessy shacks—multi rooms, double Jacuzzis, saunas, fireplaces, brass and glass—the plum royal blue suite was snaffled for a little festive faring by none other than the pops-up-everywhere Umberto Menghi. Vancouver is so small town sometimes!

And speaking of small town, Mark Angus, of _the_ Anguses, won the Whistler election and became Canada's second youngest mayor. Had brunch with the new king of the mountain, who no longer wants to be addressed as "Blue"; he has advised his nearest and dearest that "Your Lordship" would do just fine, thank you.

Nipped into the new Bruno Freschi-designed Carlton Lodge for drinkie-poos. Believe me, Babs dear, instead of quaffing Courvoisier at the club on weekends, or tinkering with the Bugatti, people are strapping barrel staves to their feet, and with a certain reverse cachet doing their financial finagling in their Bognars in the bar, when all that blow-dried apres-ski hair is let down.

British Columbia's latent Liberals got their wagons into a _very_ respectable circle for a fund-raising dinner at the Hyatt a few nights later. All the party's plumage people were there: over-worked sincere senators, glassy-eyed financiers seeking reassurance that things are indeed in hand, the small but stalwart group that forms the backbone of the party—the "non-slipped discs" who remain in place _whatever_. The Hon. Don Johnson, Ottawa's import for the night, gave his off-the-cuff remarks from indexed cards in his sock and went on ad tedium, but the after-party made up for it. On a walkabout I heard: "Well his *pre*-tax income..." "She told me her earrings weren't real, for heaven sake." "They're sort of *underground*-jetters." "Her husband is like fine wine—he doesn't travel well."

My absolute fave—said demurely over the rim of a glass of white wine: "Why, we gave each other rift certificates—the divorce goes through in April."

Must dash, Barbie dear; just one more thing. Chuck was in town. Lady Di's Chuck, you silly girl, and he really *does* seem a prince of a fellow. "H-H," as the harried security officers called him, was in and out of town *so* quickly that he left us with almost no new tidbits. But for what it's worth, he doesn't wear a wedding band (at least when he's out of town, he doesn't). He *does* wear a gold family crest signet on his royal baby finger, and what looks like an elaborate diver's watch. He is slimmer than I thought, and shorter than Phillip, and he combs to advantage over his spreading baldspot at the back.

Thanks awfully for the "Better to be *Nouveau* than not *Riche* at all" embroidered satin pillow, I love it.

Ta Ta, Darling,
Valerie

ANOTHER LEGENDARY EVENING AT MULVANEY'S

Barbie Darling,

Minced down to Mulvaney's (those Granville Island cobblestones are murder on high heels) for their 8th anniversary champagne "salute to the regulars."

Snug under the Granville Street Bridge, the New Orleans-style eatery was known from the start as a great late-night spot to let your hair down. That billowing floral fabric that swings from the old warehouse rafters has tempted more than one party-person to try a Tarzan leap from the wicker tables through the jungle of plants. And remaining upright at the standing-room-only bar in the middle of the room has always been a formidable challenge to those who dared to down the Preservation Hall Potted Parrot, the Bourbon Street Blues or the Mardis Gras Mindbiter.

It has been more homey than home to a whole claque of youngish shifters and shakers. Maggie Trudeau boogied here when she first went AWOL from 24 Sussex, and one of the city's handsomest young scions met the wife after the wife before in the lounge, and had what he calls their "first serious smooch" in the disco.

The clientele has always demonstrated a "delightful decadence," as that English friend of yours used to say of what _he_ saw in his early days, and it was amazing on anniversary night how many faces dared to show themselves again. Host Bud Kanke's charm was on full-tilt, no mean feat when your guard is never off. He greeted rowdy regulars with personalized pass cards, unavailable to the rank amateurs brought along by the pro partiers. Standing by his side was date-mate Dottie Meyers, daring in a jewel-blue item down to _there_ (an attention-getter that no doubt boosted her fashion-consulting business).

Leon Bibb, fresh from six weeks in La Grande Pomme—loved New York, hated the reviews—was natty in white-linen Bermuda shorts, knee socks and a striped seersucker blazer. Liona Boyd waltzed over in the lavender chiffon number she wore on her last album cover, but which no one recognized: it was belted this time, and she wore something _under_ it. She is sabbaticaling in Vancouver, has cut her 1960s' flower-child locks into a more tameable mane, and had just taped a segment for NBC's Entertainment Tonight.

And, while I think of it, a very nice opening it was, especially from the plush private boxes that ring the roof. The sweets for the suites included iced tarts, one in vivid green silk with matching eye shadow. She was nibbling Grand Marnier cheesecake and fresh strawberries in cream while the big cheeses devoured ripe Camembert by the crackerful. The almonds were not the only things glazed over by the show's end, but private booths being private, who's to know?

Cheery Karen Magnussen did yeoman duty to Frank Sinatra's _It Isn't Easy Being Green_ in a leaf-like outfit that did its best to disguise the trees. Toller Cranston flitted about seriously in swish lavender and silver spandex, and Carol Lawrence, whom I try never to watch doing _anything_, lip-synced her way (badly) through two costume changes, both of which I had seen twice before.

But back to Mulvaney's. A few others had joined Paul Manning out on the landing, all trying to get upwind of that plotting nightbloomer we always see at Richard's on Richards; his aftershave smells like Raid. You remember him, dear heart—he puts ice in his champagne, wears one of those cracked-wedding-bank divorce rings? And makes tiny macho moves?

The crowd, if not really "now," was definitely recent. Peter Bradshaw, late of L'Orangerie, was mingling tentatively. (Every time I see any of the eatery's past partners, I think of Jean-Claude the uncouth before he was "replaced," attacking the uncut prosciutto as though it might not be dead yet.)

Peter Brown (_are_ there parties held without him?), in beige raw-silk suit and taupe Guccis, was harboring dreams of fiscal glory at the bar, head-to-head with Downtown Dougie Gordon (Gordon Securities), who looked like a page out of *Gentlemen's Quarterly:* white pleated pants, perfect shirt and jacket, polished loafers-sans-socks and artfully disarrayed sunbleached coif. He couldn't quite remember where he got his tan (Whistler, Caribbean, sailing?).

It was one of those flawless summer nights of which Vancouver gets five a year. Yachts cruised by with very spiffy salts topside raising glasses to ours (we had switched from champagne to strawberry daiquiries by now). Faces whose names seemed too much trouble to remember murmured high-calorie nothings as the nibblies were given the olfactory once-over.

Shoot-yourself-in-the-foot award went to the fledgling legend who introduced his date to the new divorce on his right, who of course knew the name quite well as the co-respondent in her recent uncoupling, thank you very much.

David was there—dear David from Viva's an age ago. He still certainly knows who's who and why, and so does all-over-town publicity person Dale Mearns. Between them they could do a nice little local edition of the Blue Book and Celebrity Register.

The entire female staff (well, almost) of Senator Jack Austin's office was there, one of whom whined that she had to miss Chuck and Di in Ottawa. Also that incredibly beautiful couple we met somewhere political last year, who seem to make everyone around them feel inferior, because of course they usually *are*; the pair are having a fourth perfect heir, but it's not yet apparent.

That great ritualist of refracted glory Malcolm Burke was there. Malcolm usually manages to surrmount his advantages, but almost never stubs his tongue. Watching him flash a smile in his nautical blazer that night, I'm convinced that the puffed and dimpled darling blow-dries his teeth!

Mellow Mulvaneyites, fidelities intact (although some nights they are Pelican Bay expellees), still provide some of the liveliest patter current. Overheard as I slinked past the "Goodbye" cast at the door: "Love you, never change; my service will call your service and *they* can go for lunch!" Beauty is, after all, only sheen deep.

Ta Ta, Darling,
Valerie

OYSTERS AND THE ROCKER FELLOW

Barbie Darling,

There is a new *chichi boite* on the block. Actually down the alley and in the courtyard. It's called Binky's Oyster Bar and Restaurant, but rather than just a restaurant it is a "cultural endeavor."

And opening *soiree* it was littered with literati and cultured cliches among the Bluepoints, Golden Mantles and Pacifics (oysters, dear heart, oysters). The place was crawling with in-tel-lec-tu-als; if it hadn't been fun, it would have been positively threatening.

Binky's is off Thurlow in the courtyard of the Manhattan Block—you know, that award-winning heritage building? Now that the old derelict has been completely restored, it is camp to live in the apartments and so *chic* to have your business in the street-level mall.

"I dashed off a couple of stanzas before I got here," I heard someone say as I eased by Celia Duthie (of *course* of the Duthie Books' Duthies). Celia's father was looking like a latter-day Hemingway, and Allan Fotheringham was simply looking latter-day. Actually he seemed quite rested, considering that he had just cranked out another best seller for the Christmas market. *Malice in Blunderland* will have been relegated to the discount book bin by then, just in time for his new *Look Ma, No Hands.*

It's a Tory story this time—116 years of the people who would love to give the country the blues. There is only one party left for him to dissect, so at least this is part of a limited series.

I was just glancing around the room, thinking how ultra-New York it was—all glossy black-and-white-and-art-deco—when I spotted Edith Iglauer Daly, that writer for the terribly sophisticated *New Yorker* Magazine? She *did* the definitive piece on Trudeau, wrote the book on Arthur Erickson? Gave those *soirees* in New York in her Lexington Avenue apartment in the late 1960s where we all met the Buckleys and Barbra Streisand for the first time?

Edith was talking to an artsy-craftsy person in a homespun dress, and obviously just off an island. She said she was "into beads," which certainly caused a few eyes to glaze over as we moved away.

That artist with the Andy Warhol rug, whose name I can never remember, was there. I didn't talk to him, but I did notice some definite slippage; it's now encroaching on his eyebrows. He was talking to one of the few really beautiful women in the room, a blonde in a minimal mini, and in passing I heard him say, "I only involve myself with things that are stimulating, and frankly, my dear, I find you stimulating."

My fave dreamboat drifted in with an extraneous female on his arm (well, I felt she was extraneous). He was on the lam from the heat in Toronto. He had just been to syndicated-columnist Keith Spicer's wedding (remember, Barbie, Keith said "never again"?).

After their honeymoon at the Hamilton Princess Bermuda Hotel, Keith and the new frau will live in False Creek, where, I am convinced, the whole world will soon be living.

As I made my way to the bar for a spritzer, I was thinking that what distinguishes really nourishing gossip from the skimpier stuff may well have to do with a generosity of spirit. Being among the book people, I felt prone to such ills as *chagrin* and *ennui*.

"So, you have only published one small book of poetry, Alex?" I heard, as a friendly waiter passed the prawns. "History will record your *true* worth." Alex, whoever he was, was left to ponder exactly what had been meant.

"Nelson Skalbania is in my dance class," a shiny-haired brunette in a red jumpsuit was saying to her friend. "His wife Eleni is, too, but you should just see his deltoids and pectorals!"

"Please!" her friend said, without missing a beat. "Not while I'm eating oysters, dear,"

(I must say, Barbie, those bivalves were cleverly disguised, in and out of shell and batter. For some reason your aunt's reply to the waiter at the Savoy sprang to mind: "How would you like your lobster, Madam?" "Dead, with butter, of course."

Well, it wasn't tea in the Palm Court at the Plaza, but for Vancouver it was *tres* civilized.

Bopped off to Bowie a few nights *apres*—yes, Babs, David Bowie, Boy Rock Star (and the longer contemporary society thinks that 36 is "boyish," the better for all of us, right?).

Barbie, he *is* the most exquisite, androgynous creature. I mean he's beautiful enough to be a girl. Whoever dyes his hair is a master: no black roots at all, and what a shade of blond. And his makeup! So necessaire, ma chere (he is paler than his yellow hair without it, and more wrinkled than your Auntie Bess).

Backstage there was a proper portable sushi bar just for Bowie and his boys (Koji himself wielding the knives). Six little stools and six little geishas to serve.

In his pale peach suit, and later in the prettiest Princess-Di-blue shirt, he sang a whole series of songs that blended together as interchangeable ear-assaults. Musically they might have been near-genius, but since the crowd continually screams things like "Aw-_right!_" it's very difficult to know.

As I looked over to the box next door, there was Canarim's cool-cat Peter Brown himself, bouncing along with the kids in a white shirt, yellow cashmere sweater, black sunglasses (held together with a Band-Aid) and the inevitable bottle of Dom on the railing. Everyone else in the box looked as though they had just come ashore from a week or two sailing the Gulf Island: the bronzed faces, the smart stripes, the usual.

Speaking of high rollers, the Jones-boy himself (Bowie's _real_ name) picked up a somewhat chilly million for the night's work. When one lives in a _chateau_ overlooking Switzerland's Lake Geneva, and when one likes one's Lincoln Continentals equipped with TV, paintings and plants hanging from the roof, one is going to have _un soupcon_ of overhead expense, what?

Ta Ta, Darling, and Aw-_right!_

Valerie

ARS GRATIA POPULUS

Barbie Darling,

Positively galloped off to this season's sizzler, the Inaugural Ball at the courtly new Art Gallery. _Moi_ and 556 other grateful first-nighters. At 4500 a pop per duo, can you believe there was a waiting list! Vancouverites know a once-in-their lifetime thing when they sniff it!

It was a Darwinian struggle: survival of the flashiest. The picky paparazzi would not photograph just _any_ Cinderella scurrying up the Grand Staircase. She had to slip out of a limo, preferably six-door (this year's color was white), and her outfit had to evoke a hum of awe.

And those foreboding lions. You would think they were cast in stone. They practically rolled their eyes, as though by _now_ (well, since 1912) they had seen everything!

Once inside, Cecil B. DeMille could not have done better. Two-and-a-half years in the making, $20 million-plus budget, a cast of thousands and finally international-class credentials. The leading ladies came out like exotic hothouse flowers, showing it all off. We are talking a major fashion invasion here, Barbie, and the romantic leads all looked like hunk-of-the-month nominees.

The heady scent of very good French perfume was in the air, and everywhere you looked, with those discreet dove-gray walls as background each grouping was more impressive than the last. Scads of strapless gowns defied the laws of independent suspension as flutes of champagne were raised on high. There was not too much in the way of tiaras, but one nameless fashion victim had something black and spiky on her head that suggested imminent tarantula trouble.

It was vintage Vancouver. The old guard, who grace such gatherings less and less, left their cozy dens of antiquity, glanced tolerantly at what poses for blue blood these days, and sighed contentedly at being part of the previous generation.

Harry and Maxine Gelfant

You know how old money feels duty-bound to put something back into society; it salves the conscience. And this understated little zinger was easy, it was such a happy occasion.

Knowing you, dear heart, it is news of the troops you want, so I shall rummage through the yard sale of my mind and catalogue the creme de la cremers:

Almost no one was in Guess-brand labels—it was a *very* couturier tournament. In this corner we have a Givenchy, over here a Christian Dior, two Sonia Rykiels talking about that Yves Saint Laurent over there, with a steely-eyed Chloe looking on . Extravagance, just enough, not ostentatious. In Italy, as I recall, they term it making a *bella figure*—strutting your stuff in the piazza. Well, the rotunda looked like some vast coronet studded with chatting, laughing, sipping bits of glitz.

Pour les hommes, Lou Myles seemed to have trimmed the most elegant of the tuxes and tails (topping the patent Gucci or Bally pumps, of course), but I was sure I recognized ex-Governor-General Roly Michener's classic threads from our Ottawa days in the 1960s. (These joggers are such overachievers.)

Almost no clip-on ties—black satin hand-knotted, conservative one-and-one-half-inch width; dark pearl or gold studs; white linen hankie, red silk if you must; white, all-cotton pleated dress shirt, no colors or ruffles. Classic black satin cummerbund—no vests, please. Extremely old monogrammed gold cuff links, preferably handed down. Nails manicured, rarely polished. Old family watch, save the status number for lunch at the club. Cardin black-silk dress socks to the knee.

Graciously receiving their glammed-up guests were Gallery Director Luke Rombout and his wife Maxine. Luke's fine fingerprint is on everything here. "He is to perfection what Strad was to violins," mutters the bejeweled hand beside me. The serene Maxine, in an ebony dress and jacket, was chicly capped by a perfectly perched Saint Laurent organdy cocktail bow.

Corporate Kong Sam Belzberg strode in, leaving the heady scent of power behind him (or was that Aramis?) , and frau Fran floated off to his left in a perfect pleated scarlet-and-jet Mary McFadden to greet Maxine Gelfant, the Ball Chair (chair_person_, we are notified, is out). Dr. Harry Gelfant's red tie and cummerbund could not possibly draw the flash from Maxine's midnight blue Oscar de la Renta, which was topped by a brilliant, art-deco bellhop's jacket' it was a snap to spot her as she flit around her flocks, making everything mesh.

Nelson Skalbania put a shine on his _sous_—he had to cough up half-a-grand just like everyone else—and escorted the sunny Eleni through the throng. In her crocus yellow flounces, her golden hair and those big brown eyes, she was as dramatic as a daisy among the swells of black and white that surrounded her.

I passed Peter Bradshaw on the way to dinner. His mind was in the gutter as usual (he's in aluminum, Barbie, remember?). He was in fine firefly form. You know—a flash, and then nothing till he warms up again?

Chatted with lawyer Tony Pantages and his wife Diane on the way to the lower level. For the occasion her hair was tousled up in tiny curls. She had not, she assured her acerbic spouse, stuck her finger in a socket; it was _supposed_ to look like that! I thought she resembled a dimpled Colette as she swept grandly down the staircase; he rushed to offer his hand, and they finished the descent as Romeo and Juliet.

Tucking into our _filets de veau_, after we were finally ensconced in the Emily Carr Gallery, was elegantly delightful once we got there; but one maitre d' suggested that mobilizing the chatting masses to come to dinner had been like trying to get tooth-paste back into the tube. Perusing the room between courses I spotted Brenda and David McLean, she in a body-hugging chemise of black wool and chiffon, and he in his tux of course. You know, if his beard and glasses lifted off with the nose, he could be _anybody_ under there!

There was ex-_Sun_ publisher Stu Keate's son Richard, the _petit_ Keate. And jewelry designer Martha Sturdy in a high-necked Catherine Regehr, sporting a new Roaring Twenties cropped bob. A smattering of Southams (the Gordon and Ross Southams—Pia and Harvey seemed to have passed, thank you). Paul

Manning's parents, but no Paul: even fledgling legends need a night off, I guess.

Natalie Austin in her white frosted number from *H.M.S. Britannia*, with no Jack. (No, she did not leave her made money at home—the senator was elsewhere.) The Toni Caveltis; several of his jewelry pieces were gleaming around the room on throats, fingers, ears and wrists, and Hildegard Cavelti's sumptuous stamp was everywhere in the gorgeous bouquets she had done with John of Flowers by Elizabeth. Restaurateur Bud Kanke gave his nod of approval to the fancy forage done by the Four Seasons, as did Hy Aisenstat, whose sleekly chignoned wife Barbara, in charcoal gray sequins topped with a white pleated neck ruffle, looked like a Moroni portrait. Cal Knudsen's wife Julia Lee, who had on a smashing backless number, got off her best lines as she *left* groups so they could watch the dress depart.

For a potential pyromaniac, artist Toni Onley looked content. Some 427 of his prints, valued at $250,000, were safely ensconced upstairs, so he probably felt right at home. Ron Longstaffe should have been feeling proprietary, too; the Canfor executive gave the gallery a cool $1 million collection of contemporary works. Wife Jacqueline, in delphinium blue topped with a gold lame puff-sleeved jacket, could have been framed. Carol Challis from Elle International had wrought her magic again.

People were table-hopping like hummingbirds now, and I watched Malcolm Burke's burgundy bow tie dart around the room. Vancouver's answer to Henny Youngman broke up *every* table he stopped at with his well-timed one-liners. Laurier LaPierre, in white tie and tails—rented—oozed Gallic charm from every spigot. Lois Milsom in her black backless Bill Blass (try *that* 10 times, I dare you) was untanned; there had been no sun in Greece, Leonard Cohen had not been on Hydra, John Huston was back in Puerto Vallarta, and we should all go *there* to get tanned anyway! Concert Guitarist Liona Boyd, who had been with her in Greece, was not tanned either (the sun would not dare touch that fair skin), and she kept her Goody Two Shoes on all night.

I was delighted to see the charming Bonar Lund up and walking around. He sits on so many committees, I had never before seen him out from behind a boardroom table.

As I glanced up at the Emily Carrs on the wall behind me, I heard, "Well, I say, if you have it, wear it." I turned around to check, and sure enough, whoever she was had trotted out all her sparklers for the occasion.

"Totem poles for their trinkets," muttered a man who had also overheard. "Nonsense," his wife allowed. "Extravagances that awaken the exquisite creature in everywoman."

Bumped into Mayor Mike and the gentle Becky. He is feeling pretty smug about how great his city is becoming, but *everyone* seemed to be a goodwill ambassador that night. One of my dinner partners had flown in from Positano,

Italy a scant half hour before the great doors opened, and Fran (Foley) and Tim Lewis had jetted in from Bangkok; a bit of a name-drop, I thought, until I spoke to Arthur (there *is* only one Arthur, dear heart), who was fresh from Kuala Lumpur. He allowed that Sir Francis Rattenbury's ghost hadn't bothered him at all during the renovations, but then Arthur's exquisitely subtle touch showed such respect for what was already there, I am not surprised the two titans got along famously.

Diane Farris, Lauch's wife (she has the Houston-Farris Gallery with Sam Houston?), had joined us by now. She dropped that she was off to Dallas in January for the opening of the new Dallas Art Gallery, and Arthur said he wished he had gotten the design contract for that one. Migosh, Barbie, *everything* can't be his, can it?

Sondra Gotlieb, Canadian ambassador to the U.S. Allan's wife, had just announced a few minutes before that she wishes they would break ground for the new Erickson embassy in Washington. She says she still cannot find all the powder rooms in the old embassy. She kept running upstairs till she found the one in the alcove beside the front door. I am sure everyone who was at a party there during Lyndon Johnson's administration remembers when Sylvia Gould (who later married newscaster Knowlton Nash) got locked in that particular powder room. The looks on the faces of the guests cocktailing in the front hall suggested they had never heard such language, and the butler who finally got the heel-marked door open told me he hadn't either!

Fran, Sam Belzberg & Natalie Austin

Madam Gotlieb, whom I had known as one of the livelier young Ottawa wives, has become a pure delight around Washington. "Deliciously offbeat," as D.C. calls her, she has probably done more for North-South relations than the whole diplomatic corps put together. We huddled for a fast five, and Sondra, who is a very quick, very funny study, pronounced as she cased the room that the most expensive dress there was probably Janet Ketcham's—a gorgeous pale gray and gold-beaded creation that was perfection with the gallery color scheme. Sondra herself said she could probably use 14 more ballgowns than the plum velvet job she had on that night (which she got half-price in Washington; she generally tries to use a Toronto designer, because it makes everything go so easier if you are always patriotic).

As I moved to the lobby, where the band and the bar were in stiff competition, I passed two Youngish Matrons, who after being nice about a

79

third Y.M. for what must have seemed an unconscionably long time, let loose with (in the time it took to work my way past them), "She should never again speak to whoever is dressing her," and, "Right. She looks like Carmen Miranda dancing over there, but without the fruit basket on her head!"

I passed, in the foyer, what became known as the Pappas Fur Pack, a passel of three silly bunnies who wandered around all night steaming toward celebrity in $30,000 worth of mink, lynx and lamb, which I am not sure they removed even to eat.

Steven Grauer looked smoother in a tux than in his Saturday-morning Granville Island gear. His sister Sherry's witty canvas, *Former Wife on the Terrace*, drew rave reviews upstairs. And speaking of rave reviews, I was standing with one of the *Oldveau Riche* when stockster Peter Brown and his much better half, Joanne, walked by to pose for pictures at the railing of the rotunda. She was quickly voted Tiniest Waist in the House in her strapless gown of black lace over cream silk. Peter, in tails and red rose, was playing courtly benefactor that night; he and business partner Ted Turton had donated the Emily Carr Gallery, so his stock could hardly have been higher.

Caught a flash of black brocade as Diane Brady and Neil Cook whisked by; the fancy threads were on him (and I noticed Peter Hyndman, in his plaid dinner jacket, taking sartorial note, too). David Radler, that Prince of Paper Merchants and Conrad Black's boy in B.C. was just back from T.O., where he and wife Rona had dinner with Maggie Thatcher. Seems Attila the Hen is shorter than you think, and Conrad Black's portrait by Andy Warhol, owned by the gallery, is valued at $30,000, if you care.

Fashion maverick Ralph Brown, whose white vest was being held on with a piece of the string his wife Brenda was carrying in her purse (something about a missing button), was dishing out little canapes of info when my eaves dropped, as they sometimes do, to the conversation beside us. In a voice that could plane a two-by-four, I heard, "she's really all right underneath?" Pause. "Does she have an underneath?"

As I passed Gins Doolittle on the stairway up in her Scarlett O'Hara (all lace and lame and savoir bare), I wondered if, like the Miss America contestants, the blonde beauty Vaselines her teeth for a night like this. How *can* she smile all this time without her lip sticking?

Starlight, or floodlight, was cascading from the dome as I looked back at the dancers below. They resembled an exquisite ad, and the scene could have been Rome or Rio. The metamorphosis from courthouse to art house seemed complete. *Caramba!* Barbie, we've arrived.

Ta Ta, Darling,
Valerie

THE YEAR 1984

EVERYONE TURNED UP WHEN ZHAO CAME TO TOWN
Dim sum and den' some.

MAJESTIC MOMENTS
Whistler flash to Royal flush.

BEIGING MR. PATTISON
Of things sartorial, societal and celebratory on largish boats and smallish islands.

MANY A CAKE PATTED
From papal blessing to high-priced dressing—the Pope and De La Renta hit town.

THE YEAR 1984

*T*hose thuds you heard that year were a whole lot of name-dropping going on. Pierre Trudeau was out and the new Torys R Us crew were in. Mila showed great glamorous possibilities, and surely, we believed, Brian was going to goose the entree-and-cachet-people right out into the fray again. Tories in the tullies had been forcibly good and quiet for so long, it was their turn to strut. Law and P.R. firms were being switched faster than the placecards at a power dinner. And you needed a red-eye readout of the overnight change in players every morning just to keep up.

Expo construction fever was at full pitch in False Creek, World Cup Downhill came to Whistler with the requisite dash of international panache, and our resident arch-architect Arthur Erickson had a 60th birthday party.

The frisky Allan Fotheringham (whom you usually have to take everywhere twice, once to apologize), went off to terrorize Washington. Zhoa Ziang, the highest Peking official to ever duck into Vancouver came to a state dinner and the reign in Spain, King Carlos and Queen Sophia hasta la vista-ed in for drinks and tastefully prepared protocol-filled tacos.

The $41 million Mandarin Hotel opened on Howe Street with a suitably impressive kick-off line-up of hobnobbing snobs. Doctor Kissinger made a house call at the Hyatt and we all suffered through that heavy accent (heavier than it was years ago I swear) for the Kissinger kernels we knew always eventually filtered through.

The Pope and Oscar de la Renta came to town, and the words "bless me is that my dress you are wearing", were never overheard.

EVERYONE TURNED UP WHEN ZHAO CAME TO TOWN

Barbie Darling,

The engraved invitation read: "On the occasion of the visit of the Premier of the State Council of the People's Republic of China, His Excellency Mr. Zhao Ziyang, The Prime Minister of Canada The Right Honourable Pierre Elliott Trudeau (who failed to show up—more later) has the pleasure to invite (fill in the 800 blanks) to a dinner hosted by Senator Jack Austin, Minister of State for Social Development, and Mrs. Austin in the British Columbia Ballroom of the Hotel Vancouver, on Sunday at 19:00 hours for 20:00 hours. Lounge Suit. To Remind. Please present enclosed card upon entry."

These rituals of refracted glory are always absorbing. There was a loose-knit clique of regulars, but a number of early-arrival embryonic achievers glanced, green with interest, at the mink coats and silver temples sent by Central Casting. Once inside, though, the elbow-rubbing ceremonial duties of the tribe act as an effective, one-night-only leveler.

The guest of honour, the highest-ranking Peking official ever to pass this portal, governs more people than anyone else in the world, and this little B.C. piggy goes to the Chinese market to the tune of $1.5 billion. So there was *just* the right smattering of labour, business, academia and the arts (minimally), the Establishment, the Embryos and an ever-so-light dusting of Tories (a little Pacific Rim-shot there, Babs).

Rising above the happy babble of nipping, nibbling and politicking was the voice of habitual and consummate performer Jack Webster. I never did find what breed of tick was in his tam that night, but, believe me, there was absolutely *no* danger of his being mistaken for Dale Carnegie. He sailed past a small, smiling group to assault favourite target Harry Rankin, muttering, "I've never seen him at a do like this."

Former provincial Liberal leader Shirley McLaughlin was chatting with former provincial Liberal leader Gordon Gibson, while former provincial Liberal leader Senator Ray Perrault was commiserated with elsewhere. Former provincial Liberal leader David Anderson (have we left any out?) has finally grown the beard his face was waiting for.

Former Liberal (Period) Garde Gardom was flashing his *month-long* (but who's counting?) Maui tan with a neon-white shirt and dark three-piecer. The last time I saw Garde, playing in the Christmas waves with his Boogie Board at Wailea, he had the contented glow of a man who finally found what he *really* wanted to do!

Bill Bennett, runner-up for Tan of the Night Award, was in a great mood. Trade talks went tickety-boo, and for once the demonstrators weren't yelling at *him*. Outside the brocade curtains, deliberately kept closed, a screaming throng gave the evening a palace-besieged-again feeling.

J.V. Clyne (whom I always expect to say something unforgettably momentous) was looking venerable, what else? Wife Betty, sugar and steel at its best, said she was very pleased at the saving of Stanley Park entrance, in which she had a fine-fingered hand. She looked very *grande dame* in her black lace, strands of *de rigueur* pearls and unexpected little maribou-feathered cape. Rather Alice Roosevelt Longfellow.

David Radler, Conrad Black's Wild-West alter-agent, who seemed mellow after his spot of Miami sun, was of course squiring the ravishing Rona. On the other hand, Joe Cohen, of all thing, Sony, had left frau Fran decorating the posh new pad in Palm Springs, which no doubt explains that outrageous red tie.

The Brothers Mitchell, baby barrister Keith and the wily Kyle, who understand the way things *really* work, flitted in and out of little groupings with the swiftness of an orchestrated sting.

B.C. Place V.P. Paul Manning had been let out of his playpen for the evening, and Bob Bonner, full of energy even out of his B.C. Hydro office, could still work the room with lightning speed.

Just as things were heating up, the Chinese delegation filed in for the receiving-line fandango. Zhao Baby, in a tan suit and shirt—no used-to-be-mandatory Mao tunic in sight—is a tad taller, livelier, and more gracious than you might have thought. Those who met him were babbling as they shimmied out of the crowded cocktail party and traipsed into dinner that the prime guest was as cordial and low-key as a favourite uncle, a scholarly professor, or, in one charmed guest's opinion, his friendly banker (this last is hard to find, Barbie).

Passed en route to dinner two pampered darlings who knew what really mattered. One said, "You spent all *day* getting ready?" and then, after glancing up and down incredulously, added "Really?" Her friend paused barely four steps as we continued on, then offered a little tongue-on-wry herself. "As I mentioned earlier, I still can't believe *you* go to an exercise class." Those overhearing were relieved to see them split up for separate corners.

And so to table.

The ballroom was flooded with baskets of spring flowers, the glow of candles and silver, and the tightest security I have seen since Kosygin was in Canada. Faceless suits, sometimes with a row of three identifying lapel pins, patrolled the room and watched with walkie-talkies from the overhead tinted windows.

The plain clothesers, if you can call uniform-like black-silk suits plain, were either peeking or ducking throughout the whole seven courses. The rest of us had pate, soup and salmon. Or, more decorously, _terrine de chevreiul, essence de morilles,_ and _supreme de saumon en feuillete._

Governments know you can't please all the people all the time. One discontent held his glass of Johannisberg Riesling to the light and said quietly, almost to himself, "I would be ashamed to drink this wine alone at the cottage."

Whenever there was a rare between-courses pause, a handful of hard-core players would buzz off for a dilletante informational pit stop. You didn't even have to buy lunch at the club, and where else would you find an Art Kube operating solidly a mere table-hop from a Ron Longstaffe (fresh from skiing), an Ed Phillips (retired from West Coast Transmission, but being "board-ed" to death) or a Peter Bentley? Where else would you find Jack Munro, Svend Robinson (sassy as ever) and May Brown within shouting distance of each other? Or the vice-chairman of the Canadian Development Corporation, Maurice Strong, who couldn't be more international (with Hanna in all her poppy-red silk sophistication by his side), being admired by an elderly constituency secretary who had somehow never hit the State Dinner circuit before.

Natalie Austin, in a jade-green suede and leather outfit, exquisitely embroidered, bought on a recent trip to China, looked like a Botticelli painting under the head-table lights with her trademark cloud of auburn curls. She small-talked bravely with Premier Zhao through an interpreter all evening long, and promptly headed back to Kapalua Bay beach when it was all over.

Head-table-trainee Joe Clark (he still hasn't got it right), fresh from the disarmament conference in Stockholm, in mid-blue suit and wildly striped tie, was the only one I noticed smiling and nodding in agreement during the speeches. Sure, Barbie, a nice touch, but during the _Chinese_ translation? Do you know how much trouble he has with French?

Ms. McTeer wasn't there, "Off setting up her constituency office" one NDP wag allowed. Apparently _Chatelaine's_ Woman of the Year (who has said not one public nasty about Margaret) is livid about how much Mila Mulroney has set the Women's Movement back by being a happy homemaker. Now girls, be nice.

Jacquie Longstaffe, perfect chignon intact, wafted about in an off-the shoulder float of black and gold, paying her respects to the dowagers just like the well-brought-up young lady she is.

There was much sweet-and-sour discussion of pork-barrel appointments (barely enough to go around), and a few anxious faces here in the boonies were mightily disappointed when Pierre stayed in New York for the weekend—to see some "Funny Lady" he knows, maybe?

Speaking of New York, a surprising number of Big Apple eaters had just flown in—*quelle coincidence*—on the same small plane. Laurence Jolivet, who is fund-raising for the Vancouver Opera and wanted to see how the big boys did it (in dollops up to $17 million a throw), had just winged in with the swish Trish (in black see-through sequins). So had Canada Development Investment Corporation President Joel Bell, and assorted others. All professed latent opera buffery, or at least the after-party-itis that was going around (*poulet risque* with Placido?).

I swear, Barbie, the same nine people are running the country. They hit all the hot spots, whatever setting of jets that requires, and do it so discreetly that the peasants hardly notice.

Ta Ta, Darling,
Valerie

MAJESTIC MOMENTS

Barbie Darling,

Whistler is definitely a society set loose from its stuffier city footings, often with an edge of manic menace, and on this World Cup Downhill weekend there was a dash of continental spice: Swiss, Austrian, Italian and French hunks with goal posts for shoulders and as slim-hipped as necessary.

Ah, the *sportif* crowd at *apres ski*! As Eric Nicol might have said, the village was a regular Slalom and Glamorrah. The atmosphere in the glittering hamlet was enough to steam your glasses—Bolle or Vuarnet, Porsche if you must—or to put a crimp in your "mean-street-neat" clothes: leathers and suedes, a pricey pelt or, in a pinch, your designer ski jacket and perfect pressed jeans.

The First Annual Grand Ball, tickets $125 per lucky person and overseen by one-thing-leads-to-linguine Umberto Menghi, offered a five-course feast served by celebrity waiters, all legends in their own lines and all a touch boisterous over pre-dinner drinks. As their tall, starched, executive chef's hats bobbed above the crowd, one had the impression, Barbie, that maybe they had been into the sauces earlier.

The tone for our table of eight was set by our first of many garcons: the one, the only, Harold Peter Capozzi. Herb burst forth from whatever pen they were holding the simmering waiters in and offered us wine (one bottle in each hand) with a certain—let me be kind—raffishness.

His graying swinger curls peeking out from his tilted chef's hat, his starched white smock open to the navel (yes, there were gold chains), he looked more like a bodice-ripper from a lust-in-the-dust novel than your humble waiter. He was surprisingly good whenever he remembered us, though. And the new Mrs. Capozzi did look nummy as usual.

Peter Hyndman was suitably serious about his task, but affably allowed princess consort Vicky to tie his scarlet neckerchief at a jaunty angle. John McLernen (we are talking _real_ estate) never did smile; he obviously promised the Winterfest Society he would _do_ it and he darn well _did_ it.

Ken Tolmie's beard made him look like a believable chef, and Lilya Kaiser, always Resourceful, did her bit as one of Whistler's rare women-celebs. Malcolm Burke, critically unclaimed clown prince, played charming ninny: he could not decide whether to be pro- or antipasto, so he removed the whole plate anyway.

Mayor Mark Angus had taken his starched bonnet apart and was wearing it along the order of a mad Flemish nun's, which made it impossible to take His Worship seriously. Ross Southam served our quail with a flourish, but one timid soul at the table refused to eat them anyway: "They look just like baby robins on their backs with their feet in the air."

Digging in with great relish was George Cohon, president of McDonald's Canada. He ate every bit of his birdies, as did his McSon, and then passed a complimentary Chicken McNuggets' card to the Save-the-Quails lady. For a multifaceted magnate with a self-made $50 million, he sure seems like a regular guy, Barbie.

It was business at the same old stand for Peter Brown, two requisite shots of limelight a night. Except, dare I say it, he seemed "quietly responsible;" and compared to Bob Carter he was an unequivocal class act.

Carter, who was featured creature of the evening—his choice, not ours—brought the festivities to a new depth of mawkishness even for him. After pulling baguettes out of his pants, wreaking havoc with a bread knife right through Umberto's pink linen tableclothes, and serving the *salad verde* from a fresh new green garbage pail, he decided to take over the Master of Ceremonies' duties and wound up with ego on his face.

My dear, neither Black nor Decker could cut the tension. Three of us are getting together to send Sir John Lubbock's *Tact* off to the victim of the wages of macho (anonymously, of course).

Heard an aside as we were gathering our coats for the crisp night air, about Diane Hartwick, the crackerjack coquette with the clickety-click mind who is helping her mother Nan blast Powder Mountain into a Resorts Ltd. From two white-wool-panted, $600-Sweaters-by-Inga types, after glancing at Diane's smashing silk tunic and shiny chignon: "She's so confident she could try things on in the same dressing room as Joan Rivers, and not worry Joan would come away with new material."

Still full of champagne (Mr. Ronald McDonald decided our small band needed a break, okay?), we wearily rose at the crack of Race Day and flew to the top of the mountain by helicopter—there were so many whirlybirds thudding and flooding the morning air it looked like *Apocalypse Now*. That brash Billy Johnson—he is into Heavy Metal: gold—has manners you would not write home about. He speaks none of the official languages, it is all Downhill: he had the race "pretty much wired," having "nailed" the top part and "smoked" that last stretch. He would have been "real bummed" with anything other than a first-place finish. (Cute, though: a little Paul Newman with the baby blues when the mouth is closed.)

We said goodbye to Pod. People said wistfully he was "the last of the original Crazy Canucks." Not while Bob Carter is around!

Off to Jack and Natalie's little do for J.C. and Sophie. Alright—the dinner offered by Senator the Honourable Jack Austin, Minister of State for Social Development, and Mrs. Austin in honour of their majesties the King and the Queen of Spain.

The foreign press, 57 strong, and the usual pesky paparazzi added international flavour as the guests struggled through the glass-and-brass front doors of the Four Seasons lobby. I just hate that "Are you anybody?" look the paparazzi give each entry before the inevitable disdainful rejections. What should you say? Sorry, I'm not a queen?

As you know, Babs dear, being on time for the pre-dinner cocktails-at-a-walk is essential. It is almost the only time to play mix and match, because it is not considered cool to hop about once ensconced at a State dinner. You are in place from grace until the terminal toast.

The preprandial parade suggested a totally trimmed list; most faces reflected certainty they were in Societal Nirvana. Among the Excellencies, Honourables and Right Honourables were one Most Reverend (Archbishop Carney) and one Marchioness (of Mondejar) whom, if truth be told, Barbie, I must admit I missed.

But I did meet the King. The prime minister presented him around the room. He speaks very little English, but he does look right into your very soul when he is shaking your hand, which leaves your knees to do their own thing.

Very handsome. Tall—they are always tall in storybooks. The aquiline profile looks like the head on a coin, and he has all the right royal credentials: grandson of King Alfonso XIII and Queen Victoria Eugenia, who was the granddaughter of England's Queen Victoria; on his mother's side he is the first Bourbon king in 53 years.

And Sophia's no slouch while we are dropping them: eight kings of Denmark, seven czars of Russia, five kings of Sweden, five kings of Greece, two German emperors, one king and one queen of Norway and one queen of England. Also she dresses quite well—plain black top; long, green, shot-silk taffeta skirt; royal purple (what else?) sash—and her jewelry was no measly bag of agates. When she smiles she is quite the smasher. They look exactly like what a sovereign set of two _should_ look like.

Maurice Strong was one of the feasible few in the room who had met them before (in his U.N. days). As his sensational spouse Hanne (black and blonde always look so good) and I tried to set up a lunch, I demurred that I was in Hawaii or New York that week. She said that, yes, she had forgotten she was going to be in Brazil. She won.

Babbled on briefly with Carole Taylor and Art Phillips. I had just seen them in Whistler the previous week, and it was a toss-up which togs topped which. Last week it was sleek hair, black-leather pants, breath-taking red fox fur for her, jeans and bomber for him. This week it was tiny-curled halo, exquisite black and silver-sparkled floor-length sheath for her, the Marlboro man in a tux for him. Who says Vancouver has no royalty of its own?

Sam and Fran Belzberg sauntered in, Sam sensibly smug with a recent $85 million paper profit in his vest pocket, Fran sensibly chic as she again launched her red-and-black Mary McFadden from the Art Gallery Ball. There was a lot of launch-me-again fashion there that night, although Bill Bennett decided to try a tux for a change. Remember last year for _our_ queen it was business as usual? All extrava and no ganza, that man.

There were a couple of fashion *victima* gowns, and one punk hairdo, that of hair-dresser-to-the-smart-set, Derek London. I sure like what he did to the queen's locks better than what he did to his own.

At the all-frills dinner with white-glove service, John Gray told how his smash success, *Billy Bishop Goes To War*, really came about, and his quick-witted wife Beverlee *habla Espanoled* with the Excellency at our table. The only thing I could remember from my Guatemala days was, *Periodista! No dispare!* (Journalist! Don't Shoot!), which was not all that useful.

Trudeau's First-Brother-In-Law, Tom Walker, admitted he had never read the Margaret books, and then Trudeau himself, now flirting with the role of world-weary *philosophe*, got an incredible, prolonged ovation. (He told me once he preferred small meetings with no chairs, so the press *had* to say it was a standing ovation.)

Jack Austin's speech was a small, gleaming bit of brilliance. He had distilled the perfect few words, and with every reference to our Spanish connection—an explorer here, a Cardero Street there—the king's face lit up and the Spanish Conquest was complete to general huzzas (no, that is *not* one of the military contingent).

Ta Ta, Darling, and Hasta la vista,
Valerie.

BEIGING MR. PATTISON

Barbie Darling,

One can either go out there and live it or stay home and write it, and you yourself once noted that I would not miss the opening of a door. Here is a fast fill-in on a fabulous Vancouver summer, but as your aged aunt used to say, the only thing you should ever expect to get on a silver platter is tarnish.

Off to be *Drawn and Quartered* at Allan and Angie MacDougalls'. Cartoonist Roy Peterson, cut-up that he is, was launching his timely tome on the Trudeau years into orbit. Allan, of Stanton and MacDougall, and Angie, who needs no animating at all, provided the spruced-up Shaughnessy pad for the pod: yuppie to Old Guard to literary.

Squired *myself* up the circular driveway (I have reached my annual "If my kind of man doesn't exist, what kind of woman am I?" syndrome). After tripping over the lights/camera/action of the local media and muttering that Big Brother really is watching, I was greeted by white wine and Roy Peterson and immediately felt better.

With the elegantly cool Mrs. P. by his side, he takes all the time he needs to cast a calculating, comedic eye over the current scene. To him life is a videotape that needs editing.

Pia and Harvey in hot pink and black and newly crimped hair (her, not him, silly) were off to a football game, and even back then she was flirting with a return to the TV scene.

The Partons were there: Nicole, newly trimmed in red and white, Lorne in nothing notable but his—what else?—Parton shot. Pipe-smoking ponderer Ilya Gerol was surveying the scene for possible subversiveness.

The Larry-and-Sherry show, The Killams, floated about, she in a Junior League navy-silk frock (they are always frocks), he suit-ably serious, before heading off to the _de rigueur_ spates of summer at Hernando Island. Doesn't everyone?

Cindy and Steven Grauer, having well and truly altar-to-courted, did not acknowledge each other at all. As that bubble-headed friend of yours used to hum, dear heart, "There's a whole lotta litigation goin' on."

Heard the most marvellous anthropomorphic theory of partygoers as I wended my way out. "It's like a zoological park," said a nameless literary lion to the older man on his right. "There are the bears who are out there working the crowd for contacts, the giraffes who have come to rubberneck the VIPs, the leeches who go from party to party, the elephants who come just to gorge themselves. And then there are the deer. The deer are the beautiful people, racy and fast, always in the mainstream, out there cautiously gaining points and prestige."

Whoosh! And you thought life was a cabaret, old chum.

Arthur Erickson popped 'round for champagne brunch at the Orchid suite of the Mandarin Hotel. Mike Harcourt, deciding that it was time to honour the city's arch-architect, seized Arthur's 60th birthday to throw a small smash for a smattering of intimates. It was 90 minutes short, bittersweet—Arthur not being thrilled by his infinitesimal involvement with Expo—and poignant. He was hurrying off to Paris to receive an international award—the rest of the world knows what we have.

Two great lines, Barbie, one as I entered and one as I left. A woman in a yellow silk suit said to no one in particular as we were offered a first glass of champagne and orange juice, "I'd cut down on these occasions, except people might think I was dieting."

As the penthouse elevator doors closed on a fashion victim we had all noted, a voice behind me said with practiced restraint, "That dress is just not me. In fact, it's not anybody I'd care to know."

It is going to be an interesting world, Babs dear, after *everybody* has assertiveness training!

Then off to Hornby Island for the exquisite christening of Jan and Keith Sorensen's megabuck cliff-hanger domain. High in the tall timber overlooking Tribune Bay, the nearly completed chateau was the setting for the season's ultimate fete. (John and Valerie Laxton's summer blow-out in West Van was not to be sneezed at, but it is easier in town, where you do not have to transport every single thing to the site, right?)

Loads of lamb were cooking in a pit beside the one being dug for the Olympic-sized pool, and a 48-pound salmon was being decorated as 150 lucky souls arrived by boat, car ferry or private plane. Gordon Park, for one, flew in from the Park Ranch. Neighbours wandered over by foot, the high percentage of artists and potters making for a nostalgic fashion mix of 1960s redux.

Best-dressed award went to lawyer Tony Pantage's wife Diane, who wore the wild, white, off-the-shoulder number than each of us would have bought in San Francisco had we seen it first.

Loped off to Lana and lawyer Dick Underhill's Farewell to Fotheringham; he is capital-izing on Washington this fall. His 52nd birthday party was held on Bowen Island from noon to nirvana—well, until the last ferry.

Arrived coincidentally with Keith Spicer, still in seersucker leisure suit. How *does* he replace them? Where does he still *find* them?

Expo's Gail Flitton was solid and reassuring about how the Fair fares. Laverne Barnes sailed in with jaunty fedora and white deck pants on the boat of a New Zealander named Malcolm. Nancy Morrison arrived with Bruno Gerussi in the most flamboyantly flagrant Italian shirt (him, not her), which he proceeded to strip off, not for the usual gold-chain, hairy-chest baring, but because he had spilled red wine on it.

CKVU producer Emmanuelle Gattuso was all pink-and-flower printed. Her small straw chapeau made her look like a renegade from a Renoir.

The birthday boy himself ran around in a pair of flamenco-red shorts, holding his stomach in to the point of hyperventilation. Cursed with a happy childhood which inadequately prepared him for the grim realities of adult life, he wore an astronaut's hat, a tie labelled "Superjock" and a silly grin.

The blast had barely begun when Paul Manning, out of his dandiacal three-piecers and into rugby shorts and a Lacosta T-shirt, was seen hoving into view in a small, orange, inflatable dinghy being piloted by none other than one James Pattison.

Jimmy's new baby is the kind of yacht that puts luxury to shame. The 85-foot *M.V. Nova Springs* was standing idly by in the harbour while one deckhand and the unlikely duo putt-putted ashore.

Opulent, Barbie? The salon is so big you don't even notice the organ on which Jimmy played happily all the way over.

With the timing of a bumble bee, Pattison zapped each group momentarily before reboarding off into the sunset, but he left nonetheless a lasting impression:

Four shades of beige double-knit polyester—no, he does not shop with Spicer—plus beige shoes.

An undershirt shining through the beige.

Sunglasses atop a freckled, receding brow, only *one* diamond-studded Piaget watch (the other, a two-faced job that keeps Toronto Stock Exchange and Geneva-banking time, was in Victoria being repaired), and two gold-and-diamond rings.

Well, one person's chic is another's passe, and Jimmy has an image to keep up.

Speaking of image, the *only* place on Bowen is Hood Point, these weekend residents may pretend to be escaping Vancouver, but they import captive guests and have "quiet dinner parties" for "the neighbours." By owning a weekend place here, one may easily mix with expatriate neighbours unmeetable at home. One shares the common troubles of country living—transportation to and from, good help, contractors, *you* know—and racks up an interesting array of winter I.O.U. paybacks.

Peter Brown does not use his pad on the point that much, but his electric golf cart, which he drives to the tennis courts across from the Underhills', sets a nice tone with its Rolls-Royce grill.

As I turned back to look at the dwindling group on the deck, I lingered over the Foth: mugging continually, swatting one-liners everywhere, as subtle as a Hawaiian shirt. I realized how much we are going to miss him. Someone should warn the President.

Ta Ta, Darling,

Valerie

MANY A CAKE PATTED

Barbie Darling,

A mere Coles Notes-style *precis*. Still lacking in this mad whirl is a secretary to intercept phone calls, and a maid to chase dust balls.

Packed myself ever so politely into B.C. Place Stadium for the Celebration of Life. Nestled gratefully into some prime seating: center stage, only eight rows away. Proceeded over coffee—somehow "pizza with the Pope" seemed unseemly—to check out the papal people around me.

A row behind sat the soon to be great-late Vancouver Art Gallery Director Luke Rombout in jeans, blazer and great singing voice (national anthem); the beauteous blonde Maxine was all in bright blue and black. To their left sat the Tony Cavelti clan. "My parents would have loved this," murmured the jeweller-to-the-few.

UBC president George Pedersen and the elegant Mrs. P. glowed in anticipation, as did a hotbed of Socreds below them. Grace McCarthy in her new navy dress (that's three times now, Grace) and Mr. Mac, the John Reynoldses, the Stephen Rogerses, the ever-tanned Garde Gardoms, a natty Nathan Nemetz, a proud and beaming Mike Harcourt (Vander Zalm's Abbotsford triumph forgiven?), and a too-late-for-his-speech Lieutenant-Governor Bob Rogers.

As all the players climbed over each other and Davey Barrett to be seated, I was reminded of your uncle's remark: "No two issues are so far apart that a politician can't straddle them."

Two otherwise dissimilar players, Chuck Connaghan and Senator Ed Lawson, continue to insist on resembling each other. Hydro's Bob Bonner and ex-Coal's Ron Basford brought a little fire and brimstone to the scene, but Ron won "Most Likely to Recede."

Heads turned like book pages gilt-edged by waves of gold-and-white flags as the pontiff's pickup nosed into view for the Holy See. That tiny white *zuchetto* (his beanie, Barbie) circled the scene until his marvellous, famous face came within mere feet.

"He looked right at me," I heard over to my left, echoed at least 20 times by others certain they had been singled out. The JP2 licence plate reminded me that JP in this town has always been hairdresser to the chic-set, John Paul Holt of Avantgarde.

Verily I say unto you, Barbie, *never* has the *Ode to Joy* been sung with more feeling. The palpable pulse of the place carried us out into the warm night through those windy air-locks on a current of pure peace.

Traipsed off to the tribute dinner for Senator Jack Austin at the Four Seasons Hotel ballroom. Full of old faithfuls, fund-raising fixtures and close, close personal friends of.

All the talent and ego jostling for attention made seating arrangements a challenge. One found a Jimmy Pattison, in a houndstooth jacket that could jam radar, across the table from an Art Kube—awkward combo, _n'est-ce pas?_ We were not talking networking.

Jimmy cornered the floating photographer to take his picutre with the Honourable Jack while Kube hunched quietly smoking in his chair. He does that a lot.

The Peter Hyndmans swept in from a Whistler weekend, he in a great new hunkophile haircut, she in ivory satin and sorority smile. Paul Manning bounced about; electoral defeat is not new to him. I watched him charm his way around the room, unctuous enough to go one-on-one with an offshore oil slick.

The one, the only, Iona Campagnolo in claret velvet with purple-and-green-senquin shoulder accents is obviously sticking with her party through _thin_, too.

Sam and Fran Belzberg swept athletically into the room, he tanned and tennis-slender, she in a jade-green suede shift belted in black snakeskin. The Marquise de Suede huddled with Liz Nichol in jade-green jacquard silk (guess what was the hot colour that night?). Serene Senator John smiled on.

Jack Poole looked lean and busy; you had better believe _his_ business will pick up under the Tories. Darlene Young, in black off-the-shoulder taffeta and pearls, looked, well...young. Mayor Mike shook an inordinate number of hands, while wife Beckie, who wore her beige fur to the table (they had rushed in from another function) smiled benevolently.

Laurence Jolivet in perfect pinstriped yawned discreetly and uh-hummed his way through whole slices of the evening. Joel Bell, spontaneous in a carefully chiseled way, always allows his listeners a little butting-in time. He has been programmed to do that. May Brown, in a high-necked, rather Victorian Librarian black-and-red striped dress, obviously remembered that "before 6:30 and after 45 one should never show and inch of skin."

Token Tory Gowan Guest, who helped Ron Longstaffe organize the night, seemed not at all threatened among the predominantly Liberal horde. Just back from Bermuda, he mentioned that he had chatted there with the John Turners. Guest is a very secure man.

Bill Bennett and Peter Newman could not make it, so they sent witty telegrams. Well, Peter's was.

An older man off to my left allowed to no one in particular that he "did not like mucked-up foreign food," but he quite happily lit into the Canada Place Breast of Capon in Wild Senatorial Sauce. It was served with Privy Council Potatoes, and we started with Trudeau Vegetable Terrine. Get the picture, Barbie? These were political junkies being fed here.

The "Let them eat cake" cake was called Quadra Tart Slice.

Jack's wife Natalie looked nostalgically romantic in a beige-lace, three-tiered, 1930 sheath, the sleeves banded in an auburn fur that was close in colour to her own fluffy curls, and a smashing antique pearl and emerald necklace.

Jack was *so* pleased. It is amazing how you can spoon-feed flattery to a grown man. As one wag pointed out, the evening could not help but be Austintatious, and it was by no means a roast. The man was wrapped instead in puff pastry by a lot of grateful friends.

The following week Oscar popped around. De La Renta, dear heart. He flew in from Frisco and we limoed to the VanDusen Gardens in the same sky-blue stretch job that Sean Connery had used to shoot a James Bond commercial in Whistler two days before. And me in a discontinued line (an outfit I will never wear again). And *not* his perfume.

Worse still, my perfume must have leaked out of its seal and turned, because there was no denying the resemblance to rust remover. His assistant inside the limo asked what scent I was wearing, and when I offered the very good French name, she said through clenched teeth, "It's a little spicier than I remember."

Quel shame. It was to die, Darling.

As he lead me down the garden path towards the *aesculus hippocastanum* (horse chestnut to you, Barbie), I asked him where's home? "New York and an airport."

A friend who had seen it (the New York apartment, silly) says it is plush velvets, brocades, very fine paintings—he was trained as an artist in Madrid and he definitely knows what he likes.

He has a gentleman's farm in Connecticut where he keeps two pedigreed spaniels, imaginatively named Pauline and Alice, and grows flowers. He *loves* flowers. He has a home outside his native Santo Domingo, a touch-base in Madrid and a Paris apartment.

He stutters slightly and endearingly. His amber skin glows with health and Santo Domingo sun. He looks aristocratic, although I thought the way he worked all day at a rose thorn in his thumb was a little unswish.

He has great chocolate-drop eyes, porcelain teeth, baby fuzz for hair (you want to touch). In highly polished tasseled loafers he keeps very large feet. (I had insisted in the limo they must be size 13, but he took one shoe off to show me a 10. Must be a foreign measurement.)

He wears no jewelry, not even cuff links. He wears his own suits—I mean the ones _he_ designs, navy pinstripe that day.

His manner is somewhat Spanish grandee, similar to Juan Carlos. The King of Spain. Remember dinner last spring? Oh, Barbie, _do_ try to pay attention.

He made his name designing opulent, extravagant, fairy-tale gowns for the very rich, but lest one get carried away by the romance, I _do_ remember on my last trip to New York reading a floor-to-ceiling list of Oscar de la Renta companies etched on a silver plaque in his Seventh Avenue showroom. And I heard somewhere that this year's sales figures are more than 3, less than 5 (hundred million, dear heart).

As we climbed back into the limo—the driver's white gloves on the door handle left _no_ finger marks—Oscar noted that he still had two functions and a champagne cocktail party before Nordstrom's sent their corporate jet to take him to Seattle that night. And just when things were getting interesting...

Ta Ta, Darling, and Adios, Oscar,

Valerie.

THE YEAR 1985

THE GLOVES ARE OFF
From mansion-warming to moon-walking with Michael.

SEASON'S DOINGS IN PARIS AND LONDON
Euro-trashing at the top.

POLITICS AND POLITESSE
The right dinner, talk and people.

OF DISHES AND RAGS
Hearts throbbed for Michael York, and society mobbed for Jesse Jackson.

THE YEAR 1985

*T*his was the 52-weeker the big real estate blast hit the city. The all-time record for monthly sales volume hit an off-the-charts $195 mill. Of course, to those of us who care about such things, residence switcheroos are the sweetest little gauge as to what's really shakin'. Who's been dumped, divorced, defrocked, disbarred, disgraced, married or multiplied. Society is understandably fluid, but this year was a head-spinner. Arrivistes and old Establisheds divied up domains like there was no tomorrow.

Along that line, local boy makes good, Michael J. Fox did boffo box-office with Back to the Future, and that twinkling golf ball that was to become a city landmark, the Expo Centre, teed off, all 17 stories of it for 7000 first-nighters.

There is no better place to spot the pecking order than at a smallish, ever-so-swish, very high-toned dinner party at one of the city's lushest mansions. And we slipped into one of our faves, between clashes with very affected culture vultures at the Vancouver Art Gallery, and the freaked-out fans who crowded B.C. Place for a Michael Jackson concert.

I winged off to the continent for a London-Paris update, slid back into town for a dressy do with that other Jackson, Jesse, (who was flirting with a presidential nomination at the time), and in between, managed to get to an awards show at the then-so-chaud CKVU, had dinner at Spago in L.A., got to the ground-breaking Women of Distinction Awards, and sipped drinky-poos with long-time Lothario Michael York at the Vancouver Film Festival.

THE GLOVES ARE OFF

Barbie Darling,

Do you have any idea how dashedly difficult it is knitting together all the threads of tittle-tattle to form a coherent social fabric? Good. I knew you would.

Shimmied off to the Segals for the most sublime Hollywood-in-the-Thirties dinner party at Rio Vista, Joe and Rosalie's castle-on-the-Fraser.

Parked the BMW between two Rolls-Royces, while a Jaguar watched with total uninterest. Slipped the maid what until *that* night was my favorite pelt. Refused to be intimidated by the Great Hall—I have been to the Gritti Palace, for heaven's sake, *and* Versailles; I have seen a Hapsburg chandelier before. Eased my way into the *Gentleman's Quarterly* scene in the salon. Smoked salmon and caviar were floating around on silver trays while two of the hunkiest, black-tied butlers dished drinky-poos. (I recognized the duo from other splashy bashes; one cannot expect the household staff to muck about with the masses.)

High-rolling investment wizards like Edgar Kaiser and Bob Lee talked to lesser excessive successes. Rubin Stahl, developer of that mall of malls, the West Edmonton (or doesn't $70 million for a string of stores impress you?), was talking collateral and consortiums; Bill Saywell, president of Simon Fraser University, listened with glazed-over eyes as he flirted with applying those principles to *his* shop.

Mrs. Stahl, a beauteous blonde in drop-dead razzle-dazzle sequins and designer glasses, obviously equates "ordinary" with some kind of skin disease.

She was la-de-dah-ing it over on a smart little two-seater settee with a lady I called Cookies and Milk (of *course* to myself). Dealing with her was a bit like being hit over the head with a valentine. Her only flair, as your aunt used to say, was in her nostrils.

There was no need to carry a jeweler's loupe in one's beaded bag that night: all the chic little *bijoux* at collar, cuff and ear were quite real. Rosalie led us to table in a pastel sequined top, perfect pale peach pants, gold kid shoes, the *cutest* amethyst/diamond necklace, earrings, bracelet, ring and the dearest pear-shaped diamond you and Liz Taylor ever. Some princess somewhere is missing a ransom.

The dinning room, paneled in antiqued Honduras mahogany, was ablaze with candles, silver, crystal: the usual castle chattels. The table swallowed up four fresh-flower table centers before we cozied down—all 18 of us. "Ro," as Joe calls her, prefers 16 tops, but graciously made do. I did not notice any crowding myself, but...

Dinner conversation was lively, though discreet. This was a room peopled with face-savers, not soul-barers, so one hardly expects deep-dish dirt.

We toasted our hostess in champagne, the last of the five, frequently filled goblets before each place card, and retired to a drawing room that was picture-perfect. Where is *Town and Country* when you need them?

Pleased to be bit players on such a hopelessly opulent set, we mingled mellow and content until Joe, as he began showing a small group of us some of his favorite *objets*, fell into what turned out to be le *grand tour de la maison.*

Booze profits from Prohibition days built the house for Harry Reifel, but I have the feeling that these perfectly preserved porticos and regal staircase were just waiting for Joe and Ro.

Each priceless Chinese screen, each one-of-a-kind porcelain urn, each antique clock was lovingly recounted by Joe. There is a whole room just for the silver not out being used. How many Paul Storr wine coolers and silver strawberry dishes can you use at one time, *mia cara?*

To give you a hint of this collection's magnitude, I noticed last week that a pair of Paul (The Last of the Silversmiths) Storr wine coolers, *circa* 1829, sold at Christies for a cool $100,000.

There are 10 fireplaces and 11 bathrooms. Rosalie's, just off a walk-in closet Holt's should see, is sunken and silver.

The master-bedroom bed, the size of an aircraft carrier, has flanking phones, perhaps for communication. On one side is a well-worn copy of *Grits*, on the other is *First Among Equals*. One wonders who reads which?

The master-bedroom *den* (doesn't everyone have one?) is sunken. Its small, built-in refrigerator (you don't?) is stocked with Beluga Caviar. Our modest host says with a twinkle he got a deal on the caviar, so we can rest easy.

There is a ground-level ballroom which once accommodated 120 for a Children's Hospital sit-down benefit. A full-sized tavern. An antique billiard table, the surrounding walls covered in suede, *à la* Arthur Erickson, and wool tartan—for the McSegal clan?

Behind the three, arched, stained-glass doors is a wine cellar worth a separate tour. "What's that jeroboam of Dom doing here?" the tour master asked in mock horror. "I distinctly told Martha to serve that, it's ready!"

Did I mention the complete health spa, the darkroom, the 20-by-40-foot, Last-Days-of-Pompeii indoor pool and the library with its secret wall panel concealing a walk-in toy room for the grandchildren? How about the Italian waterfall outside, the tranquility ponds, the night-lit gardens with trees trained into various animal shapes by Joe himself?

(I ask you, if you purchased most of your showcase silver from the Duke of St. Alban's collection and sold the too-large candelabra to the late Shah of Iran for $250,000, wouldn't you just die if someone said you had chosen the same Fortuny of Venice wallpaper that Margaret Trudeau had put in the dining room at 24 Sussex Drive and Maureen McTeer had taken off? Well, I *didn't* tell, Barbie. Honest!)

I barely had a chance to check out Lily Lee's black-striped silk chemise and her new pearl-and-diamond birthday ring before it was the witching hour and time to face the real world outside. Joe brought me the most beautiful double-headed white orchid from the conservatory, so a little Hollywood made it out of there that night.

To the ridiculous. "The President and Board of Trustees of the Vancouver Art Gallery request the pleasure of your company to celebrate the first anniversary of the new gallery." All well and good, my dear, but no one was there. They let just anybody in, and worse, they came!

It was pouring buckets out, I did not really want to go, and just walking in one knew these were the kind of people who put ketchup on their sushi. Who if they wear designer fashions cut the labels out to avoid seeming affected.

Otherwise there was one architect, Bruno Freschi; he did not look happy. One writer from the *New Yorker*, Edith Iglauer, who is a friend of Jack Shadbolt and wrote the book on Arthur Erickson. Lauch Farris, president of Fargo Oil Corporation, who came without the gorgeous Diane, was leaving as I was arriving. Hard to fool oilmen, Barbie; he knew this gusher was not going to get off the ground.

Besides the usual leftover 1960s' crunchy granolas in tie-dyed, hand-painted velvets or pottery beads by Belinda, no one, as I say, was there. Oh, Fran Belzberg was. In her tux. Again.

To the ultimate in ridiculous. Crammed myself into my Spandex pants, black leather jacket and thigh-high boots to trot off to Michael Jackson's opening night. When I saw what I looked like I changed.

The ultimate P.R. lady Dale Mearns was just back from Southeast Asia, looking very tanned in a sort of wide-shouldered Mongolian shepherd's coat. Herb Capozzi was saying he would not have missed it for the world. The Preem was concoursing it (election coming up!). Odd to watch a grown man trying to moonwalk in tie and dark business suit.

Michael Cytrynbaum was there with his wife and *kinder*. I hear his old boss, First City, financed the Eastern part of the Jackson tour: strange bedfellows, what?

A pipe-smoking Ron Longstaffe and his delighted six-year-old daughter Brandy watched from a private box as Rock's reigner did his thing on stage. If that pelvic thrust is shy, deliver me, my dear.

He has a nose bob your Auntie Beth would kill for and does his makeup better than she. Should lengthen his pants a little; I know a tailor who could help. Needs a shave: probably just flashing that he can too grow hair on his face. Very nice teeth. Harry Rosen would *not* approve of those socks. Something more conservative in an executive length, perhaps?

I lost one of my black leather gloves at some point. Unfortunately everyone else wore only one. As we filed out shoulder to shoulder, I felt so common.

As for His Hotness Mr. Jackson, can anyone who loves Disney World and owns his own jeweled scepter be on the wrong track? He is small, scrappy, lives in a Hollywood-style dream home, loves flashy jewels and toys and earns millions. Joe Segal would love him.

Ta Ta, Darling, it's been Thrilling,

Valerie

SEASON'S DOINGS IN PARIS AND LONDON

Barbie Darling,

Positively *flew* off to Paris for New Year's Eve, but plane schedules being what they are, found myself somewhere over the North Pole at the Witching Hour. What a way to launch the Nouveau Yeareau, *non?*

During the briefest little plane change at Heathrow, a strange, six-foot apparition leaving the book store ahead of me was apparently Boy George. Bundled like a bag lady swaddled in scarves, white wooly cap, coat—with a skirt peeking out?—black wool pants and carrying its own two canvas bags, it was apparently waddling on its way to Jamaica.

And, said the book-store lady smugly, you *just* missed Walter Matthau, who had a full black beard, a trench coat and a yellow Olin ski cap, flaps up, that made him look quite like a mad Russian.

The George Cinq was full, sank' eaven, because my little *pied* on the Left Bank left me with enough *monnaie* to hit the couturier sales.

As you know, dear heart, profound, bred-in-the-bone superficiality is my thing; the view from my second-story balcony was such a Hemingway Moveable Feast that it was hard not to just stay in and spy.

Gendarmes two-by-two with caps like open soup cans, the lids still attached, carried baguettes under their arms as long as their rifles. (the prime minister was in residence or in office or whatever in a rather grand-looking _palais_ at the cross street).

Brisk-walking mademoiselles wore their Hermès bags slung diagonally (beware le pickpocket). Movie-star handsome young men wore knee-length cashmere coats muffled with bright designer scarves, the label _always_ showing—Christian Dior should be paid by the National Health for preventing the nation's sniffles.

Off for a late supper in the Latin Quarter with friends from Oxford, me a little subdued by the platefuls of student presumption, given my French and their intellect.

The oysters gave Binky's a run for it, but the rest of the meal could be duplicated at Le Pavillon in our own Four Seasons. The waiter, black-tied and a Robert Redford miniature, continually let us know that _anything_ was preferable to waiting on the dreaded _Anglaise_.

After, our car, as small, chic and unaccomodating as the waiter, refused to start in one of the coldest nights since the 1950s. At least it was still on the sidewalk where we had left it; the streets are too narrow to drive, let alone park.

To the Louvre (I am not ashamed to be a tourist, Barbie; I just never flash a camera, and walk as though I have some highly personal mission) and then it was only a short walk to the Louvre des Antiquitaries: three whole floors of small antique shops with outrageous prices. It was here I saw my first Arabian Express card.

Found myself in the vicinity of Maxim's, Pierre Cardin's new little _bijoux_ on the Rue Royale, a few steps from the Place de la Concorde. The other Pierre, Maxim's smiling doorman, was on the street in his smart braided cap and gold-buttoned coat, but lacking a reservation, and Parisian condescension being what it is, I kept walking.

Besides, Roger Viard, the maitre d', knows each of the restaurant's 1,600 most faithful habitués by name, and from my one previous visit would not know mine; I would probably have been seated in the very _outré_ grande salon, which may just as well be in the flower shop next door.

By the by, Barbie, Jackie Onassis was often seated at the same Maxim's table her husband and Maria Callas were given mere days before. The waiters call this "une petite blague"—a little joke.

Invited to have a kir royale for old times' sake at the Ritz Bar, where Coco Chanel cocooned, and Hemingway drank, and Wallis Simpson was courted by a king, but the Paris fashion sales were on, those once-a-year, 75-percent-off bargains. _That_ is how the shop girls dress so well and look so _courant_.

At Gucci there was an out-the-door-and-up-the-block line-up of men and women, a few with tots in trendy training. Momentarily considered picking up some shoes for Peter (Brown, of course), but by now he must have 80-odd pair for his extra-wide little feet. Heaven only knows where he gets his hats fitted!

Slinked off to Sulka's *Solde Monstre* (Big Sale), but not for the famous men's silk pajamas (could not remember anybody I liked $400 worth), nor the silk shirts and ties. I just enjoyed watching the handsome hunks who shopped there.

Did Guy Laroche's crowded mini-*magasin*, staffed by sour-faced shop women who were obviously baronesses and marquises in real life, and were there to *serve* you only by mistake. And Valentino's, where at least one Vancouver senator's wife I know got her red silk shirt with the little Vs all over it. And Galeries Lafayette, where acres of the most incredible French-lace lingerie supply every femme-fatale fantasy one might wish to play out.

To Au Pied de Cochon for lunch. Touristy but *fameux*, and close to the Beaubourge's Georges Pompidou Center, where I had gone to see a Miro exhibit. The waiter—older, twinkly—never stepped out of character: part comedian, part philosopher.

It is a funny thing about the French. They really do not care what you say, it is how you say it.

Ask for "moutard," they will say, "Non, Non Dijon."

Have a bill split "Demie/Demie," and they insist it is, "Moitie/Moitie," like half-and-half milk.

Ask them something they do not know, and they get furious at you for asking.

As I left, this overheard comment in the stairwell from two Englishmen: "That food was so incredibly good, old chap, I'm surprised the church hasn't gotten to it!"

Paris in the coldest winter since whenever: people passing 10 abreast on the wide Champs Élysées sidewalk.

Sainte-Chappelle, the tiny Gothic chapel hidden away in the law courts, the sun shining through its stained glass and *almost* taking away the breath of two Texans: "Boy," they whistled through their teeth, "these Frenchies shore do windows!"

Less Halles, the old covered market that is coming to life again but still flashes ads in the windows for "sweet girls."

The Quays, rows of gray wooden stalls all boarded up: no booksellers, painters, strollers, just the icy Seine looking on, waiting for a little spring warmth.

The Tuileries Gardens flowerless, deserted except for the inevitable lovers (it really *is* their city), strangely exciting in the postcard-cliché twilight haze.

I remember, after my very first trip to Paris, a dinner party in Ottawa, just before Jules Léger was made Governor-General. He had loved his former posting to Paris, and I told him how "his" city had affected me.

"Well," he said, in his tolerant, measured way, "we have had centuries to define and redefine."

Off to Jolly Old by Hovercraft. Never tried that before. Never will again. I do not have anything against two-meter-high waves in their place, as long as that place is not under me. All I could think of—besides keeping my last marvelous Cafe Muniche lunch down—was how many bodies must be at the bottom of that English Channel after centuries of shipwrecks and wars.

Weekending in the deepest English countryside lacks the snob appeal of _le weekend_ across the Channel. Under Louis XIV, Versailles was one long weekend. He did not want his guests to go to their own country houses for fear they would plot against him. The French, consummate snobs, continue the practice by heading every Friday to the Seine-et-Oise area near Louis's place; being seen in Paris on the weekend is a social kiss of death.

The Brits, on the other hand, do not go to the country to be chic; they tend to _live_ there. They pretend their miserable work days in the city never really take place, that this country-squire stuff is reality. They get themselves invited round for a spot of port—and inordinate amounts of gin—and stand around informally rosy-cheeked and terribly tweedy, talking about shooting, hunting and (interminably) dogs. And about port.

At the end of one Sunday marathon, my first and I hope my last, I had learned what the last days of the last Raj in Sarawak had been like from his son. And exactly how naughty British-gossip guru Nigel Dempster had been as a small schoolboy from the man who had taught him. (Very). And that the reason English countrywomen appear so calm and warm when _your_ chattering teeth may never again be still is because under that silk shirt or single sweater they wear wooly vests and tights.

Everything in the country is covered with dog hair, so you better learn to like it or tough biscuits and goodbye. And one must participate in how frightfully horrid the weather has been.

God knows what the landless gentry are left to do with their weekends. Do they get away with calling the little woman a "silly old moo?"—affectionately, of course.

However, it positively dropped into my lap that Vancouver's Dick Sandwell is one of the newest members of the esteemed Royal Yacht Squadron. Stockholm's Royal Swedish Yacht Club also counts him in, and L.A.'s Transpacific Yacht Club. A knighthood next? Sir Percy Ritchie Sandwell does not sound half-bad.

So sorry you had bogged off to Botswana or wherever, Barbie dear, but I soldiered on to London anyway.

Had planned on *pied a mer*-ing it aboard a 50-foot ketch at St. Katharine's Dock in the Pool of London, but the *Lord Gulliver*, as beautiful as it was, nestled in the Thames across from Antarctic explorer Scott's *Discovery*, had frozen water lines. So it was the Tower or no shower. (The Tower *Hotel*, silly. The Tower of London's been *done*; besides, it's so grim!)

Cabbed it off to Knightsbridge just down from a chichi little flat called home in the ever-so-old student days. Mr. Chow's was its usual late-night elegant. All shiny black and mirrored, filled with sprays of pink and white orchids, incongruous Italian waiters (the cuisine is gourmet Chinese) and Sugar Daddy/daughter duos in corners "canoodling," as the English call smooching.

Half of upper-class twitdom was there, too—so Monty Python I almost forgot the Peking Duck.

"Did you know that the divorce rate among dukes is 30 percent higher than the rest of the nation?" I heard behind me.

"Yes, it's the dry rot that does them in—the damp and the drafts. In the country homes. Young girls from London just can't take the endless struggle, you know, and so they leave."

Moved out of the Tower the following morning into a friend's posh Caroline Terrace town house and proceeded to Harrods for The Sale. Europe's largest department store (214 departments) racked up £4.2 million just the first day. Fought through the Middle Eastern interests who were harvesting everything in sight and up to one of the 4,000 staff, a large lady in a black military suit and horn-rimmed glasses. When I asked the price of a beaded sweater, she reacted as if I had requested the precise date on which she had last kicked the queen's corgis.

Did Marks and Sparks, too. Full of elderly Arabian ladies in black burnooses with only their eyes showing, snaffling up lacy scanties for the young women back in the harems.

To Marc Chagall's stunning show at the Royal Academy. People went into private reveries, but I was following two lovely old souls in tea-cosy wool hats. They seemed just ahead of me at each new painting, and I picked up such a lot on the royals.

Cannot vouch for the accuracy, but for what it is worth: "Princess Meg does seem to have gone through a bad patch with her lung and all. Sixty ciggies and two quarts of spirits a day will do that, you know. So nice of the children to drop 'round to Brompton Hospital to see her. Funny how Viscount Linley looks like 'er and Lady Sarah looks like 'im. H.M. the Q. should've let'er marry Townsend. Never would've gone off to Mustique with Roddy Llewellyn then. And Anne and Di not talking and all. Poor Queen has 'er 'ands full wif'em!"

To Michaeljohn's in Mayfair for a quick hairdo and the very latest as to who is in town. Sophia Loren and her old flame Dr. Etienne Baulieu were rendezvousing; does Carlo know? Peter O'Toole was seen at Heathrow seeing off his wife Karen and his two-year-old son, but the pair are reconciling (have not seen him since Puerto Vallarta).

Margaret Thatcher sold her Chelsea house for £400,000, certainly more than the £28,000 she paid. And the Sultan of Brunei has bought the Dorchester for £50 million, though it has never been the same since the Liz-and-Dick days.

(And I thought Bryan Adams posters everywhere for his London concert was news. And that Vic Chapman, once with Trudeau and now press secretary to the Queen, lasting through Princess Di's frequent staff firings was hot!)

To Brown's Hotel for very proper, very Victorian tea. Cathy Jenkins, a Vancouver architect working here now, popped in for cucumber sandwiches and a spot of. She says several Vancouverites, including Dougie Gordon, _always_ stay at Brown's, tra-la.

While doing the scones with Devon cream, I recognized an old friend from Toronto in an alcove across the way. He waved rather tentatively, and soon rose to leave with a lovely blonde creature definitely not Mr. Friend's wife (herself a lovely blonde creature). They exited wordlessly past our table, eyes fixed ahead as though their skulls were attached to ceiling strings. I thought no more about it. What could be more innocent than afternoon tea!

However, Cathy Jenkins had a view of the lobby and reported, "Your friend has been pacing up and down for the last 15 minutes."

Next he appears over my shoulder, babbling incoherently: What am I doing in London? Because what he is doing in London is buying some very fine wine, which with the devalued pound will practically pay for his trip in savings, and where do I live now? Not in Toronto, he guesses, and how often do I manage to get Back East anyhow?

Good heavens, he seemed pleased that I live in distant Vancouver. It was just tea, wasn't it?

A totally smashing last night in London, courtesy of a bright and kindly young stockbroker (for Richardson Greenshields), whose three-year-old son is already registered in that Rolls-Royce of public schools, Eton.

To one of the great inns, The Stafford, its bar terribly twee and filled with people of that ilk. Did you know, Babs dear, that there really is a Sir Iain Moncreiffe of the Ilk? The last part of his name is The McGillycuddy of the Reeks. But his friends call him Sir. Well, it beats Sir Gregor MacGregor of MacGregor or Princess Petronella Farman-Farmian.

But back to the Stafford bar. Tony, and very nautical—flags and caps and American accents. Wealthy Americans pick their English experiences very carefully.

To Le Caprice for dinner. La Pretence, as it is also known, is billed as a haven for anyone who had outgrown Langan's across the street. (So what does Michael Caine know? I saw him there *last* time, anyway.)

To the Casino at the Ritz—Private Members Only—which was flowing with high-rolling Arabs, and Japanese in Italian and French couture. Only the "ordinary rich" were playing that night. Such legendary plungers as Adnan Kashoggi and Gunther Sachs have moved on—Scotland Yard can be *so* touchy. Lord "Lucky" Lucan is still missing.

While winging about saw several renegades from the Sloane Rangers, insufferable Young Upwardly Mobilers who take their name from fashionable Sloan Square. Effortless rightness is their watchword, and you spot them by the green wellies (rubber boots), the crumpled Barbour (waterproof jacket worn for "the shoot" or riding in the country), "the crucial pearls," the burgundy cashmere sweater from the Harrods sale, and the Bally low-heeled black patent pumps.

The Rangers' name for Harrods is Rods. Bell's is Annabel's. Fred's is Fortnum and Mason. Fast black is a London cab. Taking the Woller for fodder is driving the Rolls to dinner. If you get a stiffy imploring you, "Come *do*, because *actually* it will be good fun," you have probably just received an engraved invitation to a fête worse than death at a "cottage in the country" (four-or-more-bedroomed, detached house in the Green Belt outside London, to which you bring your green wellies and Barbour, in case you tie one on and must play away (stay the weekend). Gag me, *do*.

On to Annabel's, after 21 years still *the* late-night, after-hours club. I remember being here in the late 1960s, watching Trendy Trudeau, as the Brits called him then, dancing with a young blonde named Felicity Cochrane in crocheted mini-dress.

It is in an 18th century house on Berkeley Square, filled with mirrors, candlelight, good paintings and great cartoons, packed with Lord Rights, wealthy Almost Acceptables with old Etonian or Harovian credentials. POWs (Princess of Wales look-alikes), the odd MP, and I do mean odd.

Also the Noovoos, as the English call them, and those of the Ancien Riche who are still players. Suave commodity dealers wear "the uniform:" Jaegar blazer and trousers, Turnbull and Asser shirt, Hermès tie, Gucci belt and loafers, a Ferrari watch and a Cartier cigarette case for lighting the ciggies of brand-name heiresses.

Mabel in the Ladies' is a font of info, and one hears it is best to stay on her good side. While we were chatting up Mabel, a large lady in a 30-year-old, impeccable Chanel suit sailed past us like a giant powder puff, and said to the mirror, "I did try to get the Annabel's membership in the divorce, and now I shall have to rely on the largesse of others."

A long, last lovely lunch at Claridge's with James Clavell's lawyer. He is worldly and terribly British and wears red-striped suspenders under a Bond Street pinstripe. Totally charming, knows everyone, but so dashedly discreet!

As the top-hatted doorman put me in my cab for the airport, and we roared past Grosvenor Square (Don Jamieson has a new gray limo), I felt like I had taken the High Life and Scandal Tour, but it was positively wizard, old bean. An absolute corker!

Ta Ta, Darling, and a Bientôt,
Valerie

POLITICS AND POLITESSE

Barbie Darling,

Chop-chopped off to din-din with the Jean Chretiens and a whole cadre of Chretien well-wishers at the arch little Ambleside Inn. Keepers Willy and Martha were hosts last year to Juan Carlos and Sophia, and a very-pleased-with-his-fish-dish Jimmeh Carter. Of _course_ on separate occasions, Barbie: what would the King and Queen of Spain talk to a peanut farmer about?

Aline Chretien was in the very short, very chic hairstyle that became her no-nonsense trademark during the leadership campaign, and a _très expensif,_ très safe, white wool suit. She is as down-to-earth as in the early Ottawa days, happy to talk of the joys of being a young grandmother: daughter France married a Power Corp. Desmarais. As for the feisty little guy from Shawinigan who almost became prime minister, he is writing a book about his trials and triumphs—in English, yet!

Linda and Ross Fitzpatrick popped round. The president of Westmount Resources is becoming more John Forsythe every day with his silver thatch and courtly ways. Linda's lean good looks lend themselves to those little couturier numbers she picks up in jaunts to Europe—three trips this year already, or is it four?

Lots of Dow Jones and Dow Janes: the business community does like to keep its political options open. A lawyer or two, including the everywhere-you-look Frank Murphy and also new Q.C. Walley Lightbody, a barrister jazz musician as cool with Basie as he is at the bar.

Your basic Browns, Ralph and Brenda, had their Hawaiian tans topped up with a weekend or two at Whistler, her waist whittled with the newfound joys of weight lifting.

Our front-running Love-to-hate-her was there, Barbie. She was smiling with almost all her own teeth—well, two caps and a small bridge flashing, nose job aloft, silk shoulders padded high. She still puts "sort of" before everything and "ish" after. She gives new acquaintances a card with only her business address!

Slithered off to Kitsilano, s small, artsy dinner party full of designer-water quiche-eaters.

My host, fresh from his fitness class, whisked me first into the living room, where I found Expo (Special Events coordinator Margaret Steley) talking to Ballet (promoter David Y.H. Lui) over oyster paté (Susan Mendelson). Then into the kitchen, where my hostess, just back from the Granville Island Market, was preparing pasta primavera—so Manhattan *nouvello cuisine*.

Playwright John Gray and his wife Beverlee slouched in even later than I did—I do so hate being the penultimate *anything*!—so there was a merry group of clever minds and motor mouths just chomping at bits about Sherman Snukal's new play, Walter Learning, and the lack of ballet. The hostess, whom I long have labeled the Ironic Woman, got off some of the best lines, and I myself learned a new word for phony glamor: "Bullchic."

Clicked into the CKVU Awards Night in my highest rhinestone sandals. I find that my feet killing me helps my eyelids deny boredom and stay where they should. The *Sun*'s Nicholas Read's poignant "Please God, not another awards show" went totally unheeded by the folks at M-I-C-K-V-U, as the revolving door's mousketeers have dubbed chaos city.

The first and threatened to be annual awards show was a punishing, fanny-numbing two hours. This is not a station famous for having a sense of humor about itself, and the pompous ceremonies were trite and true.

"Night of A Hundred Egomaniacs" started with limos and black tie; true, Umberto did wear a white dinner jacket and parked his own lipstick-red Ferrari, but he has always marched to a different piccolo. Laurier, who fawns better than Bambi, greeted guests with a Klieg-light smile and told each and every one how *mah*velous they looked.

Lois Milsom, who has been everywhere several times, was just back from Sikkim. She hugs on spec anything that moves, and bravely fought off a vacant look as she tried to remember where she last met the huggee. Also mahvelous in a slim, long, black skirt, sequined blouson top and silver tourmaline necklace, she greeted the glory children of the moment as they filtered into the studio in full Kabuki makeup.

"Darling, you haven't changed a bit."

"Thank you."

"Why?"

The exchange above was between a paste-jeweled, floor-length, lemon-chiffon number and a redhead in a belted "big dress" which turned her into two sausage links.

"I don't drink wine during the day, not even a little. Otherwise the rest of the day is an apology," said a mustachioed French hairdresser to a cameraman as they swished into the Green Room.

Overheard in the powder room, from a creature with lips outlined in black and sinister objects dangling from eight holes in her ears: "She's so pure her compact has stained glass."

CKVU has a way of making first-time events so...retrograde. The studio was done in Steve-Reeves-movie-still, black faux-marble pillars, draped in man-made fabric. The public preening rivaled the stage offerings; like dancing in a disco, _ma chère_, you never know whom you are going to rub the wrong way.

There were small murmurings about seating. Out of camera range was worth no points at all. Smiling—the first half-hour was "this gum for hire" time—is so unrewarding if one's efforts are not seen by the folks at home.

Award recipients, who looked as if they were at a wedding where no one knows the bride _or_ groom, were mercifully brief in their speeches. Mock-of-ages Gordon Shrum said simply that it took him 89 years to get his Lifetime Achievement award, and he hoped to do more.

Eric Nicol, tongue permanently in cheek, was grateful both for the Literature award—he said he didn't know what he did was called that—and for the rented tux.

CBC's Vicki Gabereau, wearing the black-and-blue sequined jacket she wore to the Actra Awards a month earlier, says she got her teenaged daughter Eve to come along by lying to her that Bryan Adams would be there. Bryan Adams! Migawd, Barbie, Daryl Duke knew enough to stay away, and the show was his idea!

Anna Wyman was in black and white, Iona Campagnolo in rose silk, Bill Vander's Mrs. Zalm in black moiré, Terry David Mulligan in red shoes, CTV's Tony Parsons was in the wrong station and Tiger Williams ("whose face is so flat he can bite wallpaper") was not in at all.

The air was supposed to be rarefied while the nominees got deified but I am afraid we all got nullified. Maybe next year they will offer a Get A Celebrity To Show Up award.

Off for a Evening of Eleganza with Giulio. Giulio Terzi, the tall-dark-handsome-mid-30s-single (my favorite combo) Consul General of Italy.

Moi and almost 300 _fantastico femmes_ and a smattering of smashing men headed off to the Four Seasons Park Ballroom for an exclusive showing of one of Italy's foremost fashion designers, Renato Balestra.

This crowd did not look like it was running out of means to live beyond at all. One's Secret Serviceman's eye swept from an Yves St. Laurent shoe up a Wayne Clark pant, raced sideways along a custom-made lizard belt and fixed on a Russell Davies gold-and-diamond pendant. Life has a way of keeping women auditioning all the time.

People interpreted a 6:30 p.m. event to mean any dress style was acceptable. Some 1940s glam, for example, included one little number—there is always one—who oiled her body to slide into the type of dress that draws whistles from construction sites. Other old beauties with strong, original noses and brows and real gray hair wore their good and unadventuresome Jaegers. You know the type: first wives good enough to keep.

Arthur Erickson flew in from Toronto, of all mundane places. He, old-friend-from-Rome Balestra, Lois Milsom and Laurier went for a late-night dinner after the show.

The Vancouver Aquarium's angelfish, Dr. Murry Newman, glided around the room; he always looks as though he is moving underwater. Lawyer David McLean and wife Brenda in brilliant blue silk flashed that dynamite duo: fitness and Maui tans. Philip and Brita Owen looked remarkably relaxed and unscarred. The alderman "who ought to be on council" probably will be next time.

Jeanie Southam oversaw the room, much like a Ming vase setting a tone. Mary Butterworth, who still could, says she has no time for modeling now that she is so busy with the VanDusen Gardens.

The show itself? Barbie, I have things in what I call my attic "costume trunk" that I like better. The audience was incredibly subdued, except when they remembered that Balestra himself was there after all. A minimal number of outfits drew a two-ooh limit (for garments cut more peek than boo) and several a polite clapping, but when you think of it, this man did Margaret Trudeau's White House-visit wardrobe: remember anything from that? And although his own navy blazer was fine, his gray velvet pants were badly enough cut to have been borrowed.

The fortunate senora who won the door prize, an outrageously expensive Balestra original, rose hesitantly and muttered something about renting it out. Now *that's* making a fashion statement!

Ta Ta, Darling, and Ciao!

Valerie

OF DISHES AND RAGS

Barbie Darling,

Inched my way off to Expo Center's explosive opening. When I tell you everyone was there, believe me, _everyone_ was there. The Fair's fair media mandarine Gail Flitton assured me that the preem had asked only 3,000 (and change) of his closest and mostest, but a staggering stampede of 7,000 were there for showtime.

The one-year-to-go group mingled, when they could manage to move, at the Robson Square Media Center. They willingly boarded buses in their glad rags (Ron Longstaffe's Jacquie in a sunshine-yellow cocktail coat, Phillip Owen's Britta in black-and-white, Jimmy Pattison in black _outré_suede, just-turned-60 Herb Capozzi in a '60s outfit), were happily herded on to two six-car ALRT trains (the first trip _ever_ on public transit for a good 40 I can think of) and crammed into a 17-story glittering golfball.

Once there they ate 35,000 nibblies, guzzled 3,500 bottles of pretend champagne and watched a canapé-tossing movie on a wraparound screen nine times bigger than normal that swallows viewers whole and spits them out into space shuttles, jet planes, roller coasters and runaway trains. Try telling guests they _have_ to do this for an evening and watch the flack!

Wended my way into the 1985 Women Of Distinction Awards with a wary eye to just how many males would show up. The first person I rubbed shoulders with (mine white raw silk, his navy cashmere) was Bruno Gerussi, the second was Jack Webster.

On a break from beachcombing, Bruno has a new haircut so New York the Gibsons folk will never buy the tugboat skipper bit. Of course he was with ex-judge Nancy Morrison (they are as close as crossed fingers) plus an older woman who had gotten herself up to look exactly as she must have done during WW2.

Pin-striped and newly slimmed, Webster was moving into False Creek bachelor digs (isn't everyone?) after a golfing trip to Portugal and a popover to Britain.

OWL was definitely represented that night—Older Women's League, silly—but the BCBGs were there in force: the _bon chic, bon genres_ as young upwardly you-know-whats are called in France. There were female stockbrokers, investment counselors and icon-manipulators who, if they _had_ ever entertained Barbie doll lifestyle thoughts, had traded in the Dream House for a computer, calculator and platinum card. No Ali-Blah-Blah and the Forty Sieves here, as that uncle of yours used to call any random gathering of women. I heard a great dignified snipe from a teal blue Wayne Clarke silk suit to a Sonia Rykiel white knit: "I have been told that in real life she is a wonderful woman, but I only know her professionally."

Some very heavy-duty women had a part in the second-time event. Pat McGeer's wife Edi was nominated, but didn't make it. Blanche McDonald did with a win in the Business and Professions category, but didn't make it to the awards; Sam Belzberg's wife Fran helped judge the winners; Jack Poole's ex-wife Marilyn was a donor; the Hon. John Nicol's wife Liz, who owns the Equinox Gallery, was a contributor; May Brown won in a category not usually honored, Public Affairs.

Flitted into the Fourth Annual Vancouver International Firlm Festival at the Orpheum, all aglitter with klieg lights and flashbulbs as Michael York arrived. That little Nikon-holder who used to be at all the openings was back on the job, still head and shoulders below the rest, toupee permed and dyed, complexion cleared but pushy as ever, with the same positively carnivorous look about him.

As Laurier and Lois Milsom arrived I heard over my left shoulder pad, "I swear he'd take a limo to the loo if he could." Lapierre's launch was topped by a *non-rented* silver-and-black Rolls-Royce that pulled in just behind. Lois, ever trying for that balance between eccentric and classic, opted for a pre-1970s black lace pantsuit.

No one hot enough to pop corn, but the cameras kept clicking. Marlene Cohen, who heads the festival board, was the only near-Hollywood glamor, flashing the kind of gold-lamé decolletage, white pearly teeth, ever-present dimples and blonde coif that *Dynasty's* darlings do.

Vancouver's pair of impresarios, David Y.H. Lui and Hugh Pickett, were as disparate in duds as in dealings. David looked totally trendoid in a white Casablanca dinner jacket, a lapel flower and a new, spiky punk hairdo that plays up the tiny perfect mole on his left earlobe, where others have to resort to a gold hoop or a diamond stud. Hugh, who learned legend-making a long time ago, was tuxed in black, his only nod at flamboyance a lipstick-red bow tie. Since the featured flick that night was *Marlene...A Feature on Dietrich*, and since he and the 83-year-old former glamor queen are "close, close personal friends," he was very much on his preferred turf.

A marvelous mixed bag mulled about. Camilla Ross, whose Artscope International is behind the opera's new look, had honed the guest list to have Mayor Mike mixing it up with movie maven Bill Forsythe, one of the best movie directors of his time, and fashion pasha Gabriel Levy in a bright-yellow-and-black dinner jacket dotted with tiny white sunglasses standing next to Vancouver Art Gallery director Joanne Birnie Danzker, the picture of decorum in a little black number. Camilla, the perennial Auntie Mame in striped chiffon knee-length britches and top, was just back from a Japan jaunt and off to the Shaw Festival.

There were bubbleheads galore among the hysterics and hoopla, young sparkers and glamorous trash. A very unnatural blonde elicited this from two gender-benders, one in a Tina Turner fright wig: "I'm not saying that dress is skimpy, but I've seen more cotton in the top of an Aspirin bottle." "Well, it hardly matters. She's so thin she has to swallow a walnut to hold up her pajamas." Not to put too fine a point on it, Barbie, but one of the flaxen filly's detractors once rode an hors d'oeuvres tray down a flight of stairs, amusing few.

Back to the dead dishy Michael York. Unfortunately, the rather washed-out blonde in black skirt and white blazer who stuck to him all night was _Mrs._ York. I hate it when they are happily married _and_ they bring the wife with them, don't you?

York, whose real name is Johnson, is 43, looked much younger with that boyish hank of unruly hair, the broken nose and wide, elfin grin. He underplayed _all_ the time, and appeared absolutely seamless in his Giorgio Armani gray-striped suit. In mahvelous Oxford tones he allowed that he was based in Monaco and moving to L.A.: "I'm in a sense a man without a country." Poor baby. He does not think of TV as the film's lesser cousin. Good thing: the recent _Space_ series doubtless dropped a pound or two in his pocket, and the currently shooting _Dark Mansions_ with Joan Fontaine must be well worth his while. (One hears that Mrs. Y. is a royal pain on the set, telling the hairstylist how to do Michael's hair, the cameraman how to shoot him, monitoring all press questions...and _of course_ he didn't tell me this, silly!) The Yorks and the Forsythes headed off to Bridges for a bite while Evelyn Roth, a tall red feather on her head, took a small band across the mall to McDonald's for a milkshake party. _Chacun a son goût, wot_?

Wended my way to the World Affairs Dinner to break bread—petits pains aux graines de pavot; i.e., good old poppyseed rolls—with the Reverend Jesse Jackson and 600 other $150-a-plate diners. All the right stiffs were there. Most of these charity functions were inherited from the participants' parents, and certain rules go along: hit the cocktail party on time and work that room; once you are stuck at your assigned table, table hop; when someone asks how you are, have an upbeat line or two prepared. No one cares how you _really_ are (my ex-father-in-law used to open our conversations with, "How are you dear, fine?" and that said it all). If you are thin, eat dessert; it makes people nervous if you don't.

At the Jackson victual ritual Carole Taylor was all a-shimmer in a snakeskin sequin suit, bubbling happily about her switch from TV to Expo minutes on radio. Taller half Art Phillips, sartorially splendid in a shawl-collared tux, was basking humbly in his first success as Minister of Critical Industries (or Critical Injuries as a BCTV newscaster slipped). Sir Ronald of the Longstaffe, whose hair gets more salt than pepper all the time, was puffing away on his favorite Gold Block tobacco, just brought back from England for him. A totally flushed and radiant Jacquie was by his side in hot pink shirt, skirt, shoes and cheeks. She had managed a five-minute conversation with Jackson, who is billed as "the greatest living orator" by the International Platform Association.

Pia Southam swished in, toe-curlingly beautiful and seriously bronzed—"Electric, my dear. Who has the time?"—in a red Spanish off-the-shoulder item by Zonda Nellis. Power-at-player Bob Lee eased around the room with his movable assets: wife Lily in turquoise silk and the best bijoux about, plus the lovely Lee daughters.

The tall, dark (what else?) and handsome Jackson was very expensively dressed in impeccable tux, his watch and cuff links gold. He has beautiful hands, half-again-as-long fingers and professionally manicured nails (clear polish). His store-bought top teeth likely contribute to his lisp. His speech was platitudinally preachy, but he was so theatrical you really felt that maybe the "new world order" would "impact upon" you later.

Peter Brown's rendering of the closing expression of appreciation relied upon extensive quotes from *The New Republic*, which left several listeners wondering who had read *that* for him. He was forced to put on specs, which simply reaffirms what we have always known: aging by denial just doesn't work!

Ta Ta Darling,
Valerie

THE YEAR 1986

AN UNBROKEN CROWN
Simply everybody turned out to remind Jack Webster what a swell fellow he is.

CHECK YER ROYAL
If you weren't invited, you pretended to be out of town.

NO BUSINESS LIKE IT
Off the screen and onto the runway.

IACOCCA NUTS
Chrysler's King wheels into town.

THE YEAR 1986

top-of-the line twelve-monther if ever there was one. Vancouver was having its one hundredth birthday, and a world-class gaggle of globetrotting gadabouts descended to help kick off Expo. Bill Bennett opened the gates alongside a tiara-free, straw-hatted Queen Elizabeth, a spotlight savouring Pierre Trudeau, and the currently deep-in-doodoo Duke of Edinburgh, who, to those in the know, was in semi-scandal mode even then. And that old brown-bagger Bill ("it was not a bribe") VanderZalm closed it.

Sandwiched in between we had all sorts of crowned heads pop in. Chuck and Di, still talking then, whenever she stopped fainting long enough to, graced the glitzy little gala that Brian and Mila threw at the Pan Pacific. A strappy-sandaled Princess Margaret teetered into the Bayshore for a nice nosh with a privileged few hundred, and Margaret Thatcher who considers herself as close to royal as one can get, condescended to tea with we lucky few.

The Fifth Annual Vancouver International Film Festival pulled in all sorts of bigtime Hollywood hotshots whom we have hardly seen since. The Baroness de Rothschild "did lunch" at the Four Seasons, liked what she saw and has come back to the city almost every fall since. That was also the year the clout-heavy, wheely big Lee Iaccoca came to Vanland and tried to tell us everything we ever wanted to know about free trade but weren't ready for.

I myself headed off to Blighty that summer for an up-close-and personal, in the Abbey, I-spy-with-my-little-eye looksee at the Andrew and Fergie nuptials and brought back (after the dearest dash to the South of France), enough international dish for all of us to choke on for months to come.

AN UNBROKEN CROWN

Barbie Darling,

Wiggled off to Webster's wonderful wingding with 700 other C-note-a-plate revelers hell-bent on pouring a little sugar on the oatmeal savage's parade.

John Edgar himself, all rosy cheeks and silver thatch, played reverse-Santa as he raked in the goodies - slightly toasted accolades and gelt-and-sterling plaudits.

Billed as a testimonial dinner - for a man notorious for unabashedly shooting off his mouth - is it any wonder wee Jack was nervous about becoming cannon fodder for the big guns gathered to take their best shots? If one's heart were set on household names, the Hotel Vancouver Ballroom was the place to be this particular night.

Head-table guests, sponsors and a select some rose like cream to the Royal Suite for a little imbibing before being forced to rejoin the others pouring themselves through the doors and into their posts. State-of-the-art videos flickered from all four corners of the vast expanse so that those well below the salt could keep tabs.

Jack Of All Trades (union leaders, business biggies and publishing poobahs abounded) looked even more like himself than usual as he was piped in and applauded. "By the time you're his age,

_Staff Sgt. Don MacInnes,
Sgt. Ian Millman, Jack Webster_

you've learned everything; you only have to remember it, " offered the man beside me as we tucked into our baby salmon and mousseline of pike with sauce Noilly Pratt.

Pierre Berton, of the white-cement hairdo mastered ceremonies throughout and between courses. Barbie, one is quite safe in saying "Loved your book" to him. He almost never asks, "Which one?"

As I was noting how Lieutenant-Governor Bob Rogers looks more like Cesar Romero all the time, while Expo Commissioner-General Patrick Reid, a silver fox as tall as redwood, is not far behind in the movie-star department, the owlish Edgar Kaiser rolled in, stylish Judy by his side, just back from Tokyo for the launch of his $10 million, 148-foot yacht. After 20 months at the helm of the Bank of B.C. and with some tricky steering around the rocky reefs of

Bay Street ahead, he may wish he had named his buoyant baby boat *Sayonara*.

Spotted Fran Belzberg shimmering in a sequin suit, but missed Sam. He had made a $1.86 billion - oh those zeros! - offer for Ashland Oil that day, so if he was preoccupied elsewhere, nous comprendons, non?

Despite runs in *both* her stockings, my dear, Eleni Skalbania looked ravishing - her *only* look unfortunately - in a Sheena, Queen of the Jungle one-shouldered, leopard-printed sheath. She was accompanied by Attorney-General Brian Smith until the late Nelson arrived, at which time it was cake and champagne all around. Wheeling dealer Nelson looked marathon fit on his sixth wedding anniversary, though he continues to smoke those Cuban stogies. "I thought they still celebrated *month*-iversaries," I heard over my shoulder, "though I must say they *do* look happy."

Jack Poole, whose $2 billion debt restructure seems to have taken a load off, looked peaceful and pleased as Darlene Young floated about him in a

*Pierre Berton, Mayor Mike Harcourt,
Chief Justice Nathan Nemetz*

silver-sequined backless top and satin pants.

Various lit wits appeared to have enrolled in Strutting 101, and several speakers accused each other of line-stealing, thereby proving that even gray minds think alike.

Charles Lynch, who one day will be, seems to be going to Weedeaters for his haircuts. He spoke and played his harmonica in the same style, too. The IWA's Jack Munro, attempting to control his rouge mouth, got off some of the evenings best lines, endearing himself to all by allowing that he always enjoyed eating with rich people.

Allan Fotheringham, in a burgundy velvet bow tie, spent much time defending Sondra Gotlieb's slap and his lack of coverage of it. He later earned his place in the gaffology record books by saying that Webster's great gift was his making complicated issues understood *even* by Burnaby housewives. When the audience booed and one woman suggested from the floor that he leave, he looked genuinely baffled. "Rich feminists," he allowed later.

Iona Campagnolo, in magenta silk with pave-diamentes, and Davey Barrett, rumpled and ready even in a tux, managed to avoid any minefields in their homage to the humble Scot.

J.V. Clyne, his specs slipping endearingly, had so honed his praise-be-to-Jacks he glided through his piece with the timing of a Shakespearian actor.

Meanwhile, forced into honesty by his entire family's presence, Webster of the elephantine memory sought to clear up as many self-myths as time would allow.

While almost everyone moved around, some clearly had their black belts in table-leaping. Peter Brown, down from five packs a day to gum, and lighter by 25 pounds (but not an ounce of ego), zapped those worthy with the speed and accuracy of a B25 bomber, Young mayor-to-be Gordon Campbell, in a tux right out of _GQ_, campaigned hard between the filet of lamb and the rosewater souffle glace. Paul Manning, former reporter, PMO office boy, Liberal candidate, Trudeauphobe, B.C. Place exec, BCRIC batboy and now author in progress, fluttered in from California with a delectable deb named Deborah on his arm, and they worked the room as a duo.

MP Mary Collins, just back from Ethiopia and resplendent in raspberry silk, was in a head-to-head with energy wise Pat Carney in a cream-and-jet combo. Watching them was columnist Marjorie Nichols in rainbow sequins, while overseeing them all was beauteous publisher Anna Porter, who had taken a leaf from husband lawyer Julian Porter's book to dress all in black with a touch of white at the neck. Ever book-bound, Anna arrived in town, contract in hand, with a mock-up of a tome-to-be for Webster in case he still thinks he has any choice in the matter at all. With best sellers from Foth and Chretien under her belt, Jack will be "The Pen That Roared" by Christmas.

Joanne Brown in white ruffles, black silk and jewelry the auction houses call "important," was knee-to-knee with Lily Lee (in hot pink and black), whose own baubles could give heart palpitations to the healthiest bank balance.

Peter Newman would have thought he had died and gone to _Acquisitors_ heaven. Within feet of each other were Bob Lee, Peter Brown, Nelson Skalbania, Edgar Kaiser and Jack Poole, and over there Herb Capozzi, Herb Doman, Frank Griffiths and Chester Johnson, In _this_ corner Peter Bentley, Joe Cohen, Bob Wyman and John Laxton. One could do that with newspapers (besides the local brass, such national nabobs as Paddy Sherman flew in), with the law (from twinkly-eyed Nathan Nemetz to prickly Peter Butler), and with TV and radio (from bearded Bruno Gerussi to take-me-as-I-am Vicki Gabereau, whose wiring always seems to be slightly frayed). A chandelier falling anywhere in the room would have led to serious regroupings of whole segments of the wheels of whatever.

As it was we were all left to rub shoulders, elbows, noses and palms with practically everyone we ever wanted to. All because one Jack E. Webster, who chose to settle here some 35 years ago, had touched so many lives and was so eminently worthy of all the hoopla.

Pranced off to the Pan Pacific and a small smash for the press secretary to the Royals. Of course, most of us knew Vic Chapman, Canada's bucko at Buck House, when he a B.C. Lions kicker, and later in Ottawa when he called Trudeau "the boss." No one ever messed with Trudeau when Big Vic was defenseman between Pierre and the pesky press. Now assigned to the Chuck and Di show, he was in fine form as he bearhugged such old friends and footballers as Bob Brady, By Bailey and Primo Villanueva.

Herb Capozzi slid in, looking so good Jack Webster checked behind his ears for facelift scars. Herb heads Expo's new "accommodation" committee, and the Pan Pacific was being checked out as a possible Royal Roost. The elegant Ellen Capozzi, mid-term in a 17th century French literature course, which I am sure she will use daily, chose royal blue and white for her outfit just to get into the mood. Vic sidled up to Ellen, who is tall and blonde, and pronounced authoritatively that she is exactly Di's height.

So what did I find out that I did not know about Her Royal Di-ness? Quickies only, such as her shunning real furs in favor of fakes. Do you care? With her family trust and housekeeping money adding up to some $34,000 *a week*, who can blame her if "shopping is her life?" And she is currently reading Judith Krantz's *Scruples* from way back then. Racy but passe, what?

Bopped off to Boboli, the chic new South Granville boutique, for champagne and smart canapes (Susan Newson of Glorious Foods). David Vance directed the store's design, so it works wonderfully well. It is owned by Catherine Hayes Guadagnuolo and Margaret Ross, each a spiffy, young bizwiz, who owes her body to Dana Zalko and her duds to the exclusive-in-Vancouver likes of Max Mara, I Blues, Albinea, Blumarine and Pellini jewelry. Twice a year they make for Milan to buy what Vancouver will just *have* to have, display it like fine art and wait for everyone from the old guard to young city strivers-not-faint-of-wallet. "He dresses like a cross between Don Johnson and Ward Cleaver," I heard over my shoulder pad. "If only Boboli did men."

"I'm almost sure she doesn't set out to be obnoxious," said a chrome yellow cocktail hat to a head of black pleated hair. "And always the right occasion, never the right dress," the hair answered back.

"I've borrowed Nanny's jools," I caught while beelining through the bubbling crowd for night air. "They look ever-so-much better on a young neck, don't you think?"

Vancouver is definitely ready, and Boboli is certainly able.

Loped off to Lizzie Nichols's Equinox Gallery for the launch of artist Robert Michener's latest works. Rode the elevator to the penthouse-with-a-view showplace with living legend Bill Reid, who of course knew Michener's precise pastoral scenes well.

First person I ran into was Establishment-man Gordon Southam, who has always looked to me like a state-of-the-art person. The only thing missing whenever I see the sterling-silver marcelled hair, the stern jaw, the Olivier-like bearing, is a top hat, white tie and tails, and just maybe a red-satin-lined cape.

Wife Jean perused the four-figure paintings in the large salon while he and I talked scions. Son Harvey is still up to his ears in *Equity* (the *magazine*, Barbie), and daughter Nancy was leaving for dindin at the White House with the Mulroneys. At this point Lois Milsom moved in, fluttering in a charcoal-gray pantsuit and wearing a ransom in Bill Reid adornments. She had on a gorgeous gold frog and a three-dimensional gold bracelet - "One of his first," she cooed. Iona Campagnolo told me later they are priceless.

Lois, who looks like she does her Jane Fonda *every* day, was about to board for London and Paris (I am still waiting for her next trip to be somewhere like Moose Jaw).

Those two are a match made in purgatory," I heard as I picked up my Perrier. I waited for more, but that seemed to be the end of it. Do you have any idea how annoying that is to me? Never knowing who?

No time for more, dear heart. World Cup at Whistler will just have to wait, and Yves Saint Laurent and champagne at the Mandarin, too.

Just remember, you can't have everything. Wherever would you put it?

Ta ta Darling,

Valerie.

The Prince and Princess of Wales greet Kenny Rogers, Sheena Easton, Howie Mandel, Bruce Allen, Carol Reynolds and Scott Smith

CHECK YOUR ROYAL

Barbie Darling,

It has finally happened: I have gagged on galas, suffered the wrath of grapes, been bedazzled by ball gowns and bubbles, and find myself longing for life before Expo, Centennial and the palpitating posturings of The Royals. Regarding the latter, Old Bean, those who were not invited to meet your titled twosome at at least one regal wingding might just as well have closed the garage door and pretended to be out of town.

The gala-vanting started within mere hours of Their Royal Aitches' arrival, with Brian and Mila's nervy nosh for the Nine Hundred. It was a Tory sight to behold, Barbie. Every patronage payback possible was there at a state-of-the-trough munchdown that unearthed enough Easterners to give one geographical vertigo.

Conservative premiers and mayors you never heard of were there. Such establishment elite as Charles Bronfman and Paul Desmarais nose-to-nosed it with the Errol Flynn of Finance, Michael Wilson. Pat Carney, who will one day finesse the finance portfolio herself, admonished anyone who tucked in her errant dress label to leave it: "For what this dress cost, the label can stay out!" Peter Newman and the third Mrs. N, the comely Camilla, in black velvet and rhinestones (and she dresses on a boat), searched the room for fresh literary fodder. "One for each wife," he said of the medals across his chest.

Mr. and Mrs. Jacques Ferriere, Mr. and Mrs. Joseph Segal, Mr. and Mrs. Gerald Gales, Mr. and Mrs. Joseph Cohen

Ontario premier David Peterson and his smashing actress-wife Shelly, in Tory-blue satin, rested on their Liberal laurels having two nights earlier given the week's best party to open the Ontario Pavilion at Expo.

Edgar "A Boy and His Bank" Kaiser and wife Judy, in regal red-and-gold, felt no overdraft as they floated alone about the room. Hollywood's Gordon Thompson (Adam Carrington) barely noticed local dynastician Gordon Southam, wife Jean and heiress-to-the throne Nancy as they established territorial rights at their table. The John Turners and Lieutenant-Governor Bob Rogers and Mrs. Rogers - who called themselves "The Almost-Not-Inviteds" - grouped for slighted comfort together. It was not a cold shoulder - he wore a kilt - that Tunagate's John Fraser worried about while Prime Minister's Office boy Bill Fox stumbled over *O Canada* as though B.C. were a foreign country.

David Letterman's leader-of-the-band Paul Shaffer head-to-headed it with local Grammy-grabber David Foster as Bruce Allen watched the steady stream that came to fan Bryan Adams's ego. (in honor of The Royals Mr. A went formal in black suit, black T-shirt and a Canadian-flag pin.)

Jimmy Pattison, whose freckled-face head could be seen smiling from ear to shining ear, beestung each tony table with the accuracy of a turnstile click.

Testing their chestsful of medals were Expo's Patrick Reid - "I got them getting *out* of Ireland" - plus the princely pair's pressman and former B.C. Lion-backer Vic Chapman who got his "for football," and head table boy Charles of Wales who more than earned every one for sitting through dinners like this with the likes of Billy B. and Brian of Mulroney.

The practically perfect princess who gets wolf whistles everywhere she goes? Well, she wore the off-white, backless lace number we saw in Washington last year, plus her fave *chapeau*, that diamond-and-pearl number from Queen Mary that mum-in-law Betty lets her wear if only she keeps the Walkman hidden. (Mila was bareheaded, but the sum of what sparkled on her fingers, wrists, neck and ears would give that tiara a run for it.) The glamorexic one herself was up to her usual Di-jinks, pushing the essence of quail around her plate but eating *all* her veggies.

With barely a breather, it was off to the Orpheum for the Opening Gala of the Royal Bank/Expo 86 World Festival.

Bustling past theater-front limos stretched to the max, I bumped into Carole Taylor and Art Phillips in beige lace and headband (of course *her* - pay attention Barbie or I'll stop these royal rah-rahs right now). Teck Corporation's Norman Keevil Sr. looked over the lobby's teeming platinum people as though considering a lab report. To get to their seats Jack Poole and Darlene Young scurried past Herb and Ellen Capozzi; Helen and Garde Gardom (who is looking more vice-regal daily); the Centennial Commission's Michael Francis and wife Daphne in an orangy-gold brocade; lawyer Peter Butler, who looked like himself only better; and John and Jill Turner. "No seating after 8:20," the good-as-gold tickets warned.

I'm afraid I lingered too long in the lobby (screams and flashes hinted that "they" had arrived, so I traded the Fanfare Overture for a just-about-nose-to-royal-nose). *She* was in a smashing hyacinth-and-pink, polka-dotted ball gown. He wore a red dress-bandage on his injured index finger, and of course a tux, silly. She has a small mole on her left cheek near her smile line. He has a scar I had not noticed before on his left cheek, and wears two pinky rings on the same finger. She has no dark roots. He has a widening part and is obviously finding it harder to comb to advantage at the ... uh, crown. Her nails look short, though no longer bitten, and her sapphire-and-diamond engagement ring could have been bested by any number of baubles in the audience. Really, though, one has to start *somewhere*, and future prospects look promising, especially if the Duchess of Windsor's emeralds ever surface.

My former Ottawa neighbor Mario Bernardi did a sensitive job conducting the Vancouver Symphony Orchestra. Maureen Forrester and all put in yeoman duty, but I am afraid it was one pooped princess whose noble head nodded noticeably between *Le Nozze di Figaro* and *La Boheme*.

Believe me when I tell you, Barbie, that at the following night's Royal Rock Show there were several elderly boppers pretending to enjoy a decibel level they would normally never expose themselves to. Cabinet ministers who had managed to avoid their childrens' entire teen years were forced by a social coup to sit and take it.

Nelson and Eleni Skalbania slipped in, Eleni in a great, buff-colored pantsuit, Nelson in one of those belted Bavarian hunting suits from the 1960s he resurrects just when we think we are safe. Two CCs of Woodward capered in - Chunky and Carol - to sit across from Jack Poole in white bomber jacket and Darlene Young in full-length fur. Herb Capozzi - sheepskin and cowboy boots - sang *The Gambler* in my ear better than Kenny Rogers did. As the King of Crossover mingled with the audience I noticed that he and Prince Charles wore the same after-shave and that silver-T-shirted Rogers sported suspenders to keep his pants up and over that teddy-bear tummy. Daryl Duke was a Rogers rerun in his silver beard.

Stephen Rogers may not have been in the cabinet but he still made the VIP box. So did Jack Kempf (there were heaters there for that hot-tub feeling).

Bryan Adams hit the stage with his own scream machine at peak power, got the biggest ovation, was obviously loved as hometown boy, and later assured me that rumors about him and Tina Turner are totally untrue. More animated than I had seen her the whole trip, Diana made a dramatic costume change to a frilly-shirted, modified tux of her own (at least she has stopped borrowing Charles's). She blew her hair out of her eyes as she passed me - wearing Miss Dior - smiled and subtly scratched her thigh just like a real person.

Anything new about the man who would be king? Well, he was the first royal born without a "watcher" - an official witness who makes sure nobody swaps babies. His own wardrobe is not too shabby: worth more than $450,000 with 100 suits at $1,000 apiece; handmade shirts at $100 per; 100 uniforms at between $2,000 and $4,000 each; and Princess Di, tired of snuggling up to him in his frumpy flannel pajamas, has talked him into ordering six pairs of silk ones.

Careened off to the $500-*a-deux* Centennial Ball at the Pan Pacific to mark the city's 100th. My tablemate for the evening, arranged without my knowledge, was 33, tall, dark, handsome and worth $33 million. I just love round numbers, don't you, Barbie?

Governor-General Jeanne Sauve and her husband Maurice (who has changed hardly a hair since the Ottawa days) smiled through a 100-gun salute and a champagne reception that saw the *creme de la* Centennial celebrate to the hilt.

Our old friend the Baroness Phillipine de Rothschild pranced in wearing a little charcoal sequined number that would not stay done up at the back no matter how often the young man at her side zipped her.

Bruno Gerussi, bearded and looking like the head on a Roman coin, swished Nancy Morrison around the room in a knock-'em-dead little black number that was as far from her court robes as froufrou frills will allow.

Jack Austin asked all and sundry how they like his building (he was the then-minister who got Canada Place in place). Jeweler Toni Cavelti smiled as his various creations sparkled around the Crystal Ballroom, while Edgar Kaiser stood out as the room's only slate-gray tux.

Royal Van Yacht Club commodore Ron Cliff sailed proprietorially around a room in which a lot of his members were docked. Good Samaritan Joe Cohen, with the flawless Fran on his arm, waltzed in, not to be upstaged by Ed Phillips who cut a mean three-quarter-step on the dance floor.

Bob Carter appeared to be sizing up the evening much as he might scruntinize a gas-and-oil deal. His wife Sheila Begg looked sleek in a white sequined gown, but there was a rather mature Venus off to their left who should never be bare-armed. It was here a Joan Collins knockoff in scarlet taffeta gown with ruffled shoulders, there a deb in flowing gold lame shot with sparkles.

Star of the show and chairman of the ball was Jacquie Longstaffe wearing a smashing Carol Challis creation, strapless, ruffled and in the exact colors of the invitation card. At her neck was a diamond-and-gold Christmas gift from husband Ron that Diana should definitely look into.

Speaking of princesses, I frittered off to Frank (Sinatra) rather than doing the Dutch (Princess Magriet of the Netherlands) at the Art Gallery. I have met her before, but I missed Ol' Blue Eyes in Vegas, Palm Springs and Tahoe every time he or I have been there. Spotted Peter Brown in a Vegas-style silk suit trading Art for Frank, too. Like me, he was contributing to the $300,000 Sinatra cleared before boarding the Gulf Stream II jet he just bought from William Paley and flying home to Palm Springs with nary a linger.

No time to do justice to the magnificent reception at the Meridien Hotel opening. Trust me, dear heart, _everyone_ was there. Just remember your great-uncle's words: "_Seme tantum vitam vivimus._" You only go around once in life.

Thank heavens and ta ta Darling,

Valerie.

NO BUSINESS LIKE IT

Barbie Darling,

Frittered off to the Fifth Annual Vancouver international Film Festival - of *course* not to see any of the films, silly; for the Gala Opening. The Orpheum was all white-limo, red-carpet, lights-camera-action - a lot of pomp circumnavigating the circumstance. The no-longer-fledgling festival is now in full flight, witness the flocks of *rara avis* flooding through the glass-and-brass doors. We were all left rubber-necking as if at a 12-car pile-up.

First off the marquee was actor Jeff Goldblum - *The Bill Chill, Nashville, Silverado, The Right Stuff* - who slid from limo to lobby with on his arm a gownless evening strap encasing a gorgeous starlet named Geena Davis. Though each towered well over six feet - he sporting shiny black ponytail, no-tie tux and black-olive eyes - she got star billing because of the silver-blue dress that just had to have been made while she was still in it. An on-and-off screen duo, they had just finished remaking a creature-feature of *The Fly*, Goldblum playing a barely dressed man-*cum*-insect monster. "It's weird seeing Jeff that way," Davis said. "Every square inch of his skin is covered with latex and goo." This left several of us lost in our own reveries as we watched them sashay around Westcoast Hall while the snaparazzi went mad.

The CKVU staff swept in like a fractious weather front. As aging *wunderkind* Laurier Lapierre, in a white tux jacket and an extraordinary new auburn hair color, kiss-kissed his way into the crowd, the racy poseur to my right observed, "He goes to black-tie events so he can amortize his evening wear."

Daryl Duke was not far behind, alighting (he is on planes more than most pilots) with full entourage in tow. LTLL - Long-Time Lady Love - Ann-Marie Favelle, in a green-and-gold Malaysian sarong, and bodybuilder sons Brian and David cut a V you could see through the throng. *Eminence noir* Norman Klenman hovered nearby while assorted other VU-ers fanned themselves out and about.

A dimpled dumpling of a woman in ill-advised green polka dots upped herself to handsome blond character actor Winston Rekert and blurted, "Hi, I know you." In the stilted silence that followed, I edged my way closer to *Danger Bay's* Donnelly Rhodes, once married to actress Martha Henry but now to a smashing showbizzer in a sequined blouson whose name was drowned out by a jostling duo. "The worst thing my divorce did was to bring me into contact with lawyers," the first shouted above the din. "I know, 'One swallow does not a summer make,'" the other countered as they battled their way to the bar. "But two undisclosed marriages were a lot for you to swallow."

Leon Bibb looked surprisingly non-theatrical in a gray silk suit that was more *GQ* than *Jacques Brel*. MP Svend Robinson had traded in his granny glasses for the dearest little diamond in his ear (how can that help his eyesight?). Establishment man Ken Tolmie squired his leather-bound wife Patsy (red two-piece, big shoulders, white blouse, great brooch). *Her*, Barbie; *he* was wearing a tux. The late Jack Wasserman's wife Pat creamed by in a flash of off-white, while Vicki Gabereau, wearing red-rimmed sunglasses and black and white from head to spectator pumps, was book-ended by identical twins Ted and Terry Turner. Off to cover the Commonwealth Games in Britain for CBC this summer, she likely was doing a little research on local beefcake.

Former Field Marshal for the Film Festival Leonard Schein was caught cornered by Arts Clubman Bill Millerd while their collected mass of mannerisms (both are notoriously shy) were showcased for passersby to review.

Aussie-born impresario Margaret Steley, who put together the Pope Show at B.C. Place and the Expo Opening for the Royals, put herself together with the brio of a bullfighter that night in burgundy brocade cropped jacket (tassel at the back), white frilly shirt and black jodhpur pants. "Bacci's On South Granville," she

Harvey and Pia Southam and Michael Okulitch

volunteered as the appreciative critiques came her way. Not to be outdone, her blond husband Alan - "A thing of beauty and a boy forever," I calls him - sported a black leather creation hand-painted by Evelyn Roth.

As I made my way upstairs, a minor socialite with tight-tight face job and a voice that creeps up your neck and crawls in your ear, was announcing, "One reason I don't drink is I want to know when I'm having a good time." Six steps further I heard, "I'm almost sure she doesn't set out to be obnoxious," but dismissed any *possibility* of the remarks being connected. At the top of the stairs a single male peacock nearly eclipsing three frou-frou females was saying, "They served quail at the Hyatt that night, and I could no sooner eat the state bird of California than the family dog."

Better than the movies, I thought, while easing by Expo's *real* hero,

135

Patrick Reid, and his exquisite wife Alison. With those *tres distingue* looks, Central Casting would have had him play Ambassador to Europe or King of France.

Culture maven Mavor Moore moved his mate Sandra Browning around the room as easily as though he were guiding her on an uncrowded dancefloor, even though she opts for opera as a career.

"The men's thighs in the Kirov were to die for," oozed a pretty young blonde in jiffy-pop hairdo to a chap whose wimpadour had wilted. Standing between them and obviously trying to deal with this information was what a friend of mine calls The Perfect Woman: hair streaked, teeth bonded, nails acrylic, body professionally reduced by machines, tan electric.

There were cummerbunds there to circle the city, tuxedoes without the scent of mothballs, and enough elegant bugle beads tooting their own flashy horns to strike up one well-dressed band.

It isn't Cannes yet, pet, but it will do.

From cinema to chic as the Robson Fashion Park premiered at - you got it - *a gala*! All pink marble, brass, glass and a city block of curved atrium ceiling, the posh and banner-filled plant plaza cost a mere $12 million to assemble.

Predictably pricey and so European - from Laurel to Lauren, Sung to Supre Modo - the 16 swish boutiques will save those tiresome trips to at *least* Rodeo Drive if not the Via Veneto, *ma chere*.

Opening night was rehab for the chronically trendy, who were so up to the second they could have changed places with the ever-so-laid-back, artfully disarranged models on the runway. "Clink, clink," went the champagne as the fruit of the boom showcased their stuff. Crimes of fashion were being committed on all sides. With almost 2,000 look-at-mes milling about, things you thought you would never have to deal with again passed before your eyes, from Day-glo dresses to silver-leather minis, and—on my honor, Barbie—a genuine Nehru jacket.

"I swear there should be a taste sheriff," said a man with shoulder-length black mane, black suit and vampire eyeliner. He was pointing to a girl whose sunglasses frames spelled out the word LOOK.

"If we are spotted here early, let's just say we have to go somewhere else later," one vacuous cutie leaned across me to whisper to a friend. Both wore long, strapless 1950s formals, hair that looked more irritated than teased, and had sparkles all over their bare shoulders. Where on earth *could* they have been going later?

As members of the Vancouver Symphony Orchestra added some elegance to the background sound, "Pia Shandel ... oops, Southam," as she introduced herself, M.C.'d mistressfully in a bright-red, ankle-length getup and cute, new punk coif.

Antiestablishmentarian Nelson Skalbania, for whom well-enough is never alone, started his ensemble with acceptable shoes and neutral slacks, then veered into a wild-and-stormy plaid jacket and topped it off with a grass-green tie. The ever-beauteous Eleni opted for a pink-and-white dress and rose-colored hose.

Pat Carney did not make it though supposed to, but silver-haired Socred MLA Russ Fraser was there, uttering *Reader's Digest* phrases straight-arrow-style while working a somewhat eclectic crowd with a "Do these people vote?" look on his face.

David McLean, appearing most conservative for a Liberal, had the blonde Brenda at his side as he scanned the place with an entrepreneurial eye.

CJOR's Fanny Keifer reviewed the latest vogueries, but looked content in her trademark linen Katharine Hepburn trousers. Meanwhile, Boboli's Margie Ross and Catherine Hayes-Guadagnuolo took stock of just what might be competition for their elegant emporium on South Granville.

"It's harder and harder to get noticed these days," lamented one label-lover to a fashion-free-agent friend, who countered, "I think in my new life I am trying to be

Norman Jewison & Maureen McTeer

more glamorous than bizarre, you know, and it seems to be going over better." Babs, it really is in the eye of the beholder.

Tottered off to "A Tribute To Norman Jewison" at the Ridge, where celluloid snippets from a credit-filled lifetime were flashed and commented upon by the *Globe and Mail's* Jay Scott, as well as by Canada's foremost filmmaker, Jewison himself.

From *The Russians Are Coming, The Russians Are Coming* to *In The Heat Of The Night, The Thomas Crown Affair, Fiddler On The Roof, Jesus Christ Superstar*, through *A Soldier's Story* to last year's *Agnes Of God* ... you get the picture. With 22 films, 32 nominations and nine Oscars, the man deserves a tribute or two.

Ditching the Ridge we dropped down to Jim McGregor's delicious, delightful, it's Delilah's restaurant on Haro Street. Nuzzled under a West End apartment building, it is ever-so New York with below-ground entrance, ruby-velvet banquettes and painted-angels ceiling. And of course Jimmy McG, architectural designer extraordinaire and now trendy restaurateur, was there to greet the movie folk.

Huge bouquets assembled by McGregor himself was dotted in the pools of lamplight as the bearded Norman Jewison arrived with wife Dixie, who feared she was overdressed in a bugle-beaded dress and small cigarillo.

Hannah Fisher, the dynamo Film Festival director whose plans would have Cannes coming *here* next year, floated about the celeb-studded eatery in cream-colored silk, coral beads and gold sandals, overseeing the first phase of her international plan with that sweet, quizzical look Marcel Marceau's eyebrows contrive.

Maureen McTeer - no-show Joe was involved in something about SALT talks - was a picture in a white-silk, abstract, designer number and those incredible, marble-blue eyes. She says she is really enjoying her practice, and after fall is not going to write for *Chatelaine* anymore.

Grace McCarthy flounced in in pale pink and a red-turned-to-blonde halo. Asked how he had enjoyed the Women Of Distinction awards dinner, husband Ray said he thought the cast had been really great and that the show really moved along, which left us looking at each other until dear Hugh Pickett, that maestro of mello with a sixth sense for sticky wickets, rescued us both.

Actor Rod Steiger was there as large as he seems on the screen. He has piercing eyes (which used to be bigger than his stomach), a booming voice, does a great W.C. Fields impression and has a new wife, half his age and weight, who was sleek, ponytailed, tuxedoed, polished and named Paula - a china doll who did not mix once she was seated and had nothing to say to anyone.

"I believe you get what you negotiate, not what you deserve," I heard over my silken shoulder pad. It was a man I never did meet, who sat at the bar drinking "tiny little triples," as a Whistler friend calls them.

"If you miss only one movie this year, make sure this is it," came from unseen lips as we were called to dinner. Trouble is, I never found out *which* movie.

The evening was Hollywood name droppers heaven. Much more later.

Love you, lunch, and ta ta Darling,

Valerie.

IACOCCA NUTS

Barbie Darling,

Virtually *inched* my way off to the Iacocca Dinner. With over 1,200 of us eager to eyeball the possible next president, press the palm of the feisty car zsar, or just catch an earful of the legendary Iacoccanomics, there was not a lot of Leeway in the Hyatt lobby, if you catch my drift.

The World Affairs Dinner had snagged a whopper of a talker this time. Although predecessors Henry Kissinger and Jesse Jackson had not been exactly *petit poissons, this* glittering gathering was a gang buster!

It was corporate gamesmanship all the way. "There is no free lunch," as the amiable autocrat himself is fond of espousing, and this particular repast was tabbed at $150 per plate. If you wanted to raise a glass with the Chrysler Corp. chairman in the more exclusive atmosphere of an upstairs suite, you *could* buy a whole table of 10, and drop an "As-Lee-told-me" at the club for the next few months.

"Security is tighter than a diamond choker," was heard as a chockablock crowd maneuvered its way to ballroom tables. That totem with feet, Bob Carter, bobbed above the crowd with wife Sheila

Lt. Gov. Robert Rogers, Jacqueline Longstaffe

in tow in a turquoise shimmer of a dress. The city's current pincushion for putdowns always seems to enter a room warily, as though he is ready to dodge an arrow or two.

A tuxed-out Jack Poole, in business suit, and the forever-young Darlene, in white-and-black satin, bustled in as though they barely had time for all this. Conglomerateur Bob Lee and a rather ravissant-looking Lily, in a silver slash of bugle beads from neck to knee, eased their way into the fray, passing Peter Paul Saunders and wife Nancy who had arrived separately and looked delighted to rediscover each other. (Since restructuring the debtload at Versatile Corp. is currently uppermost in Senor Saunders agenda, hearing Iacocca's ideas on the national debt would no doubt be an intriguing draw).

Ross Southam, pompadour polished, tortoise-shells gleaming, looked relaxed and willing as ever to let the blue chips fall where they may. Vancouver's answer to John Houseman, J.V. Clyne, held court while wife Betty, in her signature maribou shrug, eagerly adjudicated.

A gaunt girl with chicken-wing arms, wearing a macrame dress that left one wondering what her plants were hanging in while she was out, leaned around me to an unseen ear and said, "Even if he could afford a yacht, he'd still be missing the boat, you know?" in one of those oh-my-gawd voices. I never saw the target's reaction, but the jibe elicited several chuckles - the Howe Street equivalent of laughter - from the heads it went over.

Kennedy clan look-alike Janet Ketcham held three other dynamite dresses

Peggy Iacocca, Ron Longstaffe

in thrall as they edged their way under the chandeliers past wannabe alderperson Carole Taylor who, if she had remembered her alphabet, would have run as Carole Phillips and would not be in this fine mess. Troopers that they are, the Taylor-Phillips's smile as though the key to city hall was either within Independent reach or did not matter anyway.

Relatives of the Rich and Famous, Ralph and Brenda Brown, skirted their way in - Ralph always looks as though he would rather be *anywhere* else - while *bon viveur* brother Peter, whose stock in trade is flamboyance, played promoter. Haig Farris, who suffers from being terminally well brought up, escorted the merry Mary

through the throng, passing Bill Docksteader who, with silver hair and goatee, looked ever ready to prestidigitate the car of your choice out of thin air.

Caught a glimpse of lawyer Bill Rand and ex-model wife Tracy in white silk evening pajamas - of course *her*, he was in a tux. Tall, cool and blonde, Madame Rand manages to make walking seem X-rated.

The junction of all these tuxedoes was of course, the ballroom,. and the weatherman should have issued a tycoon warning. Every chief executive officer, investment dealer, developer, corporate lawyer, successful stock exchanger and entrepreneur you *ever* was cleverly working his latest coup into the conversation, while every wife of, significant other, or expensive date-mate was checking labels, waistlines and carat quality. It was a *very* busy room, Barbie.

An impressive head table dominated the room, its occupants warming the same upholstered highback chairs the royals did last May. Grace McCarthy wore emerald-green satin, Ray at her heel with his ever-ready red clip-on tie and both smiled all the way from antipasto to truffles, her trademark cloud of strawberry confection hair nodding and waving above the filet de veau and creme de pistache.

Mayor Mike and Becky posed prettily for the city (well *she* did in white chiffon and silver beading), Tom Siddon flashed for the feds, and Jacqueline Longstaffe for the B.P.'s: swift and silken (and sullen) in silver, skinny as a sapling, and *just* the right decolletage, my dear. Ron Longstaffe, who dodges touchy personal questions with the wiles of a Hollywood veteran, and tricky political ones with the obfuscations of a seasoned senator, put his puffing pipe at peace to introduce Iacocca who, having stashed his stogie - a Monte Cristo Havana - took the stand.

Lido Anthony Iacocca, Grand Poohbah of the evening, performed for the assemblage, a crackerjack 45-minute Economics 101 lecture that was so clear-theoried he gave mumbo jumbo a bad name. A corporate counterpuncher who has smoothed his style to a glide, he tells it like it is - "I gotta tell ya" - and, as the guy in Chrysler's driver's seat, has become Motor City's most famous motor mouth. Barbie, never mind what he *said* about free trade, federal deficit, export, value added and all, let me tell you the *real* stuff.

Jane Hungerford, Art Phillips, Carole Taylor and George Hungerford

Peggy Iacocca is 26 years younger than the man she calls Lido, was a Pan Am flight attendant, they have been married only since April and he designed the engagement ring (diamonds with two rings entertwined - from Bulgari - *very* nice). She goes everywhere with him, even to visit his mother in Allentown, should you care. She is great looking - the *wife* not the mother - and is the only woman he courted after his first wife died. She cooks Italian, "pasta with duck in tomato sauce," likes crossword puzzles, especially the *New York Times*, as much as he does, and makes him "happy as hell." She wore her chignoned-hair *up* this particular night (down at lunch on Jimmy Pattison's boat earlier that day), a black velvet shawl-collared sheath, great shoes, and hugged Ron Longstaffe fervently after his flattering introduction of her new hubby. You're welcome.

141

Iacocca himself is six-one and in the 190s, has a Daffy Duck lisp that comes and goes, a ruddy oversized putty nose, a close-mouthed smile, deep-brown eyes behind gold-rimmed aviator glasses, wears a gold family-crest ring on his wedding finger, has manicures (finishing up with clear polish) and massages (sometimes in his office), works out at least 45 minutes a day in the executive gym he had built on Chrysler's fifth floor, or on a rowing machine at home, has a pet Yorkie named Koko who has *his* eyes, and was as perfectly tailored in his silk double-vented tux and patent pumps as in the pinstripe with knife-edge creases and squeaky-clean French cuffs and collar he had worn at the Pan Pacific the afternoon before.

Bob and Lily Lee

He makes $3 on every book of his that sells (that is about $4 million so far), earned $1 million in salary and bonus last year alone, and is purportedly worth $20 million that "somebody else manages because I'm up to my ears in *work*." He gets 750 public-speaking requests a *month*. On three-times-monthly visits to New York he stays in Chrysler's three-room suite at the Waldorf Astoria. He owns a condo overlooking the Atlantic in Boca Raton, Florida, with five bathrooms and a villa in Tuscany. The house in Bloomfield Hills, just out of Detroit, is like his own country club, with tennis and paddle tennis, pool and pool room, screening room, and a *salle de exercise* with Nautilus, treadmill (which he wishes he could "get off of"), Jacuzzi and sauna, and enough cars in the driveway, a friend says, to make *choosing* one a daily corporate decision.

His office in New York's Pan Am building is a movie set for a bigtime exec: corner suite with marble floors, wood-paneled walls, wrap-around windows, gargantuan chairs, stogie-sized ashtrays. His limo is Henry Ford black, with gray-blue velour seats, and the ever-ready corporate jet seats 15 and has its own flight attendant (no, Babs *not* Peggy - she's retired).

The high-torque supersalesman is *this* close to Frank, drinking scotch with him at 21 and playing Palm Springs with him at the California compound, and counts real estate market meister and tower builder Donald Trump among his bestest-with-the-mostest. (The eye-catching Ivana Trump just about upstaged the bride at the Iacocca wedding.)

Mr. Mustang has been snapped with Sophia, looking like the proverbial _gatto_ that swallowed the canary, says he found Raquel "short" and counts Tip O'Neill and Ted Kennedy among his frequent phoners. He proved to be the perfect cup of tea for our _creme de la creme_, who gave him an on-their-feet-ovation as he replied with an oversized Muppet wave. When presented with a talking stick carved by Haida Jim Hart, America's hottest industrial folk hero and perfect pitchman, allowed that Washington would have given him a _muzzle_.

All this commotion roused Lieutenant-Governor Bob Rogers, who throughout most of the _Straight Talk_ had nodded off. Official duties having done him in, the chairman of the bored stifled a patrician yawn early on and finally just gave in.

Barbara Brink, president of the Arts, Sciences and Technology Center, who along with the Junior League was the reaper of the evening's bountiful benefits, stood clapping and beaming in her black Valentino and her corona of Fergie-red hair. She had hounded the affable huckster for three long years to get him to venture north, and as a treat for her never-say-die effort, husband Russ was taking her off the following day to London, Milan and a week on the Orient Express. How's _that_ for icing on the _gateau_, cherie?

Tracy and Biill Rand

"He exceeded my expectations," a Zsazsagaborian woman with face powder caked in her crow's feet crowed above the applause.

"Speaking personally, _je regret_ rather _beaucoup_ not talking to _Mrs._ Iacocca," affected her friend, an aging habitue of a hundred beaches, her hair blow-dried to a yellow cement dome. "I have always gotten along so well with stews."

Bumped into Pia and Harvey Southam who are just about to move into Norman Keevil's impressive fortress. Pia is lyrically beautiful, preggers with a Christmas baby, swears she stopped competing with her old friend Maggie Trudeau a long time ago, and will definitely _not_ deliver a December 25 bambino. We were joined by Lois Milsom, in purple satin, who had just spent a Vancouver evening with Shirley Maclaine and entree Arthur Erickson before all assailed upon Maurice and Hanne Strong's ashram in Colorado for some

_143_

out-on-a-limb soul-searching.

Enrico and Aline Dobrzensky suauved their way out with a hand kiss -
well, Enrico did. They had spent their usual two months on the French Riviera
where the D de D daughters' dance studies had continued at the Princess Grace
School of Ballet in the moneyed enclave of Monaco. Mommy Aline was about
to slip out of her designer pumps and into her handpainted gold for evening
jogging shoes for their stroll home to Lost Lagoon penthouse. Parting is such
chic sorrow, no?

Slithered of to San Diego for a spate of sun. Well what did you expect,
Babs? It had rained *two* days in a row and the tan was starting to fade.

It was such a spree. AirCal'd it down - smooth, swift and simple - and
checked into the Del. The Hotel del Coronado on the Coronado Peninsula
across the bay from San Diego? For Heaven's sake, Barbie, it's positively world
famous! Built almost 100 years ago, it is a wedding-cake confection of a place:
tres Victorian yet so up to date. An absolute magnet for society over the years,
and the absolute innest beach resort. The scene of ever so many state visits -
11 U.S. presidents have lapped up the Grand old Monarch's luxury - and
thousands of celebs over the decades.

Foreign flash and the world-weary have dropped round for the European
charm and cuisine. King Edward VIII gave a state dinner here and later
married a Coronado housewife, one Wallis Something Simpson, whom he met
in the receiving line in the Grand Ballroom. *Some Like It Hot* was shot here
with Jack Lemmon, Tony Curtis and Marilyn Monroe, and our old friend from
Puerto Vallarta, Peter O'Toole, shot *The Stunt Man* here. Mary Pickford,
Tallulah Bankhead, and Greta Garbo delighted in the Del, Charlie Chaplin
played polo here and Sarah Bernhardt found it charmante.

Ronnie Regan's favorite, suite 3119, was just slightly grander than mine,
but checking out a living legend - the *hotel* not the president, Barbie, *do* pay
attention - was such a hoot! The stuff of which history is made.

Moving off Coronado Island and into downtown San Diego for a few
days proved fascinating. California's second largest city has undergone a
massive redo (it is all silver and bronze and black skyline now) since I was last
here, so I decided to check it out from the epicenter.

Eased into the authentically-restored-to-its-original-1910-grandeur U.S.
Grant Hotel. The turn-of-the-century landmark is positively posh after having
had $80 million spent on it. All is now mahogany and chintz, armoires and
wingback chairs, butlers and concierges, and the Grant ranks right up there
with the Beverly Wilshire, the Dorchester in London (still Liz Taylor's pet I
found out during the Royal Wedding) and the Peninsula in Hongkong.

It has a first-class wine cellar, deluxe dining, and serves a proper English four o'clock tea with string quartet in the lobby. _Tres civilise, non?_ Best of all it is right across from the fabulous new Horton Plaza where the most jaded jet setter can shop in Southern California pastel splendor till she runs out of time or tender.

Of course I went to the San Diego Zoo and Sea World. I never, ever need to go again. That blonde Joan Embery, who brings all those cute little furry things on Johnny Carson, was shooting a show at the zoo, and _no_ one _we_ know was at Sea World. However, there was one walrus who looked uncannily like that Count we met in Marbella two summers ago ...

Ta Ta Darling, Ciao for now,
Valerie.

THE YEAR 1987

ROOTS AND A CANAL
Penthouse partying with Pantageses and Puloses, then to Panama with panache.

LITTER TO GLITTER
CATS kick off and fundraisers cough up.

DRIER BY DEGREES
A winery opens and Webster winds up.

MOODS MAJESTIC
Dining with the Queen and dishing with Mila.

THE YEAR 1987

*T*his was the year Malgabarphobia, or fear of bad dressing started cropping up in the city. The better-known non-stop scene makers, were keen, it seemed, that their state-of-the-art threads not only be in, but AVANT. It led to a lot of notice-me outfits that looked as though they had been designed by a committee.

The year had its share of razzle-dazzle blitzkreigs to show off at—the Commonwealth Conference, with all those Prime Ministers and national dress-heavy receptions, "Cats" opened at the Queen E.—talk about costumes—(at the reception unfortunately)—and the Mulroneys came to flaunt.

A deux they threw a pinkies-up bash for the Queen, or "The Cat In The Hat" as we had taken to calling her she was cropping up so often. And solo, Mila asked 40 or so terribly grateful women of the world (or so we thought then) and a smattering of token men, to do lunch at Bridges.

Ross Fitzpatrick opened his very successful Cedar Creek Winery in Kelowna with a suitable bubbly send-up that involved half of Vancouver, John Turner played fund-raising tennis at the Plaza of Nations, and 800-plus party and athletic supporters flashed what they considered the latest Liberals-at-leisure wear.

The Vancouver Symphony threw a down-home-black-tie tupperwear party with natty-to-the-max Michael J. Fox and his family (Mikey wore sneakers with his tiny tux). And the first soon-to-be annual Jack Webster Foundation dinner took place with Haggis McBaggis looking as close to both well-dressed and pleased as we have seen him.

And I sailed from Acapulco through the Panama Canal on a first class Noriega-free cruise right into Puerto Rico, that other rich coast.

ROOTS AND A CANAL

Barbie Darling,

Pranced off to Diane Pantages's 50th. Of course *birthday*, dear heart. When one looks like the same giggly girl as in university, one can afford to flash one's age. Not that the dimpled darling had any choice. She is married to one of the city's all-time pro practical jokers, lawyer Tony Pantages, and *he* decided that a "surprise" party—more of a shock, *she* says—with 175 of her closest and mostest was *just* the ticket.

"Mink is my favorite fluff," I heard as a small cluster of us huddled in the front-hall foyer of a downtown office building. Like speakeasy patrons awaiting the boss's okay, we watched as a series of brass buttons and intercom passwords were flourished before being admitted to the penthouse inner sanctum of And Pulos's high-flying hideaway.

A more perfect party place one could hardly imagine: a real *garconniere*, or "pad de bachelor," as our friend Jean-Louis would say. It had the requisite vintage pool table, decadent four-poster boudoir, baby grand piano (burled walnut, *very* antique, watch your wine glass), and enough bric-a-brac and rococo kitsch to warm an antique-dealer's cockles.

Carol Woodward, Judy Geddes

"El mundo bizarro," sputtered Bruno Gerussi as he grand-toured the mazy rooms and alcoves. "A for eclectic," said the voice behind me as we both spotted the full-sized wooden carousel horse in the middle of the living room, the wall-sized solarium filled with all manner of plants—plastic, silk and real; hanging, sitting and clinging—and Robert Wagstein's colossal Zipper Lady wall sculpture all in one fell sweep of the room. Tiffany lamps shone down on overstuffed velvet couches, a wooden lion's head roared from over a doorway, leaded glass cabinets flashed antique silver collections or Victorian beaded evening purses and disembodied statue parts, and stone fountains parked themselves wherever there was room.

Rube Goldberg contraptions cropped up anywhere at all, as did a museum-quality collection of military hats, an ancient set of scales, an authentic photograph of a nude burlesque chorus line, and a statue of the Virgin Mary with candle, her eyes blessedly closed.

"Community property is just equitable distribution," came from the small claque in front of the bar. It could have been any one of the gleefully gathered. There were more than a few TOATFW's there (The One After The First Wife) and enough lawyers for a Bar Association quorum.

Carol Woodward, who had the time before been married to Andy Poulos, flashed a flame-colored silk creation, her former-Miss PNE smile, an impeccable blonde braided chignon and some "very pretty baubles," as that aunt of yours used to call serious jewelry. Husband Chunky, who is currently doing some interesting tidying up of the family store business, was as subdued and dignified as ever, and appeared no less uncomfortable than usual. Who says society is not civilized?

A solo Herb Capozzi, Ellen being in Sun Valley, sported funereal black as he ruffled through the throng, hot-wiring conversations with what in some cases were his latest zappers. "They may be one-lines," the wag beside me allowed, "but he takes several chapters to get there.

"Herb's a good guest at a birthday," the wag went on. "He's sympathetic about aging; after all, he's done all he and medical science can do to stave off the grim reaper." And we think women are catty, Babs dear.

Stock promoter-restaurateur Basil Pantages was there, of course: beige silk suit, paisley tie, pink pouf, not a glimpse of gray. I don't know what his formula is, but he is Greek.

Tonny Pantages, Roger Atkinson

Bob and Lily Lee bounced in, as depressingly up as ever. Natty in noir, Lily sported this year's must-have fitted suit, a freshwater pearl choker, a black bejewelled bow and her only slash of color, passion pink talons, as she chatted with Neil Cook's ex, Diane Brady. Touting her trademark tan—she looks great at Whistler in her silver ski suit—the world-tromping Ms. Brady was off on an African safari. When you have already done Nepal, India and China, Darling, what is left?

Harry Moll—Harry C's, Hy's restaurant's, etc.—gave the importance of being Herb a run for its money as he regaled small clusters with his comedy routines. Wife Suzy, fresh and shiny with her auburn curls, and in a smashing embroidered oriental jacket, laughed like it was the first time.

Barbara Aisenstat was looking very Chanel indeed in black with white satin collar and pearls, dark hair sleeked back in a bow, oversized glasses perched on her nose, but a little lost I thought—like the queen without her purse. Hy, as ever, was the loveable, frosty-topped walking Toby jug, as he chatted with Lee Pulos, whose apartment on the _other_ side of the building is as large as his brother's. You remember the Puloses, Barbie—real estate, Spaghetti Factories, the-Organ-Grinder-sold-to-The-Keg, land developments, etc.? And as many brothers to confuse you as the Pantages clan?

"Her looks have a shelf life somewhere between milk and yogurt," one of those make-hay-while-the-jawline-holds ladies was saying. "Yes," replied her friend, who must go through _flacons_ of her favorite scent, "but still, that look must take massive maintenance."

By now, Bruno Gerussi, upset to be one of the few in a tux, had removed his tie and was squiring the brilliantly blue-hued new Q.C. Nancy Morrison around the room. Bruno plays a moving man who drops a piano in the Candice Bergen TV show just shot in Vancouver; some days the Beach-comber must wonder what he ever studied Shakespeare for.

Lee Pulos, Hy Aisenstat

Shannon Sheppard, whose interior designs have bedazzled Vancouver for years, flew in from Fremantle, Australia, in shades of her own pastel favorites topped off with a Hawaiian lei. Rick Hansen's sister, Chris, brought the latest news of her brother-in-motion's tour, Drew Burns caught us up on his you-too-can-own-shares-in-the-Commodore, and Attorney General Brian Smith, who always looks as though he may have eaten the wrong thing for lunch, cracked the closest to a smile I've caught yet. Gastowner Keith McMyn, who has the revved-up mind of an outboard motor and who plugs his silliness into the nearest outlet and has a wonderful time, all the while dressed like the serious businessman he is, could give the AG a run in the no-smiles department.

The room was littered with ivy-leaguers grown long in the tooth who still think things are "a gas," and who were thrilled to be brought together for a love-in for one of their favorite ladies.

And the birthday girl herself? Well, surrounded by the spouse of her life, Tony, the boyish barrister in horn-rims who is Big Daddy to the Fab Four Pantages progeny, she was one tired Tinkerbell by evening's end but smiling the same crinkly grin 30 years After Campus.

And you thought the older the better was just for wine and cheese, didn't you?

You know I have been dying to see if there were any Beautiful People *between* the continents, so I finally ambled off to Acapulco, scurried aboard Sitmar Cruises' spiffy ship *Fairwind* and sailed off into the you-know-what.

Not before casing Aca, though. Sly Stallone has built a *very* swish casa up in that section near Las Brisas they call the Beverly Hills of Acapulco, near where Pierre Trudeau stays at his freebie friend's (what else is new?). Liza Minnelli stays there, too. Of *course* at different times. Oh, Barbie, do pay attention or I won't tell you anything.

Lily Lee, Chunky Woodward

We sailed at midnight, southbound for the Panama Canal: stars, moonlight, the city twinkling. Our 800-plus passengers, somewhat awash from bon-voyage cocktails and a *very* celebratory first-night dindin, were all up at the pointy end, casting coins into the moonlit bay to be dived for by those darling little urchins who should have been home in bed.

An Ocean Deck stateroom with a lounge area, TV and a steward named Francesco, who must have been living in the wall because I just had to *think* I might like something and it was there. The only problem I had with him was when I ordered afternoon tea. Coffee, orange juice, salami and cheese arrived every time, so eventually I just took it out with the others who really did get afternoon tea. Otherwise, fresh towels arrived continuously, the bed was turned up, down, anyway, and baskets of fresh fruit materialized every day, all day. Fabuloso! Wasn't this supposed to be an adventure in self-indulgence?

For the Captain's Welcome Cocktail Party, shipmates spotted at that morning's lifeboat drill in the kind of shorts, shirts, sunsuits and headgear that make tourists the laughing stock of most ports were now "spiffed to the sequined max," as your trendy cousin might say. All manner of tuxes for the men, and a respectable designer display by the dames-at-sea.

The captain himself, Nicola Di Stefano, was born into generations of officers, and dropped better lines on board than did his crew when we came alongside. He smoked a pipe, wore spotless white Gucci loafers and insisted he was "just a bus driver, back and forth, forth and back." He also gave several small chic cocktail parties, including one for the _Circolo de Comandante_—the past-passenger club—and later asked 10 or so of us to traverse the Panama Canal "in the air-conditioned comfort of the Captain's Lounge."

It was _so_ civilized, _mia cara_. He had his steward, Jose, do champagne and orange juice, smoked salmon—lox through the locks—and other delights as we doddled our way through the ditch. This took from dawn on through most of a very sticky day, and I did feel ever so sorry for the deck people who had staked out their railing space at 4 a.m. and were now looking a shade—of which there was hardly any—warm and weary.

The highest toll charged a ship passing through was $89,154.62 for _QE 2_ seven years ago, and it just serves her right for being so blessedly buxom. _We_ threaded ourselves through the eye of that very expensive needle (the U.S. alone has sunk $3 billion into it) for a third of that, and our handsome, gold-striped officers with their gold chains on their bronzed chests looked smoothly pleased.

At a sumptuous dinner that night— cannelloni gastronomica, island rock lobster and sea scallops, strawberries Romanoff—some of _Fairwind's_ more prominent passengers were noted: George Burns, Cab Calloway, Phyllis Diller, Don Rickles, Tony Bennett, Carole Lawrence

Diane Pantages

and Robert Goulet (separately, of course, they are now divorced), Allan King, Jim Nabors and old dimples himself, John Davidson. Mind you, they were not on _this_ particular passage. Noooo. We had a violinist named Maria Neglia, who may not strike a chord with you; a magician named Ward Thomas, who was a whiz-bang wonder with umbrellas; comedian Lee Tully straight off the _Ed Sullivan Show_; and four toothy singer-dancer-whatevers from _Showtime U.S.A._ Our closest claim to fame was Big Bob Francis, the vocalist who sang the theme song from _The King Of Kensington_ and had once partied with Pierre and Margaret.

We did, however, have passengers ranging from the Abiganas of Daly City, California, right through to the Zrnics of San Francisco, plus the requisite number of hopeful damsels, the let's-cruise-to-patch-up-our-marriage-brigade, almost _no_ unattached nymphets for the toupee-and-golf-hat-in-the-wind set to slaver over, and not nearly enough maritime gigolos to go around.

Pains-in-the-deck were relatively few. The graduates of 500 Arthur Murray courses practiced most days in the deserted discos, later to strut their stuff when Scott DeTurk and the Windward Lounge Orchestra finally draped themselves around their instruments. Said one frail foxtrotter, "I take these cruises so that, after I'm gone, the kids won't be driving around in Cadillacs."

Whenever we could tear ourselves away from the Olympics of Eating—10 chances a day plus an always-open pizza parlor—we would do shore excursions. None of us got off in the Panama Canal Zone, though, so we had to take the Texas blowhard's word that "it's untamed jungle, mangrove swamps, mosquitos, machetes and rough trade."

Many went ashore in the San Blas Islands, however, which is surprising given that we had to be ferried over in small tenders, there were no streets or ships and the resident condos were sea-level huts of bamboo and palm leaves. Even before the ship dropped anchor, we were surrounded by dugout canoes. Cuna Indian women in cornea-popping colors, with gold rings in their noses and babies in their laps, offered fabulous embroidered *molas* for sale, while boys and men yelled for coins to be tossed into the water so they could dive for them. "Money, money, money," echoed as we left, rather like the murmur of jungle magpies. Beautiful people, great clothes. More than one of us that night was wondering where on earth we were ever going to wear what we had bought. San Blas had been an eye-opener, though. Don't you just love a society where the women control the finances and handle the business transactions?

Then it was off to Curacao. Lillian Vander Zalm would love to ship its pastel buildings, laden with gingerbread and tiled roofs, right to Fantasy Gardens. The island is only 38 miles long, and could not be more of a Dutch treat if it tried.

The Virgin Islands eased into view next. St. Croix has Victor Borge as its Great Dane—his antique-filled mansion is in downtown Christianstaad. Maureen O'Hara has a two-tone house on a hill, with two flagpoles and a definite desire for privacy. I found out how rum is made by going through a tiresome distillery in the heat of the day—believe me, Darling, you don't want to know. And the St. Croix rainforest I jitneyed through on the way back to the ship was the location for *The Island Of Dr. Moreau*, with our friend from the Vancouver Film Festival, Michael York.

On to St. John the next day to check out the upscale crowd at Caneel Bay. Laurence Rockefeller certainly knew what he was doing when he bought 170 acres here. "Seven beaches, one for every day of the week," my driver allowed. Rockresorts recently sold it, but those stone gates are still a magnet for VIPs, and I don't mean Virgin Island People, Barbie.

In St. Thomas I helicoptered off for one of the most spectacular rides ever. "Ain't thet purty enough to put out yer eye?" the Diamond Jim Brady beside me sighed. "I'd like to drop that there Trunk Bay down there right into my back 40,000 in Texas."

A more down-to-earth shopper, who definitely knew what she wanted, was overheard as she and another stepped down the gangplank, "_You_ may be going to Mr. Tablecloth. _I'm_ going to Colombian Emeralds."

At Bluebeard's castle—"_No_ no parking," the sign says—besides catching a put-your-eye-out view of our pristine cruise liner lying in the harbor below, I learned from a sparkling-brown-eyed local source that Bluebeard was "one top lover boy—seven wives, killed six, then the last one she got him, and ever since it has been a woman's world."

There you have it, Darling. Who says travel doesn't broaden? Soo much more. No time. Reality is going to be a real come-down.

Ta Ta Darling,
Valerie

LITTER TO GLITTER

Barbie Darling,

Clamored off to _Cats'_ opening-night gala on one of summer's most sweltering _soirs_. Leaving the yacht in Desolation Sound and flying in for a show that had already got well into its nine lives in London, New York and later in trend-setting T.O. was the kind of summer sacrifice I plan to make even less frequently in future. However, the intro of a theatrical event that over 250,000 feline fanciers are expected to see in a 10-week run is nothing to caterwaul about, and the $100-per _billet_ did go to further the arts, there being no free launch, dear heart.

The Queen E. lobby was wall-to-wall la-di-da, all seeing themselves as the cat's pajamas and no one looking remotely mousey. There was a lot of neck-stretching, but the cream was easily separated: they were in black tie and sophisticated swank because they knew they would get to howl with the other fat-cats-for-a-good-cause at the after-bash.

The very Tony Parsons, having caught the production in London two weeks earlier, crept in on little patent feet with, on his arm, the bonny, blonde Pamela Masion. "He's so smooth," muttered a CBC type to my right. "If that's calculated ease, I want some."

Lifestyles Of The Terminally Introspective guru Jim Pryor, who is really a

Jiminy Cricket kind of a guy, opted for a white raw silk jacket, a black velvet bow tie and Pat Higinbotham, and importer Dale Mearns, a cat of many colors in a 1960s reprise of a multihued frock, merged with tall-blond-and-handsome Richard Murray, *B.C. Business's* main man.

Former North Van mayor Don Bell (who now relates Safeway publicly) arrived flashily happily in a white limo, while hairdresser-to-the-Kerrisdale-claque Richard Jeha, an ultracasual cool cat in a cream-stripped suit and Karl Lagerfeld ponytail, came by in a Caprice Classic convertible with CAT on the licence plate.

Pope Show producer Margaret Steley (she did the Chuck-and-Di do, too, remember Barbie?) is trying her hand at movie producing while repelling the big magnet pulling her toward Brisbane's Expo 88. (You know how those Aussies like to stay once they have had a taste.)

Staking out territory on the landing with a beauty on either side of him,

John Ketcham, Janet Ketcham, Sam Ketcham

our QC at the QE, Winton Derby, tried to convince passersby his wit well had *not* run dry. "His briefs and beefs are rare but always well done," allowed an admiring colleague.

Peter Paul Saunders, much less versatile now, stood the ever-ebullient Peter Bentley to a pipe-off on the plaza while Nancy Saunders beamed on in bright blue and Sheila Bentley in frosty white.

A *sans*-Jacqueline Ron Longstaffe sported daughters Sherry on one arm and Brandy on the other as they first-nighted it in for the first act. Multimillion-dollar music man Andrew Lloyd Webber appears to have done it again. Take very light verse from T.S. Eliot, dress 34 lean-and-lovely song-and-dancers as bits of fluff, catapult them into a three-times-larger-than-life garbage dump to cavort and pussyfoot about unhindered by a tedious plot, then lap it up at the box office—$40 million in Toronto alone. As Uncle Rodney used to say, "Money can't buy happiness, but it's a good bargaining chip for one's next venture!" Having seen *Evita, Starlight Express* and all, one must admit that Webber really is "ept" at what he does.

A newly svelte Harvey Southam clearly felt otherwise. Either that or the *deux chapeaux* he is wearing at the offices had him asleep in the first act, to be awakened only by Rum Tum Tugger's tom-cat-on-a-hot-tin-roof-solo. Terry David Mulligan—no catnapper he—whistled and clapped as the rock'n'roll tabby (Tugger, silly, not Terry) strutted and gyrated his black-Spandexed torso. Gives you paws, doesn't it, dear?

"Migawd, they all look like Evelyn Roth," the wag in front allowed of the intricate wool-tuft costumes woven to simulate cat fur. And at $1,500 per catsuit, each is work of art.

As the onstage flash and dazzle careened to a close and the cats took their curtain calls to our squatting ovations (I loved fallen glamorpuss Grizabella: just like someone we know, Barbie), we all hummed _Memory_ as we had been programmed to, and filtered upstairs for the cast reception.

Peter Brown had cooly summersuited it as most other penguins sweltered, and he looked a little more the canary swallower than usual.

The mane event pulled in Harry and Suzy Moll, who were heading off to the Med for _le petit cruise_ aboard the ultimate _Sea Goddess_. They are staying at the very nice Negresco in Nice, just in case your envy is incomplete.

Spotted a very Kennedyesque-looking Janet Ketcham bookended by her handsome and betuxed sons, John and Sam. (Who can get their sons to put on _ties_ let alone tuxes anymore?) Wearing a slim silk shirred strapless sheath (no easy matter) with a frill-of-it-all skirt, freshwater pearls and diamond chandeliers in her ears, she was just back from Washington and the White House. I mean, when _Mrs. Nancy Reagan Invites You To Tea At 4 O'Clock Saturday_, how can you refuse? Oh, all right, Barbie:

Harry Moll, Suzy Moll

Nancy was in knee-length black and white, not Adolfo, was somewhat brittle, rather cold, and not at all chatty.

It is nice to see Janet getting a little recognition for her volunteerism and her art acquisitions work, what?

The entire cast metamorphosed from furball ragamuffins to sleek chicies in their gladdest rags, just when you thought there wasn't room to swing a you-know-what. They ate like hungry alley cats—all dancers do, I'm not letting anything out of the bag—and melted into the melting crowd. I was starting to hear _Kittens On The Keys_ in my head and knew it was time to find mine, but it really had been the cat's meow, darling: a purrfect premiere.

Bogged off to Blighty, only to find you slipped away to St. Moritz. Didn't any one tell you dear one? Never in summer! Not to worry, I'll fill you in on all the European news and prattle I picked up while you were mountaineering.

That French friend we met in St. Trop' last summer was at the Beau-Rivage Hotel in Geneva when the Duchess of Windsor's jewelry was being auctioned. She said *no* glamorati showed up (they phoned their bids or sent minions). She said the only interesting male was Nicholas Rayner—mid-40's, runs Sotheby's Geneva. *Quelle* disappointment; one thought the place would have been plagued by prominent, propertied plutocrats.

Harrods and Harvey Nichols were offering copies of the collection. Yes, Barbie, I now have a large *faux* flamingo. I also had tea in the Albemarle Room at Brown's Hotel, seeing no one interesting at all; had my hair cut at Michaeljohn, where I just missed the duchess of Kent; and bought an umbrella at Swaine and Adeney as I have wanted to do since I noticed the Queen's own on board *Britannia* docked in Vancouver three years ago. I knew you cared.

Garde Gardom is enjoying being B.C.'s agent-general in London. British Columbia House on Lower Regent Street has never looked better since he and Helen (who will have lots of chances to wear her famous hats for a whole new appreciative audience) have settled in.

Peter Brown, Joanne Brown

The house that Margaret Thatcher bought in Dulwich two years ago for £400,000 is now worth £200,000 more. NeoGeorgian, it has five bedrooms and is her weekend dream home. A friend who has been a guest tells me Mrs. Thatcher made her own curtains—I *am* relieved—and collects decorative plates and copper saucepans, and that the 200-square-foot bedroom has an ensuite with gold-plated taps and Jacuzzi, and can be entered only through a security gate (the house, not the bedroom—and if Denis is as dozy as we saw him at the Expo party, that may pose a problem). Oh, and Andrew Lloyd Webber wrote her election theme song. She won.

The Monaco Grand Prix was run while I was in England, but our Monte Carlo tittle-tattler filled me in. The course is as it has been since 1929, but this was the first time a Brazilian won in a Japanese-powered car.

Anyway, that's not the news. Caroline and Albert are fighting over who will reign when Rainier resigns. What a choice: the Wimp (last summer's Royal Wedding?) or the Witch. *Nabila* the yacht is nowhere is the harbor this year, and Nabila the daughter has been told to cool her romance with Canadian Gordon Thompson from *Dynasty*. Baby Doc and Michelle Duvalier are still living in the villa near Cannes they rent from Adnan Khashoggi's son. It backs on to the expressway to the Cote d'Azur, which they hate, but has a pool, even though they try to make no waves.

Chuck and Di's problems continued when they were at the Cannes Film Festival (he didn't want to come, she didn't want to leave). They call her "Lay-dee Dee" there, and thought her pale blue chiffon dress was *"comme une grandmère"*—that's *really* momsy, ma chere—and that he was neither tall nor dashing for a prince. Oh those French!

Back in Jolly Old, Charles had one of his works on display at the Royal Academy. It was a 3-1/2" by 3-1/2" picture of a Norfolk farm building, entered under the name Arthur G. Carrick. Arthur and George are two of his names, and Carrick is one of the places he is earl of. In any case, the picture wasn't half bad, and, at that size, how could one tell anyway?

Di's Phillip Dunne scandal was still hot, and she and Fergie (less google-eyed than we saw her last year in the Abbey) behaved very improperly at *"Askit."* I am chillily informed that they did indeed poke assorted bottoms with their brollies—from Swaine and Adeney, no doubt.

"Di is behaving less like a queen and more like a sixth-form schoolgirl" I overheard Her In The Hat tell Madame With The Ankles in a tea shop one afternoon, and since I couldn't reach Vic Chapman at Buck House to deny or confirm this vile innuendo, this salacious slander, I can only suppose it is the old *Dallas* in the Palace as usual.

Peter Paul Saunders, Sheila Bentley, Peter Bentley, Nancy Saunders

Ran into Bruce Allen and Jane Macdougall at Terminal 4 in Heathrow. They had just attended The Prince's Trust. Bruce and Bryan lose a fair chunk of coin every time Di decides she wants to see Adams one more time and he is pulled off a successful tour and *Into The Fire*. All for a good cause, though: over-privileged youth for under-privileged youth this time. Besides, there is that special shoulder-rubbing with legends like Eric Clapton, Ringo Starr (Di wore a Sgt. Pepper white-and-gold military jacket), George Harrison and Elton John. He and the estranged Renate are very much huggy-poo again, and she looks a lot more relaxed than when we spotted them at Fergie's wedding.

The only other rock bits I picked up are that Stevie Wonder stayed with Paul McCartney at Paul's village home in Peasmarsh, 60 miles from London, and Stevie seems to have liked the country air enough to drop a half-million for a thatched cottage of his own.

After the concert, Bruce and Jane spent her birthday dinner at Langdon's—impossible to get in without superserious connections, remember?—with newlyweds Tom Cruise and Mimi Rogers, and ended up chatting with Dustin Hoffman, "Not about *Ishtar*," Bruce assures. I'm so sorry these birthday bashes of Jane's couldn't be a little more upbeat.

Ta Ta Darling. That's what's new Pussycat!

Valerie

DRIER BY DEGREES

Gordon Campbell, Carole Taylor, Art Phillips

Barbie Darling,

Sashayed off to Alfred Sung's fall fashion gala at the 'otel Meridien. It was couture-couture-coo the whole evening, on and off the runway—the eau-zone of heady French perfume, and mondo swank all the way. As the Purcell String Quartet played, a champagne reception in the Chateau Lafite Room gave a lot of never-looked-betters the chance to get the lowdown on the high-ups over civilized crystal.

"Haute enough for you?" asked the snoot-over-flute to my right, moving on before I needed to answer. "That gluteus maximus is considerably minimus since her trip down south," offered the voice beside me as we watched the haute-her walk away. "And that's *real* Chanel, not a knockoff," she concluded.

Fran Belzberg (sans Sam), easily one of the city's best-dressed Hall-of-Famers, blew in in the season's de rigueur short black leather skirt, which she had topped with a giraffe-patterned black-and-white peplum jacket.

"I tried that on in Bendel's my last trip to New York," offered the shopping ninja next to me, "and is sure didn't look like that on me. Do you suppose that waist of hers is *all* from tennis?"

Carole Taylor floated in in a long black off-the-shoulder knit with a bronze beaded bow on one hip (she would wear it again several nights later at the Bennett dinner), Art Phillips suavely keeping station alongside in his shawl-collared tux and flashing an antique gold pocket watch on a chain.

Close behind came Gordon Campbell and his marathoner mate Nancy, fitness freaks who frequently train for good causes. They look as good in shorts and tops as in their civvies. The mayor was wearing a bright green tie, as was Peter Hyndman, but each denied starting a new political party on a greenbacks platform.

Bob and Lily Lee blended in on the heels of Harvey and Pia Southam, the latter in one of Barbara and Martha's last little sale items, and Lily in a patterned strapless sheath highlighted by the cutest antique jade necklace.

As we all dawdled in to dindin in the Versailles Ballroom, I checked out the Mearns sisters. Dale was wearing a black lace ever-so-mini left over from the first mini era (doesn't she ever throw *anything* out, Barbie?), while Lindsay had bagged a leopardskin sheath that, according to the *sotto voce* voice beside me, looked "like the seat covers on a 1940s Chevy."

Julie Molnar, Peter Hyndman

Julie Molnar welcomed us as president of the Cartwright Gallery, to whom the evening's $7,000 boodle (at $175 per duo) would go, while we nibbled seafood terrine to the strains of Haydn. Julie's little black-with-pearls contrasted dramatically with Jacquie Cohen-Herrendorf's gold lame trapeze. "Surely Ms. Cohen can afford a slip with that little see-through creation," said a witty kitty who had taken off her kid gloves to reveal claws. "I suppose as long as she stays out of lighted doorways.."

Mama Marlene, who would soon head east to become Marlene Cohen-Wexler, looked the part of the blushing bride in something blue.

Oohs-on-cue started almost as soon as the glamor derby moved from the floor to the stage. Cameras were clicking like crickets as *la crema di tutti crema* of Alfred Sung's collection for fall 1987 ran away with the runway. "The most sophisticated collection I've ever done," the designer told me after a show that was fashion forward with a nice nod at traditional classic. By the way, Alfie Darling himself was wearing thin—just his hair, that is. Instead of his year-round uniform of beige cotton chinos, blazer and T-shirt, he wore what he said was his only suit—navy, gathered at the back—with brown loafers, white socks, snowy polo shirt and a "cameo brooch I bought in Venice."

Robson Street Fashion Park developer Peter Foreman, who with his partners sank nearly $5 million into the property, is a joint licensee for the Alfred Sung store. He and store manager Liz Coleman looked like canary-swallowing cats as the night's money-no-objectors sang Sung's praises.

Marlene Cohen, Jacquie Cohen-Herrendorf

Say what you will about it, Barbie, this crowd is *always* willing to shop.

By the time the Judy Lamarsh affair rolled around a fortnight later, dinners out were starting to look like poultry in motion. At this little clambake (would that it had been) the two poached breasts of you-guessed-it were served with strange little bones sticking out just in case it was thought the chef was trying to *poulet* a fast one.

Let's skip dinner, though (four at our table wished they had). The evening was the third held annually in a different Canadian city to honor the scrappy cabinet minister who would have insisted that a dinner in her memory be "stimulating and fun." She would *not* have been amused.

Geills Turner, fighting trim in hot pink and black, knows that good manners are what you use to conceal what you are thinking. Still, the look in those frosty blue eyes was, in your great-uncle's words, "chillier than a penguin's toenails," as she listened to an analysis of how many knives might be found in her struggling hubby's back, or to hints about Ed Broadbent's possible prime ministership.

"The view from Vancouver, Ottawa and Washington was pas-de-troised between Jack Webster, Marjorie Nichols and Allan Fotheringham. Flattery-operated Webster responded to the converted crowd like Sally Field at the Oscars, with a "they like me, they really like me" kind of glow. Foth's daughter Francesca dug a small hole in the carpet with the toe of her patent leather pump as Daddy Dear told for the 18th time (that I have heard) how he feels like Zsa Zsa Gabor's eighth husband—he knows what to do, he just doesn't know how to make it interesting—and that he is, after all, "but a small ball of putty in the great wheel of life."

Blizzard-quick Marjorie Nichols was superb, however. Personally responsible for destroying three premiers, she proceeded to wipe the Trade and Convention Center floor with her no-chance-at-all colleagues. She was so devastatingly good that Webster and lots of the frequent speechifiers in the room could not scribble down her zingers fast enough.

Actor Jackson Davies looked on admiringly as actor Bruno Gerussi performed a could-have-heard-a-pin-drop tribute to the one and only Judy. Mayor Gordon Campbell and Mrs. Mayor decided to ignore the fact that they had arrived in black tie: "No, we weren't going to, or coming from, something else." Getting almost no response from the audience, entertainer Nancy White, whose specialty is satirical songs, decided to quit while she was behind. "There's no sense advertising your troubles; there's no market for them," as grandmama used to say. Despite all this, Jack Poole gave the evening a "nine-and-a-half," leaving the few that overheard him wondering just how much he gets out anymore.

I've had a wonderful evening, Barbie, but this wasn't it.

The following night at the Jack Webster Foundation Dinner, that honored B.C.'s outstanding journalist of the year, was another kettle of...well, rolled breast of chicken stuffed with brown and wild rice. No, I didn't eat mine, but it definitely looked like a possibility. The cream of pistachio soup was superb, just as it had been at the Iacocca dinner when it was introduced here.

Joe Clarke, Maureen McTeer

The room was filled with all those faces you see whenever you turn on the news, and all those faces _behind_ the names in the paper, with big-daddy-of-them-all Knowlton Nash telling us how it really works. Journalists, we learned, are just shy egomaniacs, while _old_ journalists never die, they just lose their frequency. And history, Uncle Knowlty acknowledged, is "just one damn thing after another."

Ron Longstaffe, who had given the Quaker grace, continued to puff on his pipe through all this, while wife Jacqueline, in a red-and-white English country-girl print and a spectacular diamond-and-gold neckpiece, slipped off one red pump and proceeded to play footsie with her own husband, for heaven sakes. Can you believe it, Babs?

Pia Southam, in an up-to-the-second (though she swears it is two years old) black-and-gold-velvet short suit, put on her distance glasses to focus on the speakers. The eyes are definitely the first to go. Everything else looks annoyingly perfect.

Former Lieutenant Governor Henry Bell-Irving and his wife Nancy reminisced between awards—BCTV's John Daly won the evening's biggie of $2,500—about some of the behind-the-scenes snafus with the Queen *last* visit, reminding me that no matter how good our newshounds are, the best stuff seldom, if unfortunately ever, gets out.

Drinky-poos in the Hyatt bar after with Knowlton Knational. In his most fulsome, self-caressing tone, he imparted pseudo-profound insights to a small and lucky group. He has a two-page, single-spaced vita, Barbie, and absolutely perfect hair.

Bob Annable, Ross Fitzpatrick

Winged off to the Cedar Creek estate winery kickoff in Kelowna. Billed as The Grape Escape by its new owners, the weekend was *tres* Learjet-setty and would have dazzled your average jaded sophisticate.

Since Ross Fitzpatrick considered the Chateau Petrus Pomerol 1974 he had skewered the week before for $1,450 a "real deal," the 285 of his closest cronies venturing into the deepest Okanagan knew that the Fitzpatricks would put on a spread to rival the exquisite dinner parties they are known for at their Point Grey Road *pied a terre.*

Buses—no vans ordinaire, darling, these were full-size Greyhounders—picked up the escapees at their various hotels in the early afternoon, except for those who feel insecure without the Mercedes or the Jaguar within petting distance. Then, while various grape-stomping teams assembled themselves for a squish-off, several of us wandered from winery to lakefront, where there will be lavish, Lake Como-like living quarters—guest house, swimming pool, tennis courts—with a 20-foot, 1965-vintage mahogany Riva runabout for Ross and wife Linda whenever they are not in the South of France, at their Tuscany olive grove or any other favorite haunts. There is a resource company to run, after all, my dear, and one must keep an eye on those pesky little gold futures.

Meanwhile, back at the winery, some of Vancouver's more respected lawyers, accountants, designers and consultants had changed into outlandish outfits complete with headbands. *My* favorite was Jean Chretien in green-and-yellow shorts, turquoise headband and sockless back business shoes, while some went for Ralph Brown in a white paper jumpsuit rolled up to the knees with "Grapebusters" emblazoned on the back and a laurel wreath taped to his thinning hair. Wife Brenda, who wore her wreath front and center, looked like a deranged Lillian Vander Zalm.

A mad monk—he had been a Scott Paper VP when he arrived—named Dave Stowe and his wife in full habit, "Sister Mary," were trying to add a somewhat ecclesiastical tone to the festivities until two streakers did a full moon in the vat, as though feet in the vino were not enough.

"Just keep in mind that an ounce of don't-say-it is worth a pound of didn't-mean-it." I heard as we filed into a white-tablecloth-and-napkin sit-down dinner for close to 300. Among the other exquisite goodies served were two 55-pound golden-roasted pigs with apples in their mouths. The flushed and stained stompers had by now changed into their "real clothes," that in more than a few cases were $300 sweaters and this year's anything-but-black leather pants.

Jean Chretien, Kyle Mitchell

This is Capozzi country, and Tom was pretty in a blush pink sweater—so appropos since Ross's winery's Pinot Noir Blanc had two nights earlier won the best "blush" in the local wine festival. Dr. Mike Bell, whose winery-warming gift had been a '66 Chateau Margaux, barely took off his Australian bush hat, Diane Farris flashed her black-and-silver Martha Sturdy earrings, and Jacquie Longstaffe shone in a sunshine-yellow Roy Lichtenstein sweater, a print of which is in the Longstaffe collection at home. The post-prandial inebriation level was remarkably controlled considering that some very fine vino indeed had been flowing for hours.

Why, fiddle-di-dee, Barbie; the whole scene was just like that wonderful picnic Miss Scarlett went to just before war broke out.

Ta Ta Darling, and remember: eat dessert first; life is unpredictable.

Valerie

MOODS MAJESTIC

Barbie Darling,

Crept off to the Commonwealth Conference with *great* trepidation. The "wealth" sounded intriguing enough, but you know how I feel about the other part.

In any case, if one could avoid all those interminable sanctions and "Fiji or not Fiji," it was just possible to look upon the whole little gathering as one week-long, $19 million-plus wingding. And so international, too.

Had tea their first morning in town with Betty and Phil. (Of course *your* Betty and Phil, Barbie; she *is* the head of the Commonwealth, remember?) Well, *I* had Twinings English breakfast, and the Queen had Dubonnet with a twist. Philip had a lot more sun spots and freckles in his hairline than last trip

Isabelle Diiamond, Frances Belzberg

(not from two days at Qualicum, surely), and Susan Hussey, Her Maj's lady-in-waiting, looked even more like her mistress than she did when we spotted her at Andy and Fergie's wedding last summer. Elizabeth Alexandra Mary herself? *Very* ordinary blue-and-beige silk dress, although the zipper *was* exquisitely put in by hand, stitch by tiny stitch. Then there was a blue-straw sailor breton just like the one wee Wills wore to the wedding, and sensible navy patent shoes with heels the size of dock pilings. But, Barbie, the jewelry! Diamonds, pearls, and a robin's-egg sapphire to die for. No wonder she is happy and glorious.

I watched Jack Webster—who seems proprietorially to regard her as *his* queen—blush a deep royal red while stammering his small chat as CKVU's Daryl Duke-to-duked it with Philip. Each and every of the lucky sons (and daughters) of the empire present looked mightily pleased that "The Canadian Secretary" had been "commanded by Her Majesty to invite" *them* "to a Reception to be given by The Queen and The Duke of Edinburgh" on a forever-to-be-saved invitation heavily gilt-edged and embossed with the royal insignia. None would have missed it for all the tea in...well, you know.

Dashed off later to the duke's Challenge To Youth awards dinner at the Hotel Vancouver. No, there were *not* prizes to anyone under 40 who could fake it, Barbie; it is a funding program for young achievers.

Over 800 diehard royalists got to dine with a prince of a fellow, to contribute to a good cause, and then name-drop for ever-more bons mots like, "As I was saying to the duke over the roast duck capon..."

Carole Taylor minced in in a black velvet sheath, and ex-Teck Mrs. Joan Carlisle-Irving, whose decorating job on the house on Mustique gives Princess Margaret's pad a right run for it, swished in with fundraiser and board-member extraordinaire Margaret Ashley, whose husband has been a Canadian equerry on a number of royal visits.

Fresh from free-trading it, Pat Carney flew in with her slim twin, Jim. She looked remarkably calm considering the week she had just had. She said she had made Thanksgiving dinner for her family, and had put up blackberry jam, the two domestic things she does no matter what, so matters were under control (Simon Reisman will be so pleased).

Jeffrey Simpson had jetted in to give *Globe and Mailers* and the CBC the real scoop as he does, and the baby Bentalls, Chuck and Julie and sister-in-law Alison (Clark Bentall is on the Challenge to Youth honorary committee, the Bentall Foundation being a corporate sponsor) flashed their familial ensign.

Peter and Sheila Bentley breezed in. He wore a dashing tux, she a fur that the evening's patron—who is also president of the World Wildlife Fund—seemed not to notice.

Martha Sturdy, Catherine Regehr

All in all, the required number of debutantes (fresh-faced in froufrou gowns), dilettantes (the $150 tickets made it unnecessary to be rich and famous to hob-nob—just rich), and monarchists (hardcore types who would not for the world pass up a chance for a one-on-one gaze into those royal blues) raised $60,000 for a winner of a cause.

Lurched off to lunch with Mila the next noon. Madame Mulroney threw a small bash at Bridges for the wives of conference delegates, the 40 or so *femmes du monde* arriving on Jack Charles's luxury yacht *Hotei*—Chuck and Di bounded aboard it last year, remember?—which was definitely better than busing it.

Elegant and elaborate, the blowout had very orchestrated political overtones, with nods toward sports, society, fundraisers, fashion, the arts and even Canadians in Hollywood.

Within a narrow set of givens, such West Coastlings as tall-slim-and-above-it-all high jumper Debbie Brill flexed pecs with the likes of Steve Fonyo and Lori Fung, who wore a great suit and was quite the spiffy look-turner. Politicoquettes Carole Taylor and Mary Collins—who is more than everywhere—were tied in the marathon glassy-eyed smileoff required of busy women who know they should be in their offices rather than where they are.

Mr. Jax's Louis Eisman cast a practiced eye over the assembled ensemble while discreetly avoiding comment even over Mila's sober-as-a-judge navy-and-white combo, or Maureen McTeer's made-in-Vancouver high-risk passion purple leather bomber jacket and skirt...and shoes, and purse. Eisman himself opted for a subtle, well-cut, and very unCanadian Giorgio Armani offering.

Denis Thatcher, who had more serious things on his mind than lunching with the ladies, was a no-show, but our man in San Fran, Patrick Reid, breezed in with the exquisite Alison on his arm. "You've brought the *daughter*, Laurier LaPierre called to the ex-Expo poobah, aluding to Rick Hansen's new bride, Amanda. The mother-daughter due are sister switcheroos if ever there were.

Alison Bentall, Chuck Bentall, Julie Bentall

David Foster brought his Mom, which was safer since he is not quite divorced and that Jenner woman hogged all the spotlight at the recent Whistler celeb-fest, Margot Kidder came alone, with new henna highlights, a man's pinstripe suit and tie, looking even more fatally femme than she had in black strapless velvet at the Genie Awards or in an emerald-green Elizabethan getup at the royal family's version in England last summer of the *Battle of the Network Stars*, The Grand Knockout Tournament.

The Southams had been shanghaied for the occasion—silver-haired seigneur Gordon in a striped shirt, tie and suit that begged compliments; doyenne of doyennes Jeannie, whose quips and asides would have Dorothy Parker scrambling for her quill; and dutiful daughter-in-law Pia, smoothing the skids in the little status game we were all gratefully playing.

Madame Southam Sr. was just back from a calorie-deprived week at Maine Chance—$2,500 a week, if memory serves, for a strawberry for brekkie, a lettuce leaf for lunch and a cup of chicken broth for din din—and was convinced that the pheasant and tortellini would wipe out her whole week at the spa. Charming and disarming, she was full of ripe royal gossip; the

Queen at Qualicum and Veronica Milner's "quaint" cottage that is "so English country garden;" the duke's "you call that a beach" about our beloved Qualicum, obviously having disremembered Brighton; and the $5,000-per-passenger donations to the Wildlife Fund that it took to go whale-watching with dear Dukey.

Surrounded by silken robes, exotic hairdos and enough microphoned Mounties to more than mention, the few of us who were not wives-of were awfully pleased dear Mila had thought to include us.

Ever the political animal, the PM's much better half rose from her _Mille feuille aus baies des vents couverts de l'ocean_—never mind, Barbie, it's a _dessert_, all right?—to sail right past her guests and thank the Bridges kitchen staff. She is one smart cookie who most definitely knows which side her bread is buttered on, dear heart. And as for _moi-meme_, I now know how to say, "How are you?" in Malaysian should the occasion ever arise again.

That evening it was off to the park with the Clarks—Joe and Mo, Barbie; do try to keep up. Actually, the dinner was offered by "The Right Honorable Joe Clark, Secretary of State for External Affairs, and Maureen McTeer on the occasion of the Commonwealth Heads of Government Meeting and in honor of the visiting Foreign Ministers, "but Maureen had told me at lunch that it was to be a barbecue in Stanley Park at _HMCS Discovery_ and just wear pants and a sweater.

Pat Carney, Jim Carney

Almost no one did—there were even some sequins and long dresses—but Ms. McTeer had on the purple leather pants to her purple jacket, and an antique crown-shaped diamond pin she had bought in Victoria.

Joe wore a buckskin jacket without the matching pants, which were being hemmed, and, yes, he did wear ordinary slacks—if you are going to carry on like this, Barbie, I will stop now.

In any case, an extremely eclectic group of about 850 gathered in a huge tent pitched at the point on Deadman's Island filled with flowers, music and a bountiful buffet. The menu, the Clarks said, had been inspired by the Canadian harvest, so there was salmon, chicken, venison and everything $100,000 would buy.

The Carney twins were there, and so were UN Ambassador Stephen Lewis

(Michelle was in New York), the Patrick Reids, our mayor and Jack Webster, who hated it and beat a retreat of his own. There, too, were Bill Clarke who had had his royal fill with Charles and Diana last time; and bejillionaire Sam Belzberg, whose wife Fran was forced to wait at the gate with Isabelle Diamond while Sam parked in the park—she had the invitation, and *no* one got in without security clearance.

Then came the Peter Browns, with Joanne sailing through all smiles while Petey Baby looked unusually surly—maybe it was the five o'clock shadow. In an incongruous conversation about names, Toni Onley revealed that his dear old mum had named him Norman, and we all agreed that we liked Toni *much* better. Meanwhile, the cool and sophisticated Yukiko, in a smashing suit and hat, removed herself from our small group's impoverished witticisms and smiled above it all.

Driving home, dear heart, I wondered what the monkeys might have thought as motorcade after motorcade sped by their Stanley Park zoo cages in the middle of the night with lights flashing and motorcycles revving.

It was off to Enterprise Hall on the Expo site the next afternoon for a spot of tea and a large and impressive dose of B.C. fashion.

Hosted for the Commonwealth spouses by Mila Mulroney and by Lillian Vander Zalm, who showed up in a skirt (last year's length—forgive me), sweater and matching you-guessed-it, the show was indeed Spectacular By Design; as it had been billed.

Martha Sturdy and Catherine Regehr flaunted their finest off and on the runway, Martha had just made an appearance in Forbes magazine, which from a business point of view "beats the buttons off *Vogue, Harper's Bazaar* and *Elle,* honey," as she smugly noted.

Grace McCarthy flashed a Mr. Jax, while Mr. Jax's Mr. Eisman went with the best of the line from Hugo Boss. The Asia Pacific Foundation's (and Senator Jack's mainstay, Natalie Austin, wore a favorite navy Valentino, and Ramona Beauchamp was all soft and cuddly in cream-colored fur and fabric. Although Julie Molnar was to leave for New York that night on Cartwright Gallery business, and planned to do a little shopping there, she has been known to affect a B.C. label or two.

While local rag-trade royalty watched the runway, the real star of the spectacle was the up-to-the-millisecond Mrs. Mulroney in a black leather miniskirt, a quilted cropped matching jacket, French-braided hair with a Chanel black-red-and-gold bow, and "the best gams in the place," as one happy news photographer whole-heartedly noted.

Now, Babs, if I stop to tell you about the little shindig thrown the next day for the artistic community at Skookum Art Glass (Ken Danby is divinely handsome but unfortunately has a gorgeous wife to boot, George Pratt is as imposing as his sculptures, Carol Sabisten's massive tapestry from labels around the world is perfect art for shoppers), or about the network scrambling among city lawyers to see who could get them in to see the Queen unveil the new coat of arms at the law courts, or the cultural conniptions that went on to meet Gov. Gen. Jeanne Sauve and Karen Kain backstage at *The Merry Widow*, then I will not have time to tell you about the latest on Betty Windsor—all right Her Majesty—and the stars in town for the Film Festival.

The night before the Windsors flew off to the Prairies, Bill and Lil gave a little fest for the faithful. Never have I seen such blatant political paybacks in my entire, Darling, but just let me give you a quick scoop.

First of all, it was at the B.C. Enterprise Center: people do love pulling up in limos to the old Expo site. Lillian, if you can believe it, looked absolutely exquisite in a silver frilled fantasy of a dress, and enough sparkles on her headband that you could mistake it for a slipped crown. Jack Webster was Pat Carney's date, and looked bemused to be sitting at the head table with Their Royal Haitches, the LG and the mayor and all, with the international press—perhaps a chap or two from Glasgow—looking on.

Ann-Marie Flavelle, Daryl Duke

Norman Keevil black-tied it in, followed by a pair of Jacks, Austin and Poole, with their wives, and the Belzbergs, Fran wearing the dearest diamond choker and a short handkerchief-hem that raised a few stodgy eyebrows. Fran Cohen sparkled in an emerald green Zandra Rhodes, and Rona Radler was in the jettest black.

There were more cabinet ministers than ever show up at the legislature, and enough fundraisers in the room to finance the takeover of Kiribati.

The Queen wore pink—nice hat but the emeralds a tad splashy—and you could tell she was still rinsing the royal curls with Chocolate Kiss, leaving a touch of gray on the temples. And I have it on good authority that she still does the makeup in zero-five: thin layer of foundation, powder, dab of blush on each cheek, unplucked eyebrows. The reddish-pink lipstick she applies at the table might be called garish by some, but it photographs well in black and white.

As she did her "Thing kew fah ian-vatin' may. Freight-flay nayce," I thought how the antics of the young royals and *Dallas* at the palace had not done her in at all. She just rules Britannia, and sails above it all.

Flitted off to the Film Festival, that was tied to the Commonwealth this year and was so international and full of stars it was almost too much.

Sean Connery and Ursula Andress popped round. Barbie, it does not matter than he is losing his hair, he is gorgeous. And as for Ms. Andress, if we can look like that at perilously near the big five-oh, there is hope *cara mia*.

I did not see Sarah Miles, but I hear she is as spacey and strange as she was in *The Sailor Who Fell From Grace*...Helen Shaver was quite sweet and shy considering the steamy scenes and the velvet voice, Katharine Hepburn seemed fragile but sharp, Richard Dean Anderson was just a regular, down to earth, outrageously handsome guy, who told me he loved living in Vancouver, "because it was like Minnesota. "What did I care what he said, Barbie, so long as he kept talking? My favorite, though, was Timothy Hutton, who really was *Made In Heaven*. Trust me.

Sooo much more. No time.

Ta Ta Darling, an exhausted,

Valerie

THE YEAR 1988

PICKETT'S LINES
One for the heart, and one for Hugh.

ACADEMY PERFORMANCE
Jostling for immortality at the Academy Awards. No wonder the Oscars are wild.

HI, ART!
Off the wall and into L.A.

DEJA VU
Reviewing the "new VU" and Diane Farris's everything's up-to-date-in-canvas-city.

THE YEAR 1988

his was the year the city's night life really began a huge changeroo. The flashy galas, designer-in-attendance fashion shows, and big name tribute dinners started leap-frogging over each other, and the same string of put-upon sources were being asked to dig deep into their silken pockets to fund everything from the arts to disease-of-the weekers.

Before that, big-buck charities had the black-tie beat all to themselves. In the late eighties, you scratched a local hospital or a struggling arts group and you found a gala-evening-wannabe. It was becoming ever-so apparent that a little of the old glitz and glamour could boost a budget bigtime, and "names" were becoming to fund-raising what designer labels were to haute couture. It was easier to get corporate contributions, fundees found, when the evening guaranteed canapes with Kissinger or escargots with Iacocca, or a seance with Shirley.

And if a board of directors flashed a blue chip executive or his same-connections spouse, their in-common cronies appeared to cough up more cheerfully. But all of this slap and tickle with celebrities had to happen before January, because social seasons being what they are, these golden geese flew south by then.

Being buffeted by bejewelled bosoms and beady-eyed blue-chippers was a 3 or 4 times a week thing that year, and at two or three hundred dollars a ticket — barely a money quotient quiver for most of these mere-drop-in-the-budget-eers — some were becoming a little testy about having to penguin-suit up on every other night of the week.

We reeled from the Heart Ball at the Four Seasons to the Arts Club, to the Playhouse's gala wine auction at the Trade and Convention Centre, to the Art Gallery's dress-to-excess "Art After Dark" party. From one of the city's first black-tie bachelor auctions to Martha Sturdy's opening on Granville to Suki's warm and fizzy tribute party to Arthur Erickson's sleek new salon for her.

Diane Farris opened her New York-cool gallery off South Granville that year, the Opera Round Table held a marvelous mansion-toasting at Joan Carlisle-Irvings', and even though the movie industry was Hollywood-Northing on our very streets, I headed off for my first ever-so-close personal peek at Oscar and the Academy Awards in L.A.

PICKETT'S LINES

Barbie Darling,

Hurtled off to the second annual Heart Ball at the Four seasons ballroom with 350 other palpitating patrons. Easily the hands-down winner in the season's glitterati sweepstakes, the now-annual fund-raiser is the perfect showcase for that frisky little formal or that drop-dead de la Renta that either Santa or the sales may have crammed into your closet.

Billed as "An Evening After Your Own Heart," if the champagne reception did not jump-start it for you, the lively white tie, tails and sneakers of the Vancouver tuba quartet would have.

The first of the season's megabuck melees ("the fat checks/worthy causes/tax deduction tango" as your great aunt used to call them) had a natty nautical look to it that must have had a *deja done* feel for several of the hearty corporate hot-shots. I ran into six sea worthy souls who had spent their mid-winter break all decked out on cruise lines and another four who were soon-to-be Caribbean bound.

As soon as the chinchillas were checked, the who's-up-to-what mass mingle started. Joel Bell slid in with his heart on his sleeve - fiancee and guitar star Liona Boyd. The former president of the Canada Development Investment Corp.

Hugh Pickett, Mitzi Gaynor,
Adrian Anzyloviich

was quietly playing articulate guru on all things global and Liberal, and held small groups in thrall as he stung like a bee and she floated like a butterfly.

The beauteous Ms. Boyd wore one of those 1960s recreations she is so fond of that allows one who looks like an angel to straddle a guitar, legs daintily akimbo, and still look very much the First Lady of the classical strings. She was flying to L.A. the next day to debut on a show - appropriately enough for this particular evening - called *Throb*, and in July she says she is off to exotic Istanbul. (If only we had all practised when our mothers told us to!)

In the dual of the jewels, Jacquie Longstaffe was right up there in her new gold-with-the-right smattering-of-karats birthday necklace. "It was almost worth turning 40 for," she beamed as Sir Ronald of the Big Heart and clever Toni of the Caveltis looked on.

177

Cartier's canny couple, the Feuermanns, joined them; Daniel, a heartbreaker with dimples so deep you could mine them for diamonds, and the bonny Ani, in emerald green taffeta, black velvet, freshwater pearls, four rings, a bracelet, watch, gold earrings, and waistline small enough to really annoy. (*Some*body was wearing Chopard's "Happy Diamonds" - $220 an ounce - I never did find out who. In this crowd it could have been anyone.)

So nice of the Houstons to pop up from Palm Springs for these little dos. It gives Jim a chance to birdwatch (his Red Robin restaurants, silly) and the ever-effervescent Jackie to flash those great little numbers she wears down south for drinky-poos with Ron and Nancy (of *course* the Reagans). Nancy just loves staying at Walter Annenberg's little *pied* in Rancho Mirage. It's *so* much more "her" than that tacky White House.

There were enough Zlotnicks there for a quorum (I counted at least six) but Marty and Penny were the Zeniths of the Zs I guess, and three of the four Mearns were there. Dale wore a flaming red sarong (from Cuba when she and Liona popped down to see Fidel?), but sister Lindsay stuck with her trademark leopard spots.

"Awfully nice to see almost all of you," I heard over my shoulder as a black tie-breaker nodded to a backless, strapless, peplumed, long-gloved lovely as we moved in to dinner. I noticed he continued to gaze as they grazed on a romantic gamut that ran from consomme, terrine of wild mushrooms, veal loin steak, red bliss potatoes to fruit floating in red wine. She did not touch her seven-grain roll or her corn oil margarine so she probably ended up with less than the master chef's planned 800 calories for-your-heart's sake that the rest of us heartily consumed. Master of Ceremonies (and his own fate) weatherman Phil Reimer, predicted a ridge of high pressure as he added salt to everything but his Chardonnay.

The old boat network continued as real estate raj and captain of the cruise Paddy Couslon graciously thanked contributing guests and corporate sponsors and, with a composure that would have gladdened Miss Manners' heart, the wrong bank.

Canada's oldest living heart transplant and move-star handsome artist Daniel Izzard danced up a happy and grateful storm with wife Denese while an Alaskan cruise and his-and-her Cartier watches were sumptuously door-prized. All told, I thought the whole shindig showed real state-of-the-art heart, no?

Minced off to Martha Study's (these new tight skirts are murder) where she launched her new spring line of wearable sculpture for the out-all-the-time crowd. The gloriously gutsy Sturdy, the big stores/fashion mag's darling who gives a personal spin to everything she does, was obviously in a mellow mood as she unveiled her favorite heart motif.

Her new multi-monied South Granville atelier was splashed with showcases full of hearts in silver, wire and red acrylic in every possible playful combination.

Long-legged glossie Denise Taylor (she was born a model) allowed her barely-there torso ("a prime example of the new *fam*ininity," sniffed one meaty matron) to be draped in everything from Martha's paint-box bright translucents to the frivolous and much-adored hearts.

Blonde and beautiful Dale Bonsall-Jevning (who owns Taffeta evening wear, and is always turning the other chic) wore all black so she could showcase a different dizzying design every few moments.

Lawyer Peter Hyndman who bustled in in a camelhair cashmere coat acknowledged lawyer John Laxton in a navy cashmere coat (do they check?).

Artist/weaver Joanna Staniskis, nodded at designer Katharine Regehr (who was almost-wearing one of her own backless numbers). Art director Susan Casey flounced in with whirling dervish fashion editor Tracey Pincott, who lapsed into fashionese with the *Province's* Renee Doruyter and the *Courier's* Stevie Mitchell making sure everyone was relentlessly up-to-the moment. Ms. Mitchell, Vancouver's own shrieking violet, does zap all and sundry with some of the *best* zingers.

Pamela Martin, BCTV's glossy-haired girl-on-the-news obviously remembers that frowning causes tiny lines between the eyes because she remains perpetually smiling and happy over the champagne, oysters and string quartet.

Latecomer Lois Milsom just back from L.A. lopped in with Hanne Strong. They sardined themselves into the shop for a quick catch-up. Hanne, who is married to Maurice Strong (the first-ever Canadian president of the World Federation of United Nations Associations, first head of Petro Canada, a director of CIDA, etc. etc. who did definitely *not* just fall off a cabbage truck, *capice*) was just up from The Baca, the 450 square hectares of south Colorado valley that she is transforming into a spiritual/business commune that pulls in Club of Rome caliber minds bent on saving the planet et al. (*And* Shirley Maclean, but she owns a very little part, Barbie.)

Heaven, it seems, has made another New Age match.

"I never repeat gossip," I heard over my shoulder as I gathered my coat and waved back at the smart and sparkly Martha. "If someone doesn't get it the first time, that's just too bad."

Heaved myself off to the tribute to Hugh Pickett at the Arts Club, Granville Island.

They really went through the old Rolodex for the invitation list.

Everyone you and Hugh ever knew was there. Every vestige left on the *ancient regime* of musical theatre in the city wound themselves up, put on their best bib and whatever and lobbed fawning puffballs at each other and the silver-tongued, silver-haired maestro of the moment, Hugh Frank Pickett. H.P. was at his sauciest best as he meshed the folks who had flow in from Lala Land with the stalwarts who has winged west from T.O., the Theatre Under The Stars originals with the scholarship babies he had just taken under his wing.

The Hugh's Who were out for the press shy, yet courting Noel Coward-clone ("*He* was a friend") - Yes Hugh, we know, so was Larry Olivier and that other Sir, John Gielgud, and Vincent Price and Elvis and The Rolling Stones and Nureyev, and most of the great woman stars of the 20th century.

"She had her face and entire body lifted," I heard as we settled in our seats for the show-and-tell tribute, "and she is now rumored to sleep standing up so the silicone won't shift." Barbie, do you think I could find out who for the life of me?

I sat beside master low-key punster and former newspaper columnist Himie Koshevoy who, when the stage lights were a tag slow coming up deadpanned into the silence, "Drags a big, doesn't it?"

In fact it ended up whizzing by. A non-stop razzle-dazzle blitzkreig of song and dance and one-liners from the pick of the Pickett pack that either got launched or stayed in orbit because of the very positive Mr. P. A solid hour of Andy Hardy-like "Come on kids, let's put on a show!" Absolutely pouring their hearts out in one long "We love Hugh" medley were Ruth Nicol and Jeff Hyslop, Charlene Brandolini and Jim Hibbard (who met and married because of him - Hugh bought the wedding dress) Susan Johnson and Sheril Morton (From L.A. and New York) Dean Regan, and Doug Alder and Rex Downey. When the house lights came up (My goodness they are unflattering!) most people could not believe they had been glued to their seats (Hugh's axiom for the successful impressario: "He who gets the bums in the seats") for an hour.

There was lots of lobby-posing at intermission. A chance for the financial and theatrical resource pool of the Arts Club to rub satin shoulders and check each other out.

Architect Blair MacDonald, as hunky as ever with the very blonde and very beaded Helen smiling smugly at his side, took a theatre breather as did thread baron Louis Eisman. (His wife Marion, who is starring in *Stepping Out* at the Arts Club was in a Mr. Jax suit - does she have a choice? "My best model," he calls her.)

Politicos Art Phillips and Carole Taylor joked that they now know how

Bill Millerd makes the Arts Club work - the seats for their $125-a-ticket numbers do not exist! Mike and Becky Harcourt worked the lobby as did Grace McCarthy, Pat Proud, and Pat Wasserman (all "good, good" Pickett pals).

Gordon Campbell (tuxless and without the chain of office) kicked off the second half of the show. He actually _sang_ his declaration of Hugh Pickett Day and for a mayor, he is not a bad singer. Radio man Red Robinson flaunted an approximation of wit rather well, then played the basking Robinson as his jokes took hold.

Kate sent a telegram (Hepburn, darling), and of course Marlene did too. From Paris, ("Pawee," says she). And Lillian Gish (she was so great at her own tribute night in New York, remember?) and dear Vincent (Price). And I am sure Bing would have if he could have.

The kindly curmudgeon hates things "chichi pooh pooh, and la-di-dah. (He despaired of friends getting "all trussed up" for this black tie affair and wore a navy blazer, slacks and shirt, a red tie and pouf, his Order of Canada pin, and as a tie clip a pearl earring Mitzi Gaynor had given him - her husband Jack Bean wears the other. "There is no doubt Hugh invented himself completely and absolutely," said a fan, "but there is no doubt his web of friends buoys the dear boy."

The glitzy Ms. Gaynor in her sassy black Scassi did a smoky "Mahwena Deitwick" talking to her husband "Wooody" (that's Rudy, Barbie) that was outrageously funny and gave the sweet and low down of what life on the road must have been like for Hugh. "A dear sweet loveable lady," he says of Miss D., "but there were times!"

Hugh himself got a chance to bat back some of the evening's accolades. He is positively a Delphic oracle of inside theater scoops. He showcased the superlative, and if the stories were not new, part of his mystique is his tireless ruthless ability to perform them as though they had just happened.

He never seems to play would-have, could-have, should-have. He always seems to like where he is _then_. Remember him at the head table as Princess Margaret's "date" at the Hyatt? (She wanted to talk about Dietrich).

Over a midnight supper, The Wizard of Odds who for 50 years had found himself in the thick of a sticky ticket wicket or trotting globally at breakneck speed seemed to bask in the glow of his Broadway babies like a kid swathed in a Twinkie wrapper.

Ta Ta Darling, life's a stage,
Valerie.

ACADEMY PERFORMANCE

Barbie Darling,

Shot off to that strobe-lit quest for glitz and glory, the 60th Annual Academy Awards. If I thought I was suffering celebrity overload at the royal wedding, or at Cannes and Monte Carlo *last* year, they pale beside this.

Picture it dear - 6,000 souls, each glowing with the unspoken satisfaction that their importance has been validated by their having been bidden to this particular spectacle.

Limos aligned, six abreast, stretched for blocks, overheating as the air-

Pee-wee Herman & date, Daryl Hannah

conditioning gasped its last in the 100-degree heat, hoods up as late arrivals bolted the final few desperate blocks so they could coolly stroll the remaining 100 yards for the flash and fans.

Helicopters whirring above in the Hollywood firmament as wall-to-wall mixed-media shutterbugged a quick-step, recording the event for what passes as posterity. Wading through the amassed masses (some of whom had camped out for two days to catch a glimpse of their favorite larger-than-life) were faces more familiar to most than their own.

The "wear-everything-and-what-you-can't-carry" school grads were certainly there, many on the arms of Buddha-bellied sugar daddies. (Scriptgirls and makeup minxes who had been ever-so-good all year?) But there was a solid core of first-class platinum acts streaming in to honor their best, too.

Charlton Heston (in surely the world's worst toupee) parted the wait-ers, as he sermonetted in, giving ominous inflection and reflection to his hallowed hellos. ("love Ben - hated Hur" is still the best movie review I have seen.) Liza Minnelli swept like Little Red Riding Hood ("Batman's wife, sniffed the mouth nearest me) in a billowing scarlet cape - Chinese red, bias-cut, Halston organza, *a la* Mama Judy - her makeup much more subdued (only one pair of lashes at a time now) than when we met her in Toronto, while Audrey Hepburn gave Givenchy her elegant all in black-and-white spots and stripes. (her face is quite "pleated" as that little niece of yours used to say, Barbie, but what splendid eyes and smile.) Just back from Ethiopia - for UNICEF - she still smokes up a storm, I noticed later, exquisitely of course.

Nail-biter (to the *quick* darling) Omar Sharif pitta-patted in on little patent pumps, gap-teeth and black-circled eyes intact. I spotted him drinking morosely alone in the Polo Lounge the night before while John Travolta flashed friends and fans at a table nearby.

Candice Bergen baby-stepped in a snug, long red strapless ("It looks like a ski sock," I overheard) with a gold mane of hair that made her look like a Roman candle. She has a great guffawing laugh that made her earrings tinkle, seems madly content with minute French mate Louis Malle and has the dearest little pot belly. What, you wanted perfection?

Daryl Hannah hove into view in a skin-tight fright of a dress - sort of a mass of shiny fish scales. Actually she "galumphed" in her silver slings, but why should mermaids automatically be able to walk in high heels? *Talk*: now that is another thing.

"I got my dress at Palace rentals," she offered. "It's 1920s." "Thirties," she was corrected. The hair, bleached within an inch of its roots was platinum, flat, and draped in a 1940s Veronica Lake screen-siren dip. The sunglasses were pure gold-rimmed 1950s, the earrings 1980s, the ratty wrap, wrong gloves and bracelet were catch-as-catch-can, and the lady

Richard Dean Anderson, Marlee Matlin

herself pure space cadet. When asked what she thought of her talented costar Steve Martin losing his nomination bid for *Roxanne*, she said she had not known because she "really hadn't been paying attention." Believe it, Barbie.

Live-wire Little Richard dazzled his way past a playful Pee-wee Herman, who was in a glen plaid tux and white shoes. Hard to tell who had more makeup on, but Pee-wee's date was definitely prettier. Little R's was obviously a bodyguard called Big Richard.

Dirty Dancing's Jennifer Grey, all five-foot-two of her, seemed to have misplaced long-time love Matthew Broderick as she bopped in with Calvin Klein jeans model Billy Baldwin. The "just friends" could not keep their hands off each other. Her spinny mini seemed little more than lace biker pants, and she completely lost the strangely suspended top of her dress as she ran for her car later. Of course I will get to "later" later Barbie.

Cuddly Dudley Moore and his new bride, Brogan Lane - a full head taller than him, but there is nothing *in* hers - seemed to have adjusted to married life rather well. "It's really nice," she pronounced about their bliss. Content that she could neither challenge nor contend with his bottomless wit well, he seemed happy to just hug her in her bright blue taffeta blitherings.

Patrick Swayze shone like a certified sweetheart, a little shy and genuinely surprised at the screams of glee he elicited. His beauteous blonde dancer wife Lisa Niemi, in a smashing cream linen designer suit, was openly thrilled for him.

Herd hysteria hit its peak as a trio of handsome Hollywood hunks appeared within minutes of each other. Mel Gibson, slim, small with piercing blue eyes and a look to go with them, arrived with wary wife Robyn on his

Victoria McMahon, Mary Lazar

arm, followed by Rob Lowe who brought his mom Barbara ("I couldn't get a date"), and newly-shorn Tom Selleck whose mini-sized missus, Jilly Mack, was in a maxi-priced ($3,150 at I. Magnin's) Christian Lacroix.

You had to swivel quickly to catch shooting stars like Roddy McDowall (skinny, hawk-nosed, silver-haired), Caesar Romero (tall, tanned, leathery, seen-it-all), Eva Marie Saint (faded but pretty in a gold lame Georgio Sant'angelo), Weight Watcher's most famous espouser, Lynn Redgrave, in a skinny black sheath and *No Way Out's* Sean Young, who wore a very sedate slate blue Bob Mackie, carried a parasol and so as not to waste the evening, an autograph book that she "hoped to fill out before the evening was over."

A subdued Norman Jewison slipped in with wife Dixie (in a black Alan Cherry, the Toronto designer Helen Shaver uses). Best Actress nominees Sally Kirkland and Anne Archer thought black was beautiful too (Sally almost bursting out of her strapless stretch velvet, Anne in a Vicky Tiel with a silver beaded cummerbund and no taste for paste in real Harry Winston jewels). Jewison's pal Rod Steiger (who is as big as a house) strode in with 40 years younger wife Paula (in red). Remember we all had dinner at Delilah's? Well, he said he is much happier than he was then and is "having a great time on the set of Jewison's *The January Man* in Toronto."

No need to tell about the show, dear heart, I am sure you picked it up over in Blighty, albeit eight hours later. Let me tell you who I ran into, and what _really_ matters.

Michael Douglas up close, has mean little eyes - you would not cross this man - the famous square jaw is getting jowly and that lip stays curled in a sneer even when he is saying things like, "I'd like to smell the roses, I haven't had a break in two-and-a-half years." Diandra, his Spanish-born wife of 11 years is quite lovely, and does not look remotely like the person in her wedding picture - in alteration-happy Hollywood, who does?

Meryl Streep was just iridescently beautiful, soft-spoken, unassuming and so shy that when she speaks to you she looks at the floor on either side, not at all like the determined pro she is when working.

Sean Connery, who spent his youth buckling swash, buckled my knees that night. Those blackbird-bright brown eyes can bond with mine any time he gives the nod. His costar in _The Untouchables_, Kevin Costner, did not have a patch on the very touchable Mr. Connery. I commented on Costner's elaborate gold-tipped shoes and we had a good laugh. His next movie is _Shoeless Joe_, Vancouver's own W.P. Kinsella's book-into-flick. Did I mention, Barbie, that Connery smelled like heather and leather? Or that his beard is solid silver now?

Cher, Michael Douglas

Richard Dean Anderson is partial to Canadians since his show is shot here, and since he met Marlee Matlin in a Calgary elevator. She dumped the frumpy look from last year (a fashion disaster, remember?) and looked marvy in magenta, hair wild and free and the glasses stashed. He said over a glass of wine that he was "thrilled" to be at the Oscars for the first time, and she showed off her six months of speech lessons saying out loud that "it was scary" to speak, and that before she went on stage, her heart was gong "pumpumpum."

That euphemism for a cyclone, Robin Williams (flying without a script - and without a net - during the show), offered later through his new mustache, that losing must be like "driving over the Grand Canyon nude. What's this hitting me in the face?"

Chevy Chase was looking handsome and healthy since he graduated from Betty Ford, and continued to ad-lib fourth-rate jokes off-stage. Even Cher said,

"You're lookin' good, Chevy. How'd you get so thin?" And he lied back, "Like you, I worked out."

Cher just knocked my sequinned socks off Barbie, she was absolutely splendid. She is not even a type, she is absolutely unique. I am sure you caught the beaded piece of blacknetting she was almost wearing. See what $15,000 buys you? The stole was extra, and of course, she and Bob Mackie argued about that. She wanted a decorated black leather biker's jacket - he won. She is five-foot-seven, 110 pounds in her bare feet, which she *was* ("my feet are killing me") when I saw her. That nifty little Greek-letter tattoo you may have spotted on her upper arm was not alone, I am sure I could see what looked like

Candice Bergen, Gregory Peck

a butterfly on her nether flank as she spun around to show what she "didn't think was too far out ... everything is covered, I don't think you can see anything." Not when she stood perfectly still, which she did not.

Her toenail polish was almost black, she wore no rings, just the cuffs and foot-long earrings Mackie made for her. She admits she had her chest done - "once, not three times" - did not have a chin implant, had her nose done twice - "I hated how I looked in *Mask*" - did not have her fanny or have her navel done either. Phew.

I remember when I was at the Golden Door Spa a few years ago, the gardener telling me how worried Cher was about her upper arms. Well Barbie, she and her daily trainer ("I've been busting my chops for the past month just in case I won") have licked that little problem.

When Paul Newman was announcing Best Actress, she knew she had won, because he "didn't take in enough breath for two names." Hairdresser to the stars, Jose Eber on Canon Drive, had done her hair ($2,000 worth of hair extensions). Her mom, Georgia Holt, is great looking, 11-year-old "Lijah" as she calls him looks just like a minature Greg Allman, Chastity is beyond help looks-wise, but trying, and Cher's bagel maker, doorman, bartender, now acting-student at Queens, Rob Camiletti (she is 42, he is 24) makes her blush when her "Mookie" comes near. They really did all go home for pizza and skip the parties.

Fortunately 1,500 souls stayed for the Governor's Ball ("nobody's ever had a sit-down dinner for that number, not in this town"). The lucky invitees who got to go to Swifty Lazar's were a fifth of that number.

Swifty and Mary Lazar's party at chef-owner Wolfgang Puck's Spago is the place to be Oscar night. Swifty is under the impression that "it is the most important social gathering of the year in a town where social gatherings play a very important role. People are panting in the streets to be invited." He may be right. A very sworn-to-be-anonymous source said through clenched teeth, that "there are people in Hollywood who would kill for those invitations, so interesting is the group who attends, and so important is it to be seen there."

One hundred and eighty went for dinner this year (champagne, smoked salmon, sauteed oysters, veal and striped bass ... none of the trendy pint-sized pizzas Spago usually serves). They watched the show on giant TV screens and later another couple of hundred arrivals flooded in.

Faye Dunaway still had the smallest smudge of makeup on her $10,000, black-and-white Yves Saint Laurent suit that she had on it when she left the Four Seasons Hotel all those hours before." She's a vanilla ice cream cone coated in sprinkles of hostility," offered one actor non-fan while another nodded. Glen Close is covered in freckles up close, Olivia DeHavilland is as gracious as an Edwardian dowager, Jackie Collins is better-looking than her sister Joan (but the black-and-silver jacket has to go), Roger Moore has dropped 20 pounds and looks great, and Gregory Peck is everything your mother ever thought he was.

The whole evening was a shindig that would have left Jay Gatsby goggled-eyed.

Ta Ta Darling, sooo much more,
Valerie.

HI, ART!

Barbie Darling,

Tarted it up and headed off to Art After Dark, the art gallery's "party of the year." It was, after all, "dress to excess" and my kind of evening, *definito.*

Hardly the social swirl's *creme de la* you-know, sweets, but a nice mincing of Shaughnessy social-lights and wackadoo, off-center street people. Watching each watch the other fit gallery director Willard Holmes' wish that it be a "coming-out party of grand scale," wherein the place would be turned topsy-turvy with floor after floor of food, fun and frolic (and a chance to mix moldy members with nouveau neverbeens). Sounds keen, right? Well the modest $22-a-head (and I use the term loosely, more later) allowed 2,000 anything-goers to play out their can't-wait-til-Halloween fantasies to the full.

"Gushy?" I heard over my exaggerated hot-pink shoulder pad, "A few minutes with her is like going through a carwash in a convertible." Since there was a great deal of cheek-pressing going on at arrival, it was impossible to know *which* geyser *where* was spouting.

The gallery's Susie Harrington was bang-on bizarre greeting all, and certainly sundry, in a fluorescent pink-net prom dress ("rented") over which she had added a traffic cop's orange and yellow vest, and a Carmen Miranda turban topped by a glowing pink Frisbee. The scarlet-rimmed glasses, she assured, were no affectation. She "can't see a thing without them."

"If only she'd worn them to *dress!*" blurted the unclear-of-the-concept bimbette beside me.

The senior Southams, just off to Stanford for Mrs. S's 50th class of 1938 reunion, sauntered in. The beneficent Jeannie in soignee Chinoise - a long lavishly embroidered coat and elaborate eyemask, while Gordon, that silvery sultan of sleek, touted a tartan dinner jacket and cummerbund and velvet and gold pumps, a "gift from Jeannie" he proudly allowed. Most *un*-Common(s) Speaker John Fraser flew in to do his part for art. "He must have splinters from all the fences he has straddled trying to be fair," offered the confused semi-wit beside me.

Vicky Russell, Bryan Adams

Pamela Martin clicked in on his heels (hers were pale blue peau de soie), saucer-sized eyes and glossy locks intact, she flashed an acid-washed denim suit from Michelle's and a "nice and kneesy mini" as your great uncle calls them.

Art Phillips and Best Rookie Alderperson Carole Taylor treaded into their umpteenth must-do of the week turning up like aces in a judiciously-stacked deck, followed unchecked by hockey-teamer Stan Smyl.

Beleaguered John Turner ("John knows what pleasure his being imperfect brings to others," a passable pundit intoned) stick-handled his way through a sea of hands. "He's up for a frequent-tryer bonus in my book," the same P.P. concluded. The glamorously gritty Geills appeared to put herself on automatic pilot for the last event in a chock-full-o'-plots week, but the sweet soul who asked for and got her autograph seemed not to note.

Gallery guru Gerald McGavin, obviously playing out some festering fantasy, aced in in Blues Brothers shades, a white suit and a gangster fedora, looking like a mob man for Colonel Sanders, while Dale Mearns did a rich dust-bowl refugee in her glad rags with handkerchief hem.

"Look, _he's_ shallow as a saucepan, and _she_ has the brains of a squid, but aren't they the cutest couple." I heard about I'll never know as I hurried upstairs for the celebrity paint-off on the third floor.

I chatted with the "Queen" on my traverse, Carolyn Sadowska the would-be reignee, who, when I confidentially asked her just _where_ she lived in Victoria, said she did not at all, but rather (in full arched accent) "in a large house in the center of London." Donchaknow?

She then pulled open her perfect-for-Liz purse, pulled out a paperweight-sized uncut stone from among a snarl of pearls and chains, and said that of course she must have it set soon.

As auctioneer Barry Scott sold off $5,000 worth of personally-painted Picasso-on-the-spot T-shirts (Willard Holmes' went for a hot $1,000), I checked out such unknowns but not forgottens as the very small woman with the very large goldfish on the side of her head. And in a fish to fowl fend-off, the beauty in black with the large white swan on top of hers. The clay-covered Aboriginal in cape and loincloth seemed keen on the smoked shark while the couple in the white full-body radiation suits (carrying _de rigueur_ geiger-counters) seemed eager to get a drink through their vinyl faceplates.

Evelyn Roth, Harold Gent

The drapes of Roth (Evelyn, dear heart) consisted of feathers and skins and a stark wedge of a headdress, that put lesser artists after darkness to shame.

Peg Steley (who put on the Pope show, and the Chuck and Di do, and is now a movie producer) pop-arted it, virtually unrecognizable in a lavender vinyl punk hair-do of homicidal proportions and striped outer-space specs. Husband Alan Manzie's white dinner jacket (Deluxe Junk, $20) was a Peg-painted canvas of moon and stars that caused many an ooh-ahh.

I passed one old jasper on the escalator down who was standing in awe as he descended, eyes glued to the vision in front of him, a rather comely creature wearing a little black dress and do-what-you-will-with-me shoes. All fine and well you say, but over this was a black lace girdle worn on top of the skirt.

_189_

Spotted an unidentified Count Dracula enjoying the live three-band music. "Nonstop sonic slush," one of the older board members called it, chummily wagging his jowls before going into free-fall rapture over how great it was to see the gallery so full of happy people.

Bumped into Bryan Adams and long-time lady love Vicky Russell on my way out. Filmmaker Ken Russell's brilliant bambino's career is based in London which makes those trans-Atlantic trysts so terribly tweet.

As I looked back at those art-for-the-people portals being rocked off their neoclassic columns, I had to agree, Darling, distance leads enchantment to the view.

Popped off to Palm Springs for the smallest spate of sun. Well it was raining here, what did you expect me to do?

It is now *Sonny's* Palm Springs, as you know. Monsieur Bono, yes *that* Sonny Bono, is the wonders-never-cease mayor of P.S. He spent $54,000 to win ("Hey, I was just kidding!") the four-year $15,000-per-annum job so that, he says, he can "give the city back to the people." And all because he got into a few bureaucratic wrangles over the size of his restaurant sign, and a retaining wall at his Spanish mansion on Crestview Drive. He thinks the city is a sleeper, and the "stodgy old guard" has got to be shaken up, and a world-class film festival, an annual marathon and revival rock concerts are the way to go. I have not asked Joe and Fran Cohen, Jimmy Pattison or any of the myriad of the other P.S. home-owing Vancouverites what *they* thought yet, but Mr. B. seems on a roll. At the only political meeting I saw (held at Maxim's where else?) Sonny told the other candidates that he didn't have to listen to them because they weren't his mother or his father. So there. His first son born shortly after victory day, was named Caesar (Chesare Elan). Delusions of grandeur, ma cher? Not at all. "It's like, my *duty* to bring class 'n stuff back to Palm Springs." The beat goes on, don't it dear?

Jim and Tammy Faye were down. They had a place in the Coachella Valley and are thinking of staging a comeback from a place called Mecca. Truth, as your ancient aunt used to say, is stranger than just about anything.

Nudged up to Newport Beach and checked into the apogee of 'otels, the Four Seasons. Those sumptuous suites are so civilise, dear heart. The party-sized living room, the dining room that seats eight of your nearest, the marble bar, the maid's kitchen, the TVs and phones - seven of them, one in each of the two swish bathrooms. It is the old casual elegance on the California Riviera; *you know*, Babs.

Edgar Kaiser's pal John Denver finds this as close to a Rocky Mountain high as he can get when he is in town. So do those designing darlings James Galanos and Oscar de la Renta. (Remember how much dear Oscar loves the

VanDusen Gardens _here?_) George Bush and Henry Kissinger gave the nod to the Newport Beach, and General Charles Yeager certainly found it had the right stuff. Year-round climate ("You Canadians seem to love it here.") and shopping to die for.

Lopped off to Lala Land (well it was so _near_) and checked into Joe and Rosalie Segal's favorite inn, the Four Seasons Beverly Hills. Fran Belzberg was staying here and so were Maxine and Harry Gelfant. ("Harry's speaking in Disneyland," Maxine spouted. "Anaheim,"corrected Harry.)

The hotel is new, smallish, and _tres_ European, and as totally stress-free as possible in a city where there always lurks a sense of "business being done."

I ran into Faye Dunaway in the lobby, poor pale darling. She was with Warren Cowan, one of the heads of the giant Rogers and Cowan, whose PR clients include Paul Newman and Stallone. I won't say theirs was a silky rapport. Something about sunglasses (hers) not being perfect. _Mommie Dearest_ had nothing on Miss D.

Crocodile Dundee put his snakeskin boots up here, and Selleck does his sneakers. Andy and Fergie popped round for a spot, Liza Minnelli calls it home-away-from when she is not in New York, Elton John hangs his hundreds of hats, and Julio Iglesias and the new 19-year-old Brazilian beauty have bossa nova'd prettily poolside.

Dynasty had their wrap party at the Four Seasons, no one came with who they were supposed to. Emma Samms came with Arsenio Hall, John James came with his new best friend, and Joan Collins swished in on tan man George Hamilton's arm.

If one hangs around poolside here you can learn to talk Hollywood. Industry heavyweights, powerbrokers, starmakers, agents, "take meetings" among the potted palms. They talk "above the line, back-end money, four-walling, house nuts, turnarounds, majors, play or pay, legs" (as in _Beetlejuice_ has "great legs" - box office longevity) and "points," until you think there really _is_ no biz like show biz.

Let me just tell you the latest from Hollyweird. There is a new BevHills gym for the tinkertoy set called Kidz-R-Cize. The club charges $110 a session, and Jaclyn Smith's two tykes (two and six), Pia Zadora's two, and Burt Bacharach's baby are all regulars. Farrah Fawcett and Ryan O'Neal's three-year-old Redmond got a midget pony for his birthday that cost $85,000 and lest you think the kids are the only ones with toys, I checked out Aaron Spelling's new 56,000-square-foot, $12 million-plus chateau in Holmby Hills. Boy are his neighbors mad. (Wife Candy wears $3 million worth of jewelry just for lunch with pals, so they are merely doing everything by the book - the bank book - as usual).

Nancy and Ronnie Reagan's retirement house in Bel-Air was just $2.5 million - practically a fixer-up at that price. It is at 666 St. Cloud, but they changed the address to 668 because of the biblical sign for Satan. Nothing is easy, is it?

Popped out to Ali MacGraw's new Malibu Adobe restaurant, Just missed her, but Dom DeLuise was feeding face and family as I arrived. He must weigh 300 pounds, my dear.

Bopped off to the ever-so-in Bistro the next night. Walter Matthau was at the next table with wife Carol (the whitest skin you ever) and friends. When a dropper-by-the-table asked Walter what he thought of his new heavily-shouldered suit, Matthau, without missing a mouthful of lamb, asked who the designer was, Schwarzenegger?

That's Hollywood for you, Barbie. Just the same off the screen as on.

Ta Ta Darling, and Take Two,

Valerie.

DEJA VU

Barbie Darling,

Clickety-clacked off to CKVU's "Hello Vancouver" celebration in the New World Harborside Hotel's ballroom. Amazing what umpteen-million dollars can do to spruce up an old face. The hotel, Barbie, the hotel. And it was amazing how many recycled VU visages were dredged up and dusted off in Phase Two's launch of *Revolving Doors: The Sequel.*

"The New VU" as the current keepers-of-the-same have been forced to christen their obstreperous offspring is still B.C.'s first and only independent television station, however, it now has a new set of foster parents.

It has been an eight-year struggle to wrest control from founding fathers Daryl Duke and the ever-there Norman Klenman. But new daddies Izzy Asper (QC, prominent tax lawyer, ex-Manitoba Liberal leader, Global TV Goliath, George Gershwin fanatic and chairman of Canwest, whose adoptee Channel 13 now *is*) and Don Brinton who is the president, "can now get down to business, and make this thing work."

"Geez, there's a lotta suits here," said a blonde stunner in a dress no bigger than a sock as she perused the myriad of business-types huddled around the room. "Let's just hope there are no *counter*suits," the brassy barrister beside her mumbled. "They've got a financial year-end review to get through, their license renewal and one more trip to court, but at least they won't be wondering _Who's The Boss?_ anymore."

"No," the sock answered, obviously warming up to it. "Now they just have to go through _Growing Pains, In The Heat Of The Night_ before they find out whether the _Wheel Of Fortune_ has dealt them _One Life To Live_ or _Jeopardy._

Spotting Joe Cohen across the room and badly in need of a down-to-earth word or two, I zeroed over to find the good doctor (honorary), ex-Citizen Of The Year, chairman of the Police Foundation etc., etc., up to his eyeglasses in election talk with Alderman Jonathan Baker. No sooner had the fate of the nation been decided, than the ballroom doors opened and an amorphous army that multiplied like rabbits flooded in, and a sort of Circus Minimus began. _Literally._ Clowns and musicians and a high-wire unicyclist parted the chatting masses who were more intent (especially the media munchkins) on buzzing about _who_ got _what._ Wet-finger-to-the-wind weatherman Douglas Miller and CBC's Sharol Josephson are hosting the new WestCoast, CKNW's Dave Abbott got the new Morningline (and subsequently lost _Nightline_ - ah, the pettiness of the open-line closed-mind radio brass). Everyone was buzzing "station profile," "local programming," "network specials" while bread and circuses swirled about them. Make that sushi and schmoozing, Barbie.

Izzy Asper and Joe Cohen

The lean and leggy Kim Blake swiveled in, peerless pearlies and polished pinkies intact. The publicist for Bruce Allen's talent stable was with her boss. He, in white shirt and beautifully-draped pants, was ever the ultra-cool dude the industry _thinks_ he is. And in a great mood for him; he did not yell at anybody once.

Flashes from the past Barbara Constantine and hubby Cash Edward waltzed in, VU veterans that they are, as did once-more-with-feeling George Froelich who in _this_ reincarnation plays the role of executive producer.

Grandmama was right Barbie; what goes around comes around. Feeling a touch of _deja_ VU, I passed a bow-tied Leon Bibb as I headed over to "Best-of-Luck" the awesome Mr. Asper.

"Izzy's a tremendously hard worker with a real vision of what he wants, and he sure doesn't need the bucks;" I overheard as I headed out the door, "You just watch him open up the West." Chapter two of The Little Station

That Could, watch for it.

Dithered off to Diane Farris's new, just-off-South-Granville gallery. *Ma chere, tout le monde* was there. Well every anybody anyway.

This move from her Gastown gallery to a 6,000 square-foot, state of the space-age lighting, 18-foot ceilings, *very* New York concrete bunker, was gala-brated by a hue's who of over 400.

The dynamo Diane who is always on fast-forward, moved with Concorde-like speed on this space. In less than eight weeks she and her friendly band of drywallers turned a do-little warehouse into a everything's-up-to-date-in-canvas-city 1980s art gallery. And by moving to West Seventh, she joins "gallery row" - Lizzie Nichol's Equinox Gallery and the Heffel and the Kupczynskis - and she can play mater-familias to her myraid of struggling young soon-to-be-well-knowns in a walk-in yuppie demographic where looky-loos actually *buy* too.

Bunting banners of flag silk were draped dramatically over the massive entrance pillars as first-nighters swept through making head-snapping entrances of their own. Art know-it-all and avid acquirer Ron Longstaffe eagle-eyed the inaugural exhibit. With that secret little smile of his, one has no hint at all whether he has already bought all 25 works, none at all, or only the ones he knows will double in value by dawn's early light.

Martha Sturdy minced in all newly-married and glowing in hot pink and orange swirls of silk designed by best pal Catherine Regehr. Catherine dressed herself in jade green with black lace pants, and to top off their trio con brio, wheeled in Farris in a passion-purple pants outfit. Of *course* they were all wearing Martha's jewelry, too. Catherine and Martha shook up Singapore last June on a junkett to show their stuff, and Di's gray and white gallery is the perfect backdrop for the designing duo's duds and doodads.

"I was surprised to see her because I thought she had used up her allotment of fame and had passed on to wherever it is transient celebrities go," I heard behind me in the crush, but by the time I, my handbag, and my very full wine glass wiggled around, it was too hard to determine just who it was that had used up their alloted 15 minutes of fame.

I spotted Lois Milsom, though, in front of Angela Grossman's *Angels Will Watch*. Since Angela has been known to put everything *and* the kitchen sink in her works, Lois was a conservative contrast in her black suit, white shirt classic. You have no idea what a relief to find that Ms. Milsom had *not* just been on safari in Africa, saffron-gathering in Kashmir, had "just had lunch with the sweetest Saudi Arabian prince, baron, head of a film studio, William F. Buckley and his wife, Givenchy, Pierre Trudeau or Katharine Hepburn." Nor had she just been to the commune property she has in Colorado. I was delighted, because she always makes me feel so "what-have-I-done-lately," you know?

"Migawd that looks _just_ like the locker room at the YMCA," one wicked wag whispered to artist Alan Wood about the most dramatic painting dominating the walls.

Attila Richard Lukacs' (Rick to his friends) massive 14-by-16 foot mixed-media monster _Where The Finest Young Men ..._ is a sort of sadomasochistic tangle of nude men, one dog (a bull terrier) and what look like bandages. It is definitely _not_ the Y, Barbie, but since Alan Wood had just spent four hours at the dentist, and could not laugh without it hurting, I saw what I think is the first neo-expressionist _expression_ I have ever seen.

Ross and Linda Fitzpatrick breezed in, concerned cosmopolites that they are. Owners of a fine and eclectic collection (mostly Canadian) they seem to keep tabs on what is going up and on in the art world. They were heading up to their winery (What, doesn't _everyone_, darling?) to check things out before their annual grape-gathering get-together.

"Gee, I find that intriguing," the timid young little black dress ventured while lost in Vicky Marshall's difficult-to-decipher _Scavenger_. "My husband and I have one of Vicky's paintings, and they really grow on you."

"Suit yourself dear," the expert allowed. "But even Graham Gillmore's _Mounted Fish Head_ over there is going to appreciate more. Mark my words. Besides the Gillmores are _such_ a nice family.":

In need of a little night air I searched out the misty-eyed Ms. Farris, and found her surrounded by friends and fans. From scholarship-winning dance student (Theater Under The Stars and the Vancouver Opera), she married a Farris, raised two sons and a daughter, found her way back into the arts via Ballet B.C. and the Vancouver Sculpture Acquisitions Committee, began her art forays as an organizer for Alan Wood's $600,00 _Ranch_ project five years ago, worked on the Vancouver Art Gallery's _Young Romantics_ exhibition, and eventually sponsored them in her own gallery when she opened three-and-a-half years ago.

Flung myself off to Alfred Sung's fall fashion gala for the Cartwright Gallery. The usual cast of characters did likewise. God forbid any of us miss the chance to ask that maitre of style, "What's it all about, Alfie?"

An unsurprising number of the chic-to-the-teeth showed up in Sungs, some purchased at the other charity affairs. Lily Lee sported the navy taffeta strapless with shawl that bountiful Bob had bid on at last year's Endeavour auction. (Endeavour arrangers are panic-stricken because this year the Lees - Bob bought Lily enough clothes and jewelry and treats to open a boutique - are in China with Jim and Jackie Houston on Endeavour night.) Organizers just might have to skip a year.

Julie Molnar beautiful-peopled it in a song Sung blue too. "She does such a great job on this and the other events she organizes," groused husband Andrew wistfully, "I wish she'd work more in the business with me."

Sung store manager Liz Coleman one-shouldered her way in Alfred's nod at saving fabric. Pia Southam shimmied in in a coral pink snip of a dress and just-about matching shoes. "Erreuno - from Leone's." She was with her dad, Harry Sjogren, A Cesar Romero stand-in, with a sort of moussed-up mystique about him.

Alan Manzie, who never seems to mind being introduced as Margaret Steley's husband waxed absolutely rhapsodic over Sung's shirts ("the collars never shrink"), a white linen Sung summer suit that always brings raves, and went on to gloat that his time-tested tux was 12 years old (a: he must have bought it at an obscenely young age, and b: he still fits it).

Jackie Cohen-Herrendorf, sans hubby, swished in in a tiny black-and-white strapless and a huge pouf of a shocking pink stole. She is looking more like Monaco's Princess Caroline all the time, and there is *nothing* the princess could teach the heiress about black-belt shopping or setting-jets.

Artist Sam Carter, impeccable-as-ever flashed a much-admired faille tux he bought in Sacramento, while designer Jimmy Nguyen (you *will* hear about him, Barbie) opted for an all-right, all-white number. *B.C. Business's* fair-haired boy Richard Murray dusted off his tux and tie for the fourth night in a row. "It's the *shirts* that are the tricky part," he complained.

Peter Hyndman, who is on the Cartwright Gallery's board of trustees, trotted out his tartan tux one more time (I've seen *it* more than some of my relatives over the past few years) and his significant-other, artist Joanna Staniziskis.

The reception bubbled over into dinner (salmon bavarois, roast veal, truffle cake—ship-sinking calories, dear heart) and Alfie's adoring acolytes did their runway sleight-of-hip as they modeled everything from class Sungsport to the flash class of his see-through sequinned evening stuff. A veritable conga line of "I could use that" erupted all around. Actually it *was* one of those collections that you did not have to be six feet tall and 100 pounds to wear.

And Monsieur Sung himself, Barbie? Still smokes up a storm, is shy to the point you want to help him find a hiding place, has switched his clear frames for horn-rims, his T-shirt for a bow tie, and kept his trademark blazer, baggy chinos and glossy brown brogues. And obviously his sense of "What do women really want?" He should tell Sigmund Freud.

Ta Ta Darling, keep your hemline up.

Valerie.

THE YEAR 1989

BLOCK PARTY
The auction block, darling, and Endeavor's best evers.

BARRE HOPPING
Nureyev then and now.

FANDOM OF THE OPERA
Aida was big, but Lloyd Webber was bigger with the Operas' dough-see-dough crowd.

SOCIETY'S ISLANDS
There are addresses all around the Strait of Georgia just as fashionable as any back in town.

THE YEAR 1989

A lot of the twinkly people came to Vancouver that year—Audrey Hepburn and Rudolph Nureyev, Eric Clapton and our old friend from the Zen zone, Shirley MacLaine. Ritzy business all the way. The town's arty partiers got to do those intimate little crushes with name-droppees that they so dearly love to refall for years to come.

Tiny, definitely-not-perfect Andrew Lloyd Webber wheeled into town on little patent-leather feet with then-wife (soon-to-be-disposed-of) songbird of note Sarah Brightman. A gargantuan production of Aida lumbered into B.C. Place Stadium, Steve Cannell's $25 million North Shore Studios came into camera focus, and the Endeavor Auction raised a half-a-mil that year—the most it ever had.

The money is no object crowd has always loved that particular event— and it got to pick up some of those lavish doodads so hard to gather anywhere else. There were almost no bridge and tunnel people there so they could flash to the guilt-free indulgent max, dress to the nine and a halfs, and feel good about the ultimate good for a multirama of needy charities.

I got out of town that summer to take a tony peek at where some of our local notables go to get away from it all, and found a ton of native land claims showing up not surprisingly, on near-by islands. And having had one swell time the previous year at the Oscars, I headed back for a closer, second, nose-to-noser with Kim and Jack and Michael and Judy. You can never get enough of those twinkly people.

BLOCK PARTY

Barbie Darling,

Early-birded off to the 23rd Endeavour Gala Benefit Auction at the Vancouver Trade and Convention Centre. Eight-hundred-and-seventy of the town's top town-and-gowners slick-ticketed it at $175 per patron, and, with the pre-Christmas loot they accumulated, (over half-a-million) they made this the most mega-bucked Endeavour ever.

As I checked the chinchilla, I overheard two charity-circuiteers (whose hubbies were obviously stashing the Porsches) cooing over the coat (pelts-to-melt-for) of a third. "Thank you," the furry one treacled back, "my husband gave it to me for my 40th birthday."

"And it's lasted so *well*," one mouthed to the other while the envied one moved into the coat-check line.

The cavernous convention hall was a full-speed-ahead tuxedo function as some of the city's uppiest-echelon set out to do good and did well. Beneficiaries from Ballet B.C. to the Waterfront Theatre will remember the coinage from this little all-that-glitters-must-be-sold.

Ran smack into Ross and Linda Fitzpatrick at the viewing reception. The fastidious Mr. Fitz was natty beyond necessity in a pinstriped silk tuxedo. His practiced eye perused the hoi polloi as though he were gauging a stock option, and he looked content that the market was on an upswing. That tux of his had *very* deep pockets—he donated the entire evening's wines from his Cedar Creek estate winery, though if *this* group finds a wine it likes, Cedar Creek will be rolling out the barrels until this sedimental journey of Ross's does as well as that cute goldmine of his did.

Linda Fitzpatrick, Endeavour's president this year (whose skills as an organizer are becoming the stuff of legend) outshone herself in a pleated and poufed silver-and-black-baller while Most Popular Alderperson Carole Taylor flashed a sassy Liberal red off-the-shoulder number that sported a large and sparkly Republican elephant pin front and center.

Spotted this season's "must have" bronze Thierry Mugler jacket on not one, but *two* avoid-each-other-at-all-costs twinsies. Joyce Connolly and Rebecca MacKay who both looked smashing as they stayed on opposite sides of their stalls must have each thought there would be no horserace at $1,650 per set of sleeves. *What* would Liz and Joan Collins do, darling?

Impark's high poobah Arne Olsen (who was a great parker in high school, if I remember my West Van High days) surveyed the room for possible boffo bidders for his weekend retreat on Hornby Island, while supersaleswoman

Andrea Eng (she sold more than $40 million worth of condos, plazas, offices and all last year) watched the amateurs at play. She is as sensational looking as she is smart at the dynamics of buyer/seller matches. Don't you just hate that beauty/brains combo, Barbie?

Constantine Pappas outfoxed no one as he swished in in a full-length fur, while wife Sherry knocked a few silk socks off in a little mink and diamante bomber jacker.

Tory terror Lyall Knott, who is awfully good at separating the chaff from the chaff, manifested a most unconservative red bow tie as he steered wife Susan about the exhibits.

After hors d'oeuvres (sashimi to chicken fingers), dinner (smoked filet of trout, wild mushroom consomme in puff pastry, loin of lamb, chocolate shadows, you know, the usual) Gordon Campbell admonished the gathered to "bid often, bid big" and the real business of the evening kicked off.

"If I scratch my nose, do I own a Manet?" asked a hood ornament of a woman in diving decolletage. "Just let me handle it, dear," answered the mild-mannered line-of-least-persistence beside her. ("I made her wear gold lame so I could keep my eye on her at all times," he whispered to me).

Ross & Linda Fitzpatrick

The silver-haired, pipe-smoking VP of the Lignum Group paid $300 for 1,000 personalized paper lunch bags. Since one assumes Ron Longstaffe does not brown bag it to work, daughter Brandy may be name-dropping at school till she hits junior high. (Mother Jacqueline, a slim cigarillo that night in a black velvet sheath, her trademark chignon and her birthday diamonds, won a shopping trip to Jaeger's and a day's pampering at John Paul Holt's Avantgarde Hair Studio.)

The Andre Molnars (Julie causing whiplash in a little white and black beauty) were heavily into real estate as usual. They managed to snaffle a week at Joan Carlisle-Irving's villa-to-die-for in Mustique, and a doghouse. The villa ("Oliver Messen has done such a great design" Joan tells me) will be shared with Deborah and Francesco Giulini and David and Vivien Thom. At $7,000, a mere droplet in the Sea Star's pool. Besides, they can always borrow a cup of money from Princess Margaret or Mick Jagger, their island neighbours.

The doghouse, finished and handmade by designers David Vance and

Francesco Giulini has a heated marble mosaic floor, Kilim carpets (doesn't yours?) beveled glass windows, a guest room for Fido's friends, art work from Emily Carr College, a Nakamichi clock radio for when it is time for "walkies," and a few smart grooming aids. It went for $4,500 (a bargain, Babs, it was worth $7,200). Andre and Julie say they *will* get a dog.

"I was sure Susan Pezim was going to buy that for Murray," I heard to my left. (The new Mrs. P spent $1,600 for the Diane Farris Gallery party instead. Just *whose* art she is going to exhibit is unclear but rest assured it will be an off-the-wall wingding.)

An adorable English sheep dog puppy with red bow and a definite Disney movie career ahead of it, brought a wildly enthusiastic bid of $5,200. "It doesn't have to make sense," shouted auctioneer-to-all-the-best-charities Barry Scott as the crowd surged to its feet in a wild whistling burst of applause.

Cigar-chomping Bob Carter, tongue and tie loosened, took to center stage with five balloons (one with his $5,000 check inside) and proceeded to win it himself. In the flick of an ash he bounced it to Ballet B.C. (his wife Sheila Begg's favourite fund). Big Bob did go to the dogs later over a $500 purebred black Lab puppy for which he woofed out $1,500.

The Arts And Science Council's Barbara Brink (in fuchsia silk) gets to go to Hong Kong and stay at the Hilton in

Andrea Eng

the new year with husband Russell. The Ross Fitzpatricks picked up first class British Airways to London, deluxe accommodation at the Inn On The Park, tickets to the *Phantom Of The Opera*, champagne, tennis and more (worth $13,622) for a pittance: $6,700. (While they are there they may as well pop over and check on their olive orchard in Tuscany, what?). David Mooney got $12,000 worth of New Zealand for $9,000, and the been-everywhere Peter and Joan Cundill (of London, California, etc.) bought a grand style ski package at Whistler for $3,500. (The peripatetic Peter, Cundill Value Fund's *wunderkind* had just run another marathon, and the annoyingly beautiful Joan tells me *she* no longer runs—her knees are giving out—nothing *else* is unfortunately). Peter, whom you will remember, Barbie, has a brown belt in judo, sizzles as a jazz pianist, has a pilot's license besides being a marathon menace and is a mean dancer.

203

Peter Brown, "Mr-Living-Well's-Best-Revenge" to his friends, "just can't stop playing Peter" says a green-eyed cohort. In a bid of all right, he bought a Haida raven drum, for $13,500 (by Bill Reid, it is a collectors item investor piece), a helicopter trip to the Gulf Islands with brunch and Dom Perignon for $1,500, and a $13,536-thoroughbred filly racehorse for $20,000. Since this baby's grandpa "Vice Regent" just sold for half a million dollars, it looks like Petey B's stable-savvy is piggy bankable.

As the last of the 3,000-plus items hit the auction block happy cash-and-carriers either hit the dance floor or the door.

On the way out I heard a rather large lady in a bright blue Spandex-looking suit hiss to the small man beside her, "I *told* you I didn't want that fitness package. If God had wanted me to bend over, he'd put *diamonds* on the floor!"

Toddled off to check out Audrey Hepburn who was in town to host *The Gift Of Music* concert for UNICEF at the Orpheum Theatre.

What can I tell you darling? She is absolutely perfect. Holly Golightly in her favourite designer Hubert de Givenchy's *leetle black numbaire*.

Her face (though 59 now) is forever frozen in time (and looks much less pleated than it did at the Academy Awards when we met her when she was just back from that Ethiopian sun). No nail polish, no wedding ring, a small-stoned pinky ring on her left hand, truly great eyebrows, a velvet voice (though she smokes like a peat bog fire) and Eliza Doolittle enunciation that makes words like totally sound like a long, slow river-rafting "*doe-da-lee.*" Five-foot-six and under 100 pounds, she has the tiniest waist, flattest stomach, the firmest, though-hardly-any upper arms, has no need for shoulder pads, ankles like a colt, the same simple chignon dyed chestnut that sets off that sculptured jawline. The neck is still swanlike, but no longer as granmama would say "a spring chicken's," her ears are very long, pointed and with the sparkly brown doe-eyes, give the shy fawn effect that is *her*. Her teeth are just wonderful, and her smile is sweet, distant, like she is remembering snow on the Alps, or something, and she seems painfully shy, in need of sheltering.

As I remember she gave up films to be with her sons Sean, by actor Mel Ferrer, and Luca by hubby number two, that Italian psychiatrist Andrea Dotti. Well she now lives in Geneva with Robert Wolders (realtor, businessman, sometime TV actor) who is bearded, handsome, has piercing blue eyes and smells of English leather. He speaks very softly—a slight accent—and seems always aware of where ever she is in the room. You're welcome, ma chere, I know you care.

Ta Ta Darling. That's it from the colonies,

Valerie.

BARRE HOPPING

Barbie Darling,

Nudged my way off to Rudolph Nureyev and friends at the Queen Elizabeth Theatre. Absolutely *no* one you would know, dear heart, but they were fiercely loyal to the tartar star, and the critics' before-and-after carping did very little to diminish that "catch him while you can" loyalty.

Our barre-hopping boy is 51 now, an age when most primo ballerinos have hung up their tights and tippy-toed into the wings. That age—like a dog's—has to be multiplied. Thirty-five for a dancer is probably 65 for an executive, so Rudy's a little long in the tutu to be *rivoltading, high cabrioling and grande pirouetting* across the boards, even if, as one fan murmured at intermission "it's almost enough just to watch him walk across the stage."

Rudolph Nureyev

He was hardly a heartless cossack riding roughshod over his dance steppes, Barbie. He did put his best foot forward, even if his landings were a little shakey. He puffed, he panted, his leaps *definitely* knew their bounds, and at one point he looked like he was seriously considering *not* lifting Carole Arbo during Balanchine's *Apollon Musagete*, even though she most definitely appeared to be counting on it. He actually shuffled off stage once at what appeared to be an inopportune moment (Elisabeth Platel, one of the gorgeous Paris Opera Ballet *etoiles* was dancing *to* him at the time). "Miller time for Apollo?" murmured the classicist beside me.

I first saw him dance at the Royal Ballet in London in 1960-hmm-hmm. (Of *course* I was a baby at the time.) Rudimania was at its height (he had just defected from the Kirov, and believe me in his prime he was all animal virility). He danced *Ondine* with Dame Margot Fonteyn who was all sublime purity and was just as revered as a member of the royal family. This long-haired beatnik (*before* the Beatles, Barbie) was as much a part of the 1960s scene as Mick Jagger, and he partied as hard as a rock star. He smashed plates and insulted people in restaurants, he stormed off stages and left his wide-eyed pas de deux-ers to fend for themselves. He spoke of himself in the third person—

"Nureyev does not wait for taxi, he is most famous dancer in world." And when this 23-year-old carnal cadabout danced with the then 47-year-old English icon he awakened something in her that I remember at the time was almost too private to watch.

He was practically bronzed from the moment he jete-ed west, and for 28 years, he has been a peripatetic superstar centerstage all over the world—at an average 250 performances a year—more than any other dancer in history. And he takes such *great* bows Barbie. He looks inspirationally beyond the balcony, through the roof, as though he is getting really big-gun approval.

Mr. Neat-enough swept into the after-party, cape furled and cap set, with a dart-thrower's eye for the camera. The darling of "Rudolph's rich groupie set" as Lynn Seymour (who danced but did not dine) calls his international fan club, wore the same beret he wore to Lee Radziwill's wedding. So if it is good enough for Jackie Onassis's princess sister (he left it on during the ceremony as he was standing up for the bride), it is good enough for *moi*. (That hair, if you must know, is less coiffure than a slowly collapsing bird's nest. He pulls it forward a la Napoleon, but it is definitely exiting stage left, if you know what I mean.)

He is rather slight, though it is hard to tell. He was wearing a sweater, a jacket, a coat, a cape, silk pants and the beanie, none of which had anything in particular to do with anything else. Maybe he wears it all at one time so he can pack quickly.

He walks wearily like his knees hurt, or like he has been sitting too long, or has "buckled too many swashes" as that old uncle of yours used to say.

He has a retinue in tow (itsy-bitsy bite-sized ballerinas and all), but you notice only him. It is not the first-degree fashioncide either, it is those sheet-lightning eyes and a sort of power aura around him, as though he might just devour the world.

He drank his Corona beer from the bottle, spooned his *sopa del dia*, like a "borscht-slurping peasant" sniffed one observer, and dived into his *ensaladilla rusa* as though they might run out.

"He hasn't eaten since he got off the plane this afternoon..." an aide offered lamely. "He had his usual 20 cups of herbal tea, that's all."

He lives most of the year in Paris in an apartment overlooking the Seine and the Louvre. It is as ornate as a stage set, all brocade and naughty 19th century paintings. He haunts antique shops on the Quai Voltaire, collects (and wears) elaborate costumes, plays the harpsichord, reads voraciously. ("He looks like a mad monk in his fur hat and coat as he sweeps about," a friend who has spotted him told me." He has a house on the outskirts of London and a New York apartment overlooking Central Park that is "positively sumptuous," and enough friends with chalets (Saint Moritz) and yachts (Stavros Niarcho's) so that anywhere he hangs his hat is his.

He seems absolutely impervious to criticism. It is because of what he was that detractors cannot forgive him now. He will stop dancing when the public stops coming to leer. I watched him limo away into the silver night, Barbie, and thought when Pushkin comes to shove, Nureyev will still be here. Rudolf the Red knows reign, dear.

Whisked up to Whistler for a quick who-was-where, and there they all were. Bob (he helped get financing for the mountain) and Jan Annable who gave their house by the gondola to the kids and have snuggled into new digs in the benchlands were spotted high-level noshing with mountain men Hughie Smythe (Soooo Robert Redford-cute, Barbie) and Jim McConkey. Winter-faring with them were Lana and Dick Underhill and Peter and Penny Pearse, and Blackcomb's bad boy Allan Fotheringham who is off to turn out another timely tome in time for next Christmas's stocking stuffers.

The fast pack at the top of Whistler rolling into the Roundhouse for a warmup were Andre Molnar in platinum gray, Tony Parsons, as sartorially splendid in red as he is on the nightly news, Dale Mearns in a punk hair-don't, Scott Paper's big roller Dave Stowe and his gung ho wife Mary, and, downhill-all-the-way Peter Brown villaging among the peasants. Intrawest's Joe Houssian was keeping a wary eye on Blackcomb's base, lawyer John Swift and wife Laura (in fur from head to foot) strolled the town center while Murray Pezim, hating every second away from his desk, was holed up making plans to bolt from short term spouse Susan. (So $50 million can't buy happiness. How do you know till you try?)

Partied at businessman John McLean's super chalet in Alpine Meadows with world whiz-about Lois Milsom who added some fabulous Bavarian fare to the pheasant and champagne. (Besides the German count, she picked up the most marvellous recipes on her last riding trip through Hungary.)

Martha Sturdy arrived flashing her new husband, David Wardle, and a full-length mink whose name I did not catch. Eleni Skalbania called during the doings and did not breathe a word about Peter Bogdanovich marrying Dorothy Stratten's little sister in the Wedgewood at that very moment. Don't you just hate that kind of discretion, Babs? Ciao for now.

Ta Ta Darling and keeps your tips up,
Valerie.

FANDOM OF THE OPERA

Barbie Darling,

Nudged my way off to the North American premier of *The Music of Andrew Lloyd* Webber, who by-the-by has filled more theatre seats around the world than any other living composer. (And who, in true soap opera fashion left his wife, married a beautiful young chorus girl and proceeded to write showcases that would make her a star. *Much* more later. Would I disappoint *you*, dear heart?)

Andrew Lloyd Webber, Sarah Brightman

It was a sold-out performance and the Phantom of the Popular pulled all his best bunnies out of his hat. We got *Cats* and *Evita* and *Jesus Christ Superstar* and the incredibly cutesy *Starlight Express*. (Remember that night in London, Barbie when we just about lost our smart Mr. Chow's dinners as the actors whizzed up and down the aisles on *rollerskates?*) Andrew L, that iron-supplement-for-tired-musical-theatre even descended like a tiny Moses with new note tablets called *Aspects Of Love*, but the plebs all left the Orpheum mumbling *Memory*, and humming *Don't Cry For Me Argentina* after the five or six squatting ovations Vancouverites seem to give anything that resembles "international."

Webber's winsome wife Sarah Brightman wore a heavy two-foot waterfall of a hairpiece throughout the show, which kept those doe-like eyes even bigger than they are, and a deep green bandage-wrap dress in the first act that should be rerolled and buried. But can that girl take a bow, darling, and reach those arms to the rafters till the audience is in each palm? (Despite the hair, she appeared light-headed backstage as she sipped champagne from a plastic cup and put a stop to a friend's further bubbly with a "Please, you shall have us dancing on the table."

Two hundred and fifty dollars bought dress-circle seats and a swish champagne reception later at Le Meridien hosted by Joan Carlisle-Irving whose classy clavicles were tanned ("Long Island," she told me) and whose dulcet tones ("fine silver clinking against good crystal, "as Grandmama would say) always tell you the best jet-setty stuff. This was the premiere event for the _Night of a Thousand And One Dinners_ so it brought out the heavy hitters whose charity dough-see-dough see the Vancouver Opera through the season.

Investment whiz Peter Paul Saunders, a longtime friend of the arts, slipped in for a spot of bubbly with wife Nancy (in a black and flowered print) right behind Toni Cavelti and his Hildegard in the zingiest little black and white polka-dot Louis Feraud. Woody and Sherrill MacLaren flexed their social muscle—she is great to talk to with a second sure-to-be-a-best-seller (on Canadian women and power) in the works.

Condo King Andre Molnar and his fund raising femme Julie bustled in on the heels of car czar Henning Brasso and his cosmetics executive wife Kam, who had been Poole-ing resources with Jack and Darlene only moments before. Jack-be-quick, newly retired from BCE Development, had just made an announcement a few hours earlier with Mayor Gordon Campbell (who was standing right behind him at _this_ tony do) about developing new low-cost housing.

Toni & Hiildegard Cavelti

The lieutenant governor was trumpeted in, and Guus Mostart, the new artistic director of the opera was introduced around, but this was really a showbiz kind of night and chichi charityites were waiting for a flash of glam.

Joel Schumacher the director of Cousins pranced in, all six-foot whatever in his perfect shoulder length bob, a dark and spiffy evening suit and the dearest little brown dancing pumps with bows and white socks to head-to-head with actor-now-director David (_Blow Up_) Hemmings. Well, besides being an actor, Hemmings apparently was a boy soprano too, and later starred in Andrew Lloyd Webber's only flop, _Jeeves_, and he and his wife, Pru, became friends with the Webbers. They flew up from Malibu, loved it here, and are looking for a home in the Gulf Islands.

"He's so sexy, he just _stews_,' murmured the baubles-and-beads beside me, not minding Hemmings silver locks at all. (This was the same creature who moments later gasped at Webber's entrance. "Migawd, he looks like a baby hedgehog. Thank goodness he's so talented.")

Sarah Brightman wafted in pounds lighter (the hair presumably left in the dressing room) in a flower child dress Maggie Trudeau would have loved, and beige cowboy boots with straps and buckles. ("More Goodwill than good taste," sniffed baubles-and-beads before I moved away to chat with England's *other* Andrew and Sarah). I now know more about Britain's biggest cultural export than I really need to, but who knows when there will be a test?

He is 41, was married before, and has two children: a boy, Nicholas, and a girl, Imogen. He grew up in a musical family (brother Julian is a world-reknowned cellist) in south Kensington and wrote his first musical as a teenager (after becoming entranced with *South Pacific*).

He and Sarah, soon to be 29, have a 12 acre seaside estate in the south of France in St. Jean-Cap-Ferrat. His favourite restaurant is the Cafe Paloma down from Eze and just across from Monte Carlo, and he speaks fairly good French though a friend who lives there tells me they still call him the *Anglais*.

He composes on a white Yamaha upright in the guest house and it is his very favourite private place, though he owns a 60th-floor apartment in the

Joel Schumacher, David Hemmings

Trump Tower in New York that be bought two years ago for $5.5 million, a duplex in Easton Square (just across from our friend James Clavell's lawyer, Michael Lew) and a 12,000-acre estate outside London called Sydmonton Court. The Fleet Street tabs peg his wealth at several million pounds so it looks like he could afford the Palace Theatre in London's West End that he bought for $2 million. When his Really Useful Theatre Company had a stock offering four years ago, Webber netted a cool $20 mil, and how about those royalties floating in at upwards of $5 million a year? (You would think he would up Prince Edward's salary a quid or two. Lizzie's little lad started his theatrical career as "tea boy" there.)

His passion is Victoria architecture and pre-Raphaelite art, and he tools around London in a chauffeur-driven Bentley that Sarah (who walks, swims and dances to keep that five-foot-five-inch frame frisky) gifted him with. He told me he was thrilled with the Vancouver Symphony's 70-piece ensemble, that they had never played the two encore pieces before that night, and that he would love to film *The Phantom Of The Opera* in our beloved rococo Orpheum. The British tabloids peg Steven Spielberg (who lives below him in Trump Tower) as a possible director. (Bryan Adams' girl Vicky Russell's father Ken directed the video, speaking of small worlds, what?)

You can be sure, *ma chere*, that the movie when done will be an "absolutely-take-it-to-the-bank-and-cash-it-sure-thing" as they say in Jolly Old, and then maybe Hollywood will persuade Andrew L to turn in his Beatle haircut.

Aced off to _Aida_ earlier with its he-man handiwork, its drive-in theatre image, its focused firepower, its motorized mechanisms whirring special effects into gear into the rarified heights of B.C. Place stadium.

Kettledrums crashing, choruses rising, it was half-hokum, half-Hollywood, and unless I am as vague as a vacuum I was not the only one hoping for the homestretch. "Ahlan wa sahlan (Welcome to the land of the pharoahs)," indeed. I mean, "Sominex meets Valium," darling—_a dinosaur_. And the crowd? Like a convention of blind dates. Where _are_ these people in the daylight hours?

But it was the _after_ party you want to know about. Those caring souls who had paid up to $300 a ticket (to benefit the Cancer society) got to sip champers and nosh nibblies at a midnight supper at the B.C. Enterprise Centre.

Senator George Van Roggen harrumphed his way in wearily (it had been a long night, believe me, Babs) as did good sport Gerald McGavin (chairman of the B.C. Sports Hall Of Fame) and Blackcomb's Joe Houssian who has seen men move mountains (if not pyramids) before. The Italian consul general Gianfranco Manigrassi talked _Verdi_ with

Joan Carlisle-Irving

"I-just-want-to-bring-opera-to-the-people" Guiseppe Raffa, the artistic director/conductor of the big tent production. The larger-than-life Raffa really does seem to believe he is changing the face of opera around the world. From the foot of the Sphinx to right here in _your_ neighbourhood. He also says he wants to stage Bizet's _Carmen_ in a bullring in Seville and Tchaikovsky's _Boris Gudonov_ in Moscow's Red Square. All that enthusiasm certainly left _me_ feeling a little past my ripest hour.

Ta Ta Darling, notes to you and please keep to the designated arias.

Valerie.

SOCIETY'S ISLANDS

Barbie Darling,

I have been thinking about island getaways and retreats, and about those who idyll on the 500-or-so little beauties scattered around Georgia Strait. There are the "weekends only," who spend Friday getting there, Saturday worrying about the return trip, and most of Sunday getting back, and there are the "summer people," whose idea of relief from city rituals is to reproduce them elsewhere. In either case, though, the most isolated beach is washed by the detailed and devious features of city social life.

Allan Fotheringham, who year after year throws himself a birthday bash on Bowen, has intoned that "the most valuable advice any mother can give to any daughter is an age-old one: never go to a party on an island. The floating, away-from-reality aspect of an island reduces inhibitions, tosses away caution, and sweeps away sweet care." Barbie, you will recognize this as a distinct toning down of Foth's former "drunk and out of town doesn't count," but I digress.

Hornby Island has long been home to artists, architects and academics. Many of Jack Shadbolt's canvases were inspired by the summer view from his Downes Point patio. Wayne Ngan's ceramic pieces from his Sung dynasty-like kiln were sent around the world by External Affairs after Joe Clark and Maureen McTeer fell in love with them. From his deck on the hill above Ford Cove, architect Bruno Freschi has watched back-to-the-landers build their assembly-line A-frames and kit cottages as well as sod-roofed shake-and-driftwood concoctions.

Lawyer Tony Pantages, his wife Diane and various kids have spent 25 years back and forthing for the tennis and Hornby's beaches. Keith and oh-so-second wife Jan Sorensen have built an *Architectural Digest* delight on a bluff above Tribune Bay, there to host some most opulent soirees. Hornby's big party of the year takes place chez Sorensen. By boat and plane, they come, including rancher Gordon Parkes, architect Barry MacLeod and already-there ex-stockbroker Bob Phillips who was an early developer on Hornby. Those who will not spend a half-day on three ferries can be sipping that first martini having landed in a pinch at "Hornby International" among grazing Jerseys owned by Imperial Parking's Arne Olsen, whose working ranch-farm is as productive as it is breathtakingly pristine on rolling land beside the sea.

There is a crust of customs on Hornby, and everyone plays. With water, water everywhere and not too much on land, it is "two-minute showers strictly, flush only when necessary." Metal, glass and paper are all separated with a surgeon's skill and deposited, socially correctly, at the community recycling depot.

Just 15 miles east of Hornby, Lasqueti Island wants nothing to do with anything remotely citified. Access is by foot-passenger ferry, there is no electricity, and Lasqueti has for years taken the rap (it's those RCMP air raids) as pot capital of the Gulf Islands. Unlike Paisley Island, where those wishing to join such as Peter Hebb, Malcolm Burke and the Ladner clan must pass a country-club screening process, Lasqueti's tree hugging green thumbs occasionally let in straight professors and their socially prominent wives and children. Regarding which, I hear that Peter and Penny Pearce's new place is not only ecologically sound but certifiably chic.

Saltspring, of course, is another kettle of hobby farmers. Jack Webster has for years been laird of a 99-acre, sheep-riddled mountainside farm at which guests have let down their famous coifs. John Turner, who stays at Hastings House while playing hookey in our Hamptons, usually ambles over to check out the state of all unions via Webster's 110-channel satellite dish. On Saltspring, too, the Carney family, including Pat, is often to be found busily writing.

Ex-senator John Nichol and his gallery-owning wife Lizzie have since 1957 hosted pundits and prime ministers at their

The Killams Hernando

Savary Island home-away-from. Pierre Trudeau and Margaret (Justin was their only baby then) stopped by on a borrowed yacht, and the peripatetic PM spent the afternoon jumping off the dock with the local kids. Daryl Duke has a place on Savary, Norman Keevil Sr. has _two_, and the Woodwards began there before moving to Hernando Island.

Hernando is the hideaway for a wealthy and worldly assemblage of out-of-towners—Keevil Sr. again, the younger George Reifel, Ken and Patsy Tolmie, Dr. Mike Bell, Gowan Guest, Sandy Fisher, Brian Rogers, Hank Gourley—who have chosen its windswept shores for what can be a back-to-the-very-exclusive-land experience. Larry and Sherry Killam reassembled a `83-year-old Ontario barn into a Hyannisport haven the Kennedys would covet. Vancouver architect Leith Anderson adapted it from cows to kids, while Larry—who is known for his deadly eye on Vancouver's aesthetics—and artist wife Sherry created a frame-any-view vista throughout the antique-laden rooms. The dining room seats 24 on chairs retired from the Chateau Laurier, and an invitation to dinner is worth its weight in fresh crab and Saltspring Island lamb.

The closest island of all, of course, is Bowen, where a wide array of ambition presents itself in as many different dwellings. Peter Brown's award-winner at Hood Point would wash with the smart set in any New England retreat, as would his magnificently restored mahogany launch. The electric golf cart with the Rolls Royce grill for those trips to the tennis courts is...just Peter.

Fine old families—Sauder, Underhill, Rogers, Purdy, Pearkes, Malkin, Cromie—have summered here for years, and done Thanksgiving and Easter, too, weather allowing. Cabins that blossomed into respectable second homes, then got shuffled or divorced ("you take the kids, I get the cottage") have led to a whole new series of abodes a-building in the I'll-show-you-bigger-and-better style. There is no such thing as "getting away" to a fashionable place, dear heart. You must take it all with you.

On that biggest of islands, former lieutenant-governor Bob Rogers and his wife Jane have a *Country Homes* cover place at Dorcas Point near Parksville. The cedar-and-shake showcase nestles among oak and arbutus, blending into a grassy slope from the water. The Rogerses bought the 28 hectares in 1962 and have been refining it from cottage to house ever since. An invitation to a relaxed evening here tops any former formal event at Government House.

Qualicum, of course, has Judges Row, where in season one may find Gordon and Jeanie Southam (Harvey and Pia flew in from their rented Rosedale mansion; sister Stephanie was there, too, the Bell-Irvings, Victor MacLean and John Lecky, whose mother is a MacMillan. Nearby is the 41-acre, very private waterfront estate of Veronica Milner where the Royals stay, somehow irritating Jeanie Southam. Charles barbecued there for Di after arriving on Jack Charles's *Hotei* during Expo year.

Back in the city, I sailed off to Jeto and Sid Sengara's South Granville stamping ground to meet Patwant Singh, the esteemed author of *The Golden Temple*, I walked in with that jettiest of setters, Lois Milsom, who of course had met the author in India and was remembered fondly by him. The pair were updating their communal trivia exotica—just who was just where just now—as Peter Hyndman and a silk-suited Joanna Staniszkis, rhapsodizing about the book to artist Toni Onley, were joined by Leon Bibb in the most perfect GQ shirt and slacks.

Forgotten but not gone, a newly slimmed Laurier Lapierre was holding forth on his soon-to-be New Age TV show, while that Greek in sleek clothing Costas Syskakis tossed small swishes of spirits into the fire and watched the flames leap.

You know, dear: the same old list of suspects.
Ta Ta Darling, the more things change,
Valerie.

THE 1990'S

*O*ld money, as we bade a fond farewell to the 80's, was startng to mean any family booty more than a decade old. Multi-faceted diamonds-in-the-rough — some of them the grown-up babies of the boom-timers,— others with foreign names we would have to learn to spell— cropped up more and more often on the *beau monde* boards of the I'll sponsor yours if you sponsor mine.

Young philanthropists-in-embryo were starting to take control of what had always been in the hands of the Establishment. Or, in more than a few instances, were starting up brand new give-away-plans that by-passed the usual labour-heavy, cost-a-lot channels and going right to the sources that needed them. The smart, young, no-holds-barred money began raising astrobucks for charity—record sums in record time—at events that were new and different and a treat to attend.

Broadway hits—*Les Miz, the Phantom,* hit the boards for first-rate Vancouver runs and helped us feel a little more cosmopolitan. The busy, busy Baroness de Rothschild continued her once-a-year pit stops at our wine auctions. The first Molson Indy race varoomed into town (and it looks like an annual keeper.) Endeavour, Art's Umbrella's "Splash", The Black and White, and Lover's Balls kept popping up like clockwork. Art galleries continued to open and close, and to exhibit as adventuresome showings as we rainforesters could handle.

John Turner resigned, we didn't have Bill VanderZalm to kick around anymore, and Kim Campbell came and went in a millisecond. Hollywood started shooting movies here with blase frequency ("I'm at Le Meridien for two months, they're using my houise for a shoot"). Whistler continued its ascent into becoming an international year-round playground, and when you mentioned at the Oscars that you were from Vancouver—the stars you were chatting with knew where it was because they had either skied Whistler, or shot a movie around town. And they could often name favourite restaurants, shops and city landmarks. A big change from a few years ago, when if you mentioned anything Vancouverish you laid a big fat Faberge egg.

Every law firm worth its retainers still buys tables to most dinners, and because ploys will be ploys, big business still buys the perfunctory block of tickets to keep up the old image. Which means that most high-scale social events are still a fairly interesting barometer of what's up. They offer a sort of blow by blow (a million dollars today, being essentially chopped liver) of the rise and fall, and sometimes the rise again of the city's *bon viveurs*.

As a semi-last gasp on the subject, the galas don't seem to be the glitter-happy drainingly monumental events they used to be, and some should be retired because they have become, apologies aside, *fetes* worse than debt.

THE YEAR 1990

WITH GREAT RELIEF
The night the Grits rolled and extolled John Turner.

HIGH HILL, BIG BILLIES
Would Salmon Rushdie get the right table at Il Caminetto or Val d'sere? If he were in Whistler, he would.

LETTER FROM HONG KONG
Who counts for what where five-and-a-half-million citizens are said to have six million connections.

OVER THE FENCES AND AROUND THE STARS
They came to shindigs from all over town, and Shirley MacLaine from all over time.

RACING PARTIES AND FINE ART PARTYING
An Indy gala pit stop, a crumb-free Ben Gurion benefit, and Attila's Young men.

WITH GREAT RELIEF

Barbie Darling,

Trudged off to the tribute dinner for John Turner along with 700 other *very* eclectic souls, each of whom coughed up a well-mannered $250 to add their two cents' worth to a Dear John swan song that *did* go on.

With his resignation, The Right Hon. John Napier "Chick" Turner, PC, QC, MP, BA, BCL, Beta Theta Pi, Canadian junior champion in the 100- and 200-yard sprints, Rhodes Scholar and the pride of his UBC class of '49, said bye-bye as leader for the last time after a shared meal of shrimp, salmon and Cornish game hen.

Geills & John Turner

Not to get all warm and runny, Darling, but there were a few perusers-of-the-passing-scene dealing with just what had happened to Old Blue Eyes in the fast five years since he popped back into the fray. He was supposed to be a consummate smoothy, a political pro with Bay Street smarts, when he arrived back in Ottawa after nine private-sectoring years. Instead he turned out to be a rusty knight whose back-slapping, bum-patting, throat-clearing Turnerisms needed a spot of polish. And after the second-shortest term in history as prime minister, just 79 days, an electrorate up to here with Liberal-ities and Pierre's patronage legacy voted for whose-Tory-now.

"Look, he was beleaguered, but he was in a beleague of his own," I heard as I watched Turner pump hands with his two-handed grip, fixing the intended with those 60-year-old azure lasers.

From another: "I was in Ottawa when he resigned as finance minister, and that [expletive deleted] Trudeau offered him the Senate or the Bench. Then we talk him out of a cushy private law practice [one of the best four or five in the country] so his own caucus could kneecap him with palace revolts. He sure paid the cost to be the boss."

There was plenty of Liberal red and fiscal black at this jostle for John, and for one brief, shining moment querulous cliques and fractious factions seemed to be quite united under the glass-roofed B.C. Enterprise Center. As the MP from Quadra himself had said in the House of Commons, to laughter from both sides: "The good-byes are far more generous and spontaneous than the hellos." But there was little laughter in this room, Darling, and enough raw, graceless garnering of support for a new leader to levitate the roof.

Six Liberal MPS showed up to flash the flag (I always enjoy chatting with Bob Kaplan, who speaks with the air of a parent explaining to a four-year-old why the sky is blue), and several senators: Jack Austin in gray hair, gray suit and with his gray cells in gear as always; the Teamster senator, Ed Lawson; Ray Perreault, as loyal and verbal as ever; and George Van Roggen, who broke with his old friend Turner over free trade.

Iona Campagnolo, who is no longer destined to be Canada's first woman prime minister, flew out to put her Grand Damnable clout behind Paul Martin and to nod goodbye to Turner. Bruno Gerussi, who is so NDP he glows, endured Liberal doses of Meech Lake and visions of Canada while party heavyweights did their standing-ovation-imitation. Gordon Campbell was so effusive thanking "his" MP, you might have thought that Turner had owned a house and paid taxes in Vancouver.

Lana & Richard Underhill

Prospero Realty bizwig Bob Lee, motor maestro Henning Brasso, venture-capitalist Steven Funk and developer Jack Poole were among the ladened-with-loot lads lauding the leader (the last minister of finance to have two successive surpluses in his budget), while Bryan Williams, Dick Underhill, Walley Lightbody and Nancy Morrison lent a little from the lawyers.

Mart Kenney, whose band had played at Turner's 1949 UBC grad dance, serenaded supporters; Turner's longtime tennis partner Jack Cunningham smoothly handled the affusion of the evening's introduction; and Ross Fitzpatrick, a one-time Turner lieutenant who turned back his perfectly tailored topcoat to Jean Chretien, splashily supplied the "Tribute to Turner" wine from his Cedar Creek winery.

At the exclusive Laurier Club afterparty (members donate $1,000 and up to belong), Geills Turner, in a smashing gold-silver-and-blue-brocade size-six dinner suit, lit into Chretien supporter Linda Fitzpatrick and Paul Martin supporter Kilby Gibson who had been "incredibly disloyal" by working for their hopefuls *before* her husband (to whom she is outspokenly, fiercely loyal)

221

had announced his intention to step down. For the very few who overheard the controlled kerfuffle, a little flush certainly was infused into an otherwise flat function.

As for the guest of honor himself, if all the world's a stage, as Shakespeare says, and the rest of us had trouble learning our parts, John Turner never did. Through more than 20 years in public service, as in all his life, he was guided by "acceptable behavior," by an "enormous sense of mission," by the belief that dues must be paid for a good life, and that a man "owes it back to his country." Turner showed grace under fire, and was never a crybaby despite inuendo, gossip and back stabbing enough to sink a lesser man. He lost a bundle financially by returning to politics, and will need to hustle on Bay Street to make the $15,724 monthly mortgage payments on the $1.55 million house in Toronto's Forest Hill district he and Geills bought recently.

Turner played out his self-imposed lifelong role, still insists that becoming a politician instead of the priest he once said he might be was "fun," and that "winning gracefully and losing gracefully are essential civilized qualities."

Ta ta, Darling, and ta ta, Turner. He will write the next chapter himself.
Valerie

HIGH HILL, BIG BILLIES

Barbie Darling,

Upped to Whistler for the holidays, and it proved to be the *ultimate* in nouvelle lang syne. Some Armani draped snowstoppers were already back from Saint Moritz, while plenty of other mogul-hoppers in ankle-length mink, fox and lynx had already taken a powder to the pampered playpens of Aspen.

Whistler/Blackcomb showed that all the dollars ladled into its 214 major trails spilling off 5,006 vertical feet, as well as all the hands-down glitz that goes with it, can pull in some pretty hefty hitters. I mean, we can talk about "dazzling bright sun, rocky outcroppings, huge and craggy alpine panoramas, jagged pinnacles of granite surrounded by rugged snow-filled cirques outlined against an opalescent sky," Babs, or we can talk about the *real* stuff.

Priscilla Presley was there. Of *course* I mean Elvis's Priscilla, silly. She and lived-in lover Marco Garibaldi (whom Lisa Marie can't stand) were in the valley with baby-no-more Navaronne, who was taken to the Kid's Kamp at Blackcomb for his first ski lessons.

They registered at the sparkling new $70-million Chateau Whistler, of which more in a minute, as Mr. and Mrs. Garibaldi. "I'm sure you know how to spell *that* around *here*," Priscilla said, smiling sweetly with nary a line in her fortysomething brow. She was almost as fresh and wholesome as *Dynasty's* Linda Evans, who whistled up for a look-see from her Oregon home and thereby proved that her new hair-weaving had really worked: her bulked-up coif—color-by-Clairol—looked good. Linda has crinkly deep-blue eyes, a lot of freckles under very little makeup, and is long and lithe with tiny hips and enough curves elsewhere to elicit teeth-gnashing envy except she is so darned *nice*.

The Chateau was already hosting some of the 75,000 souls it expects will lodge annually under its green-gabled roof, and its 343 rooms—including 36 swank suites at up to $550 an eider-downed night—were chockablock with Vuitton luggage. Whisked from Vanland by the $225-return Whistler Express helicopter to land mere steps from the Chateau's cozy, country-estate Mallard Bar, there was plenty of time for taking off the edge with a champagne chill as a passel of porters took the bags up and the skis down.

Zonda Nellis's swish boutique was crowded with Japanese buying every woolly in sight to go with all the Gucci, Fendi, Hermes and Chanel they had bought downtown at Holt's. I looked

Pamela Martin

outside, then around the Great Hall and in the Chateau's glittering shops for someone wearing that $12,000 ski parka with the 18-karat gold zipper and snaps we saw in Vail last year, but came up only with Keith Sorensen and the oh-so-slim Jan bustling by the lobby's carved limestone fireplace on their way to the bar. Keith was ever so chatty; said his ex-sister-in-law, actress Linda Sorensen, had just gotten a part in *Murphy Brown*. Since Keith was a Whistler pioneer often found at log-cabin apres parties in the 1960s, it was interesting to see him in a loaded-with-grandeur setting. He was accompanied by Marlboro-man-handsome rancher Gordon Parkes and his sharp-as-a-tack wife Emir. Remember them from Hornby Island, Barbie? The same people seem to just flit from the Gulf Islands to Palm Springs, from Maui to Whistler, like migrating birds, no?

Bob and Jan Annable, whose big-bucks Deer Ridge development in West

Vancouver is a-building right along, gave a smart little soiree in the Chateau's Frontenac Ballroom, their table guests for duckling and dancing including Peter and Penny Pearse (remember *them* from Lasqueti?).

I know that Whistler is a place that's steep and seldom sleeps dear heart, but if you are expecting me to tell you who, or more likely what, was at Tommy Africa's, Citta's, Jimmy D's, The Longhorn, The Boot Pub, Johnny Jupiter's, Buffalo Bill's or the Savage Beagle, that foofoo juice perfume you wear too much of has gone to your head. However, I *will* tell you who I spied festifying on my search for Brave New Mountain chic. As Thoreau said, cherie: "Beware of any enterprise that requires new clothes." And since skiing is definitely one of those, personal asides aside, here goes.

The celebrity watering hole, where Siberia seating is the punishment for nonstar status, is still Umberto's Il Caminetto. You can "drink until you are legless," as grandmama used to tsk, or you can table hop like a jackrabbit.

Pamela Martin—40 now, tra-la—breezed in straight from the slopes all in lavender with main man Bruce Gordon, passing Nancy Greene Raine, who incongruously told me that she and Karen Percy have the same size feet and that "all top women skiers have small feet." Oh, that Nancy and the mountain air!

Stepped past some yupped-up puppies in apres-ski ultimates, staking out their territories. There were enough fur coats, hats, muffs and boots to fill a game farm, and enough nuclear name-dropping to busy the cellular-phone set sitting there.

Architect Ron Howard and wife Barb, just back from Maui, sported their tanlines as Ron tossed another monologue on the fire. Planted in the midst of a table of younger "outrepreneurs," Howe-Streeter Wally DeZura was dressed all in white. How's *that* for character impersonation? Maxine and Harry Gelfant said how they love-love the house in Woodridge they bought from Murray Pezim's hex-of-the-ex Susan, Maxine admitting that she finally has enough room for "all the grandchildren." Edgar Kaiser had bought bizwiz Neil Cook's splendid log mansion, Westcoast Energy's Mike Phelps had acquired—what else?—an energy-conscious also-log abode, and restaurateur Brent Davies's petit pied-a-terre was definitely *Architectural Digest* stuff. Indeed, playing Who's Where in Whistler, with its mouth-to-mouth recitation about who lives in out-of-town anonymity up here, certainly left me wide-eyed.

Sprinkled around the valley are Cartier's Daniel and Ani Feuermann, designer Francesco Guilini and wife Deborah, lawyers Tom Braidwood, John Swift and David Hossie, Judge Sam Toy and his family, Andre Molnar and Norman Keevil, architect Terry Hale, Robson Street real-estater Peter Foreman, Bob and Suzanne Brody, Russell and Barbara Brink...It went on and on, Barbie. By the time I headed off to dinner, I really *needed* that cold mountain air.

Val d'Isere is *the* new cuisine Francaise restaurant here, dear, and the one that every majestic-peaker has checked out at least once. Bjorn Borg had a tasteful little din-din there while pushing his $80-million Whistler Resort proposal, and loved everything. That 38-year-old Italian rock singer he is hooked up with was nothing but trouble, though. She barged into master chef Ron Lammie's kitchen to announce "no onions, no garlic, no this.." Well, you get the picture. The likeable Lammie, who has elan with a flan and is *very* avant gout, just took it with a grain of salt. Sorry, Babs.

Ron Longstaffe and family, who use their place at "The Gables" all year round, love the restaurant that Roger Crisp and Michel Jacobs of Le Crocodile have hatched for the haute and hungry. So did Pierre Trudeau, who was up with Justin, Misha and Sasha, and looked rested and rosy from his ski day with Bud Kanke and Bud's father-in-law Dick Meyers. Trudeau used his little half-glasses to read the menu, had the tomato-gin soup and the duck, remembered exactly where he had met Lammie in Montreal 10 years ago, and was as storm-the-mountain, gung-ho a skier as when we skied with him, and those two cute Mounties, 15 years ago. I know you care, Barbie.

The night I was at Val d'Isere, so were Margaret Trudeau Kemper, hubby Fried, and another couple. Bouncing boy Kyle and baby sister Alicia were elsewhere, and movie-star-handsome Fried could not take his eyes off Margaret, who looked so fabu, as your affected friend George would say: shiny, shoulder-length curls; great skin for a soon-to-be-42er; pristine white blouse with antique pin at the throat; those incredible big blue eyes. "I'd rather be planting my garden than doing that level of partying and living on the edge of a dream that I used to," she said. "You have to know when to exit." She looked almost like she did the day we went for herbal tea at the prime minister's place at Harrington Lake when she was expecting Justin. She was planting her garden that day, too, madder than a wet hen that some bureaucratic department or other was spraying pesticides from a plane over *her* organic produce. Plus que ca change, Darling.

Paul Storey, the full-of-finesse restaurant manager, looks like a renegade from film noir with his shock of silver hair and Godiva chocolate eyes. He is also ever so discreet in his table placements and info disclosures. Do you know how many exes are up in Whistler, dear? Maggie and Pierre never knew that each ordered exactly what the other had.

Of course I skied, silly. Two runs followed by a two-and-a-half-hour lunch at the Rendezvous in Christine's: a little onion soup, a little Caesar salad, enough Veuve Cliquot. Now *that's* skiing.

Ta Ta Darling. Do you know the way to Saint-Tropez?
Valerie

LETTER FROM HONG KONG

Barbie Darling,

Hopped off to Hongkong for a high-end look-see. Cathay Pacific's sumptuous service was one long banquet on the way to more millionaires per square mile and more Rolls-Royces than anywhere else in the world. More designer shops than in Palm Beach and Beverly Hills put together, too. And all these years I kept doing London, Paris, Roma and the Riviera!

Brenda Chau and Kai-Bong Chau

The Taipans and Tai Tais—"those rich and pampered wives who spend their way to happiness," as your friend from Jardine's let slip—were totally intriguing to watch at work. "Real life," the Jardinaire told me, "starts for the typical Tai around lunchtime, when she meets friends and starts her daily prowl of the big-label boutiques, nips into Wardley's banking hall to check share prices for an hour or so, then back to the main business of the day—trying on jewelry and watching what the competition is buying." Sounds great to me, Barbie.

Someone who combines a bit of a career with this *perfect*-sounding pastime is Brenda Chau, a glamorous little number who wangles her way into society and both gossip columns—*never* in the same ensemble. Brenda is a lawyer married to another one, Kai-Bong Chau, and they are stinking rich. She rides in a pink Rolls-Royce with a pink-clad chauffeur; her designer clothes, hats, turbans and rubies are often pink; and she writes the local Chinese equivalent of the rich and famous, which she calls *Through Pink Glasses*.

Robin Leach told me last year in Vancouver that Brenda and Kai-Bong, who attended Cambridge university and qualify for "regular" British passports, are "the most ostentatious, excessive couple" he has encountered in his travails. *Everything* in their gilded cage, Villa D'Oro, is 24 karat gold. Walls, ceilings, doors, chairs, tables and most of her 33 fur coats are sprayed gold, and their two Rolls-Royces are flecked with gold-dust. The only things ungilded are life-size paintings of themselves, studded with diamonds, emeralds and rubies.

Sniffed a not-so-successful financial-sector crony over XO brandies: "They have carried China's poetic name—the Golden Mountain—to new lows."

Dame Lydia Dunn, the senior member of the Hongkong Executive Council, is quite the opposite: classy and cultured, with a finely sculpted face and flawless British accent. On the two times I spotted her, she was wearing sienna. Her signature color is that shade of priceless Chinese lacquer that is usually impossible to duplicate. Oodles of where-withal, but subtle, you know?

Hongkong may be "five-and-a-half million people with six million connections," as the saying goes, but connecting the dots for this "foreign devil" was an exasperating Chinese puzzle. Many of the often-titled tycoons who have made it big seem to play their cards, if not up their sleeves, very close to their chests.

Li Ka-Shing should have been easy, no? Twenty-billion big ones of his own, and he controls five times that—15 percent of the Hongkong market's total value—but no flash at all, Barbie. If you thought the ex-Expo lands owner's profile was low around Vancouver, it is a mere hen's tooth higher in the colony.

"K.S." surfaces discreetly, almost shyly, at the wedding of friends' children, for instance. Wearing his usual navy blue

Michael Smith, Margaret Defensor, Berton Woodward, Phielle Woodward, Sean Toplis

business suit instead of formal attire, he was one of a thousand guests at the spectacular fall marriage of Christina Lee and prominent doctor Samson Sun's son David. He did go formal to the royal opening night of the cultural center, mind you, but was the unassuming host for the preconcert cocktail party. I stayed part of my time in the Hongkong Hilton, one the world's top hotels, but did not find out until later who owns it. K.S. also owns the Hongkong Bank and the Hongkong Electric Holdings, and on and on, but associates say you would never know by his exquisite manners that he is the colony's richest Chinese businessman. A friend calls him a "plain quartz watch in a city of gold Rolexes."

Then there is Macau gambling czar Stanley Ho, a smiling, sideburned foxtrot fancier who keeps one wife in a 25-room Toronto mansion and another in the Portuguese colony (old laws, darling—it was allowed). Called "the decadent tycoon" around H.K., he seems to enjoy freewheeling it as much as making it. Although self-confessedly belonging to "one of the wealthiest and oldest Hongkong families," he seems never to forget his youthful "losing of face" when his mother, a great beauty, had to pawn her jewelry to keep the family going. Scratch the Mercantile Bank, Jardine's or the Shanghai Bank, though, and you will find a Ho or two.

"Of all the mighty magnates who are moving their money to Vancouver," a wag-about-the-colony told me, "Ho's ancient, honorable family is by far the most colorful." Ho bought the Meridien hotel and the next-door La Residence three years ago, but the hotel's Karen Hall says he has only dropped by once.

Eldest daughter Pansy Ho makes the social columns almost as often as father the flaunter, frequently giving the welcoming address at charities of which papa is a patron. The under-100-pounder's clothes and jewels are detailed to the nth: Pansy at *The Nutcracker*; Pansy at the Ballet Ball, in rubies and diamonds and designer duds; Pansy introducing Karl Lagerfeld at his first H.K. appearance. Meanwhile, Ho the Elder launches the $100,000-initiation-fee Dynasty club for those who have "achieved standards of living and lifestyles quite different from those of their fathers." These opulent sons meet in a HK$110-million four-floor beauty with bars, billiard rooms, restaurants and petite private dining rooms. And s-o-o-o privee, ma chere.

One hard-to-ignore woman, whose name crops up in Vancouver as much as in H.K., is Sally Au Sien. She controls the $150 million Sing Tao Group—a little publishing, a few apartment blocks here and in Toronto, some pharmaceuticals, part of Imperial Parking, a Richmond shopping center. Spice-of-life stuff, you know. And that reminds me: she is also heir to the Tiger Balm fortune, which makes her, at 56 or so, the world's eighth-richest woman. Tiresome, what?

I was at the Clearwater Bay Golf and Country Club (corporate membership is Hk$1.5 million) for lunchy-poo on one of those fine, jasmine-scented days with the South China Sea islands visible, when a name or two just dropped into my linen-clad lap.

"Did you know," my ever-so-knowledgeable host inquired, "that Sir Run Run Shaw [I *love* that name, Barbie] and Sir Y.K. Pao, the shipping magnate [I knew *that—Fortune* listed him as one of the world's 100 richest people], both raised large sums of money to found this spectacular club?"

In any case, Sir Run Run, who must be in his mid-80s but barely looks 50, is showbiz all the way. A movie mogul turned TV titan, he shows up at the opening of an envelope, flashing his glad-to-be-here smile. Movie stars are big on the social scene here, too. "Jackie Chan applied for membership at the

Clearwater Bay," my accommodating host dropped, "but he is too busy to play." And cropping up at the odd party *with* Jackie Chan is former kung-fu actress Michelle Poon. There's more, though: Michelle married Dickson Poon, who is heir to a $1.8 billion windfall, Dickson Concepts Ltd., and she is *very* pretty and therefore an up-and-coming force.

However, I promised you some colonized Canadians, didn't I, dear heart? Let me start with ex-Vancouverite Berton Woodward, who has been here for over 10 tightly packed years. His mother is Lucy Woodward, who is Pierre Berton's sister. Shirley Grauer, who was married to B.C. Electric's Dal Grauer, and later married Lieutenant Governor Walter Owen, who is Alderman Philip Owen's father (artist Sherry Grauer is Shirley's daughter who is married to architect John Keith-King), whose brother-in-law is Steven Grauer, who was married to Liberal queen-pin Cindy Grauer, is Berton's father's sister, making Shirley Berton's aunt. That is perfectly clear to me.

In any case, Berton Woodward is eastern region editor of the very influential *Asiaweek*, and told me that Hongkong is "the *only* place to be as a regional hub for Asia-wide operations."

His wife Phielle—they were married in Vancouver and their two-year-old, Catalina, was born in Hongkong—is a director of Trading Places Limited, which specilizes in finding just the right chichi niche for expatriate executives.

Cathay Pacific's Ian MacDonald was promoted from Vancouver to a 15th floor office in Cathay's Swire House overlooking the harbor, but rarely sees it because he is always flying off somewhere. Wife Shelley Milne, a marathon runner like Ian, left her ICBC corporate-lawyer job and is becoming oriented at last. Speaking of lawyers, practically every Vancouver firm now has a branch in H.K., Bull, Housser & Tupper being one of the heaviest weights.

Getting a Hongkong posting is a much-desired coup, and New World Harbourside sales director Deanna McGonigal, among others, was thrilled to move to the company's home base. Accepting responsibility for five major Far East properties just snaffled a nice little six-digit salary for Deanna in hardship pay.

The major hotels here are among the world's most cosmopolitan, and almost always the opulent backdrop for major charity events. The Regent is a favorite, and the new Grand Hyatt is worthy of its name: sweeping staircases for those grand entrances; soaring marble columns for debonair leaning against; and cascading fountains in which to drop those pesky cocktail toothpicks.

My most memorable evening in this most memorable of cities, however, was last-night late dinner at the Peninsula Hotel. I already knew it as a discreet retreat for everyone from Imelda Marcos to Paloma Picasso, and remembered Rudolph Nureyev raving about it to me a year ago: "One is ensconced in a

229

cocoon of attention—every guest is master."

My gracious hosts (and they *were*, Barbie—dinner for one can run HK$1,000) were absolute fonts of info, and I do hate duck out just as I am Peking. More over the months.

Ta Ta Darling. Kay-Wai Lay.

That is my Chinese name; it is said to mean intelligent and charming. Or not.

Valerie

OVER THE FENCES AND AROUND THE STARS

Toni and Yukiko Onley

Barbie Darling,

Sauntered off to Southlands for the Summer Show '90. It was hardly Harringay, dear heart, but for this mere novice it was a busy, hoof-thumping romp through the homegrown horsey set. Besides, one had hardly *any* invitations to the Hamptons this year. The show has been running in one form or another for 30 years. That I have so far managed to avoid the sweating, wild-eyed beasts—the horses, Barbie, the horses—is just ruddy good luck, I say. Nonetheless, neigh-sayers be damned, I learned more than I'll ever need to bring up in smart conversation about all things equine, and had a jolly time to boot.

The riding club's 18 ever-so-manicured acres are snuggled down between the Point Grey and McCleery golf clubs, and for this summer's four-day show, its huge white marquee was cheek-to-wither full of Southlands members and oh-so-vital corporate sponsors.

"The linking of equestrian sport and corporation sponsorship behooves, so to speak, both parties in a fashion that can't always be easily measured," offered one stiff upper lip in a tie that blinds. "It works both ways," he further pontificated. "The harvests they reap from the mutually beneficial arrangements are similar—more possible Olympic medals, more banking, more flying, more buying, more investing. This is a very upscale sport, and that suits a lot of image-questers."

Did you know, darling, that the typical show-horse owner has an executive-management job, owns a home and two or more horses and cars, takes two or more trips annually, is university educated, and participates in skiing, water sports and other fitness activities? No? Well, if I have to be bothered, so do you.

Although the lofty tent shading dollar-drenched devotees from the noonday sun was no Royal Enclosure, the undaunted marked their fashion turf with a vengeance. Everything from designer duds to demideranged gaucho outfits ponied up for hors (what else?) d'oeuvres, champagne and those spiffy little tea sandwiches that permit simultaneous munching and mumbling. One can stuff oneself, it appears, and spur on nags with names like All Or Nothing, Earn Your Keep, Count The Jewels, Aged In Oak or, impossible, Keep The Change. And nod at such owner-fillies as Fritzi, Willie, Natasha, Catya, Samantha and Tamara, whose parents named them just *knowing* they would one day saddle up to do horse trials and mock hunts.

Allison and Isauro Flores

Artist Toni Onley, one of the show's benefactors, pranced in with his smashing wife Yukiko, he groomed to the nines in blazer and tie, she in a Di-would-die-for-it organza hat, a short linen skirt and a flowered silk blouse that was perfection. Toni had just overflown the Stein Valley in a helicopter once owned by Fernando Marcos. "Beautifully done out, it was," said the artist. "There were absolutely *no* old shoes left around, and it ran rather well."

Joe Houssian jockeyed into position in a black silk bomber jacket and silk slacks, the silver curls and black shades making him a picture of foreign intrigue. Wife Joanne, who is a steady and supportive player on the charity circuit, wore all white as they posed with their sponsored horse, meanwhile keeping the Houssian children out of the spotlight.

Nan Nicholls, all jodhpurs and Irish knit sweater, cantered in on foot with daughter Tish, fresh from a morning's ride. "We have two horses on Sea Island," Nan chirped as she headed off to do something or other in a paddock beyond the gentrified goings-on. Stockster David Ward, late of the Carter-Ward brouhaha, watched this horse race of a different color, while weatherman Phil Reimer, who through the Adventure Syndicate owns a piece of pony called Tarzan, predicted which way the wind would blow for his fleet four-footer.

Well-shod two-legged thoroughbreds were being pointed out everywhere as I trotted about: "now, there's David Lyall; he's Gordon Lyall's son and he married Jill-whatever who is a model, and that's their son Michael. And there is Robbie Ross; he is Bob and Sheila Ross's son—they are *very* involved down here—and he has an investment company with Graham Dawson—Duncan Ross Associates, I think—and Sheila is a Graham. And there is Vicki Gourlay, who is Victor MacLean's daughter, who was married to David Graham and is now married to Hank Gourlay; her family used to own half of Hornby Island. Oh, and Joe and Fran Cohen's daughter Lori is a show patron. And, of course, Gorgeous Willie McDonald over there's husband is a stock promoter with Noramco Capital, and those two adorable children beside her and hers. Now, Betty Lou Sully's daughter Tracy—is she Westchester or what—is a much-ballyhooed hunter/jumper event winner; she is an apprentice judge today, but you watch, she'll be a senior judge in no time. And over there is George Tidball's daughter Laura; she's Laura Balisky now—got to the 1988 Olympics, is currently sponsored big-time by Toshiba, and just won $30,000 in the Chrysler Classic."

Shirley Maclaine, Micheline Carriere, Arthur Erickson

As I took my leave and climbed into the only horsepower I care to associate with, thank you, I made a mental note to tell myself that "dressage," should it *ever* come up, has nothing whatever to do with what one is wearing.

Sailed off to South West Marine Drive to one of the summer's swishest soirees. Set amid the Gatsbyesque splendor of John and Rebecca MacKay's splendid great house, the evening was called Ole! Flamenco, and was spectacularly Spanish from the first sip of sangria to the last strains of the flamenco guitars. The stone house at the end of a long, winding driveway is right out of *Casa y Hacienda* (that is Espanol for *Town & Country*, dear heart), and from expansive hallway to oak-and-leather library, each room could be framed and filled with exquisite movie extras sipping champagne. Of course it was and they were. As grandmama was fond of saying, it was that combinacion rara of the impeccably dressed, imperially slim and immensely wealthy.

232

Patrons of the arts—this was a money-gatherer for the Vancouver Museum's Panache exhibition of 200 years of clothing, which will open to the public on November 27—looked utterly matadorable as they slipped in wearing their variations of lace, fans, flowers, sombreros and boots.

You know the mix, dear heart—old establishment, new-money tenderfeet, hotshot power brokers and bizwiz big-wigs. And for spice, a few titles. Count Enrico and Countess Aline Dobrzensky made a palpable pit stop before heading off to Monaco for the rest of the summer. The countess's sister, Princess Patricia de La Tour d'Auvergne, passed, but Baroness Heidi von Pfetten nodded in. Mayor Campbell showed up without his chain (which is ornate enough to have fitted in perfectly), and Mr. and Mrs. Howard Phipps III, from the old, old New York family, were as cause-concerned and low-key as always. And the art world was fated to be mated to this frameable scene: Diane Farris aced it in lace and never looked better; Daniel and Denese Izzard and Zbigniew and Eva Kupczynski posed prettily whenever—*they* understand composition.

Kerry and Lynn Dix

Savvy senoras Andrea Maw, Deborah Savoie Giulini, Lynn Dix (in the hautest sombrero there-o) and hostess Rebecca MacKay, along with Carole Taylor and Vivien Thom, all looked as though they could have been whisked to Madrid to fiesta with the finest.

Spotted Joe and Rosalie Segal reminiscing over this sybaritic setting—the view of the river, the house sparkling with lights, the dancers, the band—as well as how a very young and eager John MacKay, whose casa we were chatting in, had, for peanuts, painted their first house. Turning to look back in the wee small hours, I was certainly convinced that *that* was one ladder that went right to the top.

Little did I know that mere evenings later, the more-than-magnanimous MacKays would lend their stellar setting once more to the arts, this time for Ballet B.C. Under the patronage of Arthur Erickson, the event was billed as an Evening With Shirley MacLaine, at which 50 special souls (her favorite kind) got to sip Veuve Cliquot champagne and discreetly chow down on the best West Coast salmon. Meanwhile Shirl—we are all this close now—giggled, jiggled and batted those lashes (they never came unglued), and told us stories of other times, other places.

I will tell you quickly who was there, Barbie, and then I will get to Ms.

233

Mac. Arthur, of course. Shirley had sung and talked most of her show (so fabu it was) to him the night before; she just adores him. David and Brenda Mclean were there. I wondered if Shirley knew that David owned The Landing—you never know when that might come in handy for her next extraterrestrial trip. The Giulinis materialized, as did Daniel and Ani Feuermann, Bob and Lily Lee's beautiful daughter Carol, real-estate extravaganza Shelley Lederman, Kerry and Lynn Dix, and that jewel of a couple, Toni and Hildegard Cavelti. Joan Carlisle Irving flew in from wherever, as did Baroness von Pfetten, who prefers to be called just Heidi. The effervescent Eleni Skalbania had her daughter Elpie along from London, while Nelson, in red turtleneck and shoes

Diane Farris, Cathy Rauser &
Dottie Kanke

(of course he had a jacket and pants on, Barbie), looked like a renegade sea captain as he bid on a pair of Shirley's shoes at auction. They had been made for her in 1973, she danced in them for a full year, and Nelson bought them for $1,000 a shoe. Eleni did not look thrilled; she is probably not an eight-and-a-half B.

Warren Beatty's sister is a great stew of contradictions. To have lived through all the incarnations she claims to have, she would have needed the lifespan of a tsetse fly. Her perm and curls—sort of a carrot mousse—make her look like a Botticelli baby. The eyelashes are devastatingly dangerous—both pairs. The nails are Lee Press-Ons, and the hands are from her life as the Ancient Mariner. The legs are unequivocally great, even the one with the knee brace. Her teeth are quite pretty, her jaw line is firm, and her neck...well, skip her neck. She wears, count 'em, eight crystal earrings of different lengths. Her outfit was obviously thrown together during a carbohydrate rush (that evening she ate like a dancer— enough dessert for three), but she has a great slim figure on that five-foot-seven, ballet-disciplined frame. She speaks in sort of prissy locutions, suffers fools not at all, is always busy scoping the scene, has a sort of vinegary zest to her, and announced that her dinner, done deliciously by the wizards at Caffe Veneto, was "the best I have had in 10,000 years." I just knew you cared.

Ta Ta Darling, and like Marco Polo, I only wrote half of what I saw,
Valerie.

234

RACING PARTIES AND FINE ART PARTYING

Barbie Darling,

Varoomed off to the first Molson Indy Vancouver gala at the Hotel Vancouver, where the well-heeled wheeled in for a good cause and a chance to rub shoulders with some of the most celebrated monikers in motor sport. Move over Monte Carlo (remember when we watched the Monaco Grand Prix two years ago from our hotel window?): $1,750 bought a table for 10, caviar with the aces of the races, and that huggy-all-over feeling that came from knowing that the proceeds from the sell-out crowd were all going to Children's Hospital and Sunny Hill Hospital For Children.

Darlene and Jack Poole

White tuxes mingled with cream-colored deck shorts; the mayor wore a white lab coat borrowed from a hospital, and the waiters all wore pit-stop caps and coveralls as they raced around pitching victuals and vino to the revved-up crowd of 600.

Now Barbie, if you think I know a Lola-Cosworth from an Alfa Romeo, you have obviously piled up the Porsche one time too many. Ditto if you think I would stay in town to watch a bunch of brightly-colored blurs whirring by on blistering asphalt while I breathed engine fumes and sported earplugs. But this _was_ the World Series of auto racing, an audacious undertaking for the city, and the Indy gala _was_ the peak party of the surrounding celebrations. Anyway, Paul Newman was rumored to be fast-tracking it in. Turned out he passed this time, but Mario, Emmo, and Danny-o dropped by to meet and mingle. There was a definite smell of methanol and money in the air.

Danny Sullivan (he hardly ever uses the III after his name) shows up everywhere on the cocktail and media circuit. The pretty-boy promoter—and he is, Barbie—was named one of the top 25 sexiest men in the world, lives in Aspen and L.A. when he is not circuiting the world, has a six-month-old son named Daniel O'Driscoll, and looks not quite as nummy as he did on his flash appearances on *Miami Vice* and *All My Children*.

Emerson Fittipaldi, tiny and talented (he skis, speaks five languages, but English is not necessarily one of them), told me that driving the Indy was not work at all, but "an act of love." Much safer he claims, than driving the streets, particularly in the south of France. Oh, those Brazilians, Barbie—so romantic. He even "loves" owning a Mercedes dealership. He thinks it is "fantastic."

Edgar Kaiser

As cute and compact as Emmo was, Mario Andretti (who is two inches shorter) made even more of an impression. As he crossed the floor to make a few remarks to the racy poseurs gathered for the high-velocity fling, Jone Fraser, the wit-to-spare second wife of cabinet minister Russ Fraser, was heard to mutter into her potato amandine that she had had "one of those on top of my wedding cake, didn't I?"

John Frasco, the Michigan based promoter of the Vancouver race—lawyer, former CART director, and a genius in the marketing field—thought Vancouver had "the best viewing racecourse anywhere in the world." He also must have been impressed with the bizwiz biggies the evening pulled in, after a "little strong-arm twisting" by Molson Indy chairman Jack Poole, as I heard repeated by more than one deep-pocketed source.

Sam and Fran Belzberg slipped in, making a rare social showing. She looked as sparkly fresh as she does after having whomped a tennis foe, and he as unperturbed as ever, even though his $6 billion First City Financial Corporation Ltd. dropped $27 million during the first half of this year.

Edgar Kaiser came down off the mountain (he has been living in the wilds of Chartwell since his spectacular house fire) to hobnob once more with his old high-octane crowd.

Nelson and Eleni Skalbania, developer Fred Stimpson and his wife Gerry, and Darlene and Jack Poole made a pit stop that night. They were all heading off—some as soon as the next morning—on one of those dream trips they so frequently take. *You* know, darling—fly to Rome, do Venice for a week at the Cipriani (the Skalbanias were doing Rhodes, Greece), fly to Rome, then all meet in Harry's Bar. The Hotel du Cap was in there somewhere—my ears glaze over with envy sometimes. In any case, it was all chateaux, villas, champagne and smart evening clothes laid out each night. Did I mention it was a _bike_ trip?

I digress. Back at the bash, Bob Kadlec, president and CEO of B.C. Gas, and his wife Bobby were doing the first few laps around the dance floor, which was painted like a huge black-and-white checkered race flag. Kam and Henning Brasso, he of MCL Motor Cars, were right in their element with this car-azy crowd. Bob and Lily Lee (partners with Henning and Jack Poole in all things auto) were basking in congratulations for Bob's Order of B.C. medal.

You would have thought "Gentlemen, start your engines" was an election call, Barbie. The room was awash in Socreds. Environment Minister John Reynolds was obviously picking up a few pointers because he was scheduled to green-flag the loud, monotonous consumption of high-priced fuels that would be the Indy race mere days later. A bumpy mid-evening ride around the room revealed a Stephen Rogers here, a Claude Richmond there, a Walter Davidson right under your nose, plus lawyer-campaigner Lyle Knott with Brenda Kinsella, wife of top gun Patrick Kinsella. Scarier than the race, to be sure. I decided it was time to put the pedal to the metal myself at this point. I had Indy-gestion.

Hurried off mere nights later to the Harrington Galleries for a Gala Art Benefit for the Ben Gurion University of the Negev. It was the opening night of an

Diane Farris, Attila Richard Lukacs

exhibition of oils, acrylics and lithographs by Lea Avizedek, most of which I would have happily hoarded given the chance. She is well-known from Tel Aviv (where she lives) to Toronto, where her sort of Toulouse-Lautrec-meets-Chagall work does rather well.

The swish Harrington, according to suave owner Ken Swaisland, although only a year old, has in fact exhibited Chagall, and this evening, in the silent auction, there was a Rembrandt etching at $5,600, and two Pissaro's at $8,000 to $12,000.

"Purchasing art endows status. It's like owning a Rolls or a Rolex, particularly if it goes up 300 percent like two of my pieces have in the last five years," I heard in front of _Still Life With Guitar_. "And it's so much more fun than stuffing a stock certificate in a safety deposit box." The dark and doughty pair continued their rounds.

Roberta Beiser, director of Business and the Arts, little-black-dressed it in with her sister Julie Kamin (who used to live on Old Brompton Road in London, as I did) and their equally smashing mother. Bertie was in the middle of running for an aldermanic nomination, and husband Morley was elsewhere, campaigning for her while she did her patronage committee duties at the gallery.

Max and Anita Shnier swept in on the heels of Sheila and Gerald Stern. They both seemed intrigued with sculptor John Sund's beautiful bronze bust, but I was far more interested in hearing from Sheila about Maxine Gelfant's plastic surgeon son Ben's wedding.

Newspaper nabob David Radler and wife Rona (she in a cropped white military jacket, slim black skirt, and great, spiked, I-mean-business shoes) sampled Susan Mendelson's sumptuous buffet which, Susan told me, was "country elegant with no crumbs" by the gallery owner's request.

"Art," I recalled Tom Wolfe writing, "certifies wealth, and provides its owners with spiritual legitimacy." He added, "No one in his right mind pays the kind of money that's asked, for something he simply likes." Unless, I thought as I drove away, it is for a good cause.

Rona Radler's military duds would have fit in just perfectly the next night at the Diane Farris Gallery preview champagne reception for Attila Richard Lukacs. His latest series of paintings, grouped under the title *To Interested Young Men*, depicts American military cadets because, he says, he "always liked looking at catalogues from places like West Point and Valley Forge," and would have gone to Royal Military College if he could have. (Dad Joseph said no, thank heavens.)

The evening was the two-year anniversary to the day of the opening of Diane's new gallery, and the shindig attracted serious money. Canfor's Peter Bentley, who is known for his contributions to the arts, was there, along with Vancouver Art Gallery do-gooder Gerald McGavin, lawyer Mitch Gropper, the Playhouse's Larry Lillo, and bigbuck realtor Malcolm Hasman. Also, artists Alan Wood, whose association with Diane goes back to his *Ranch* project, and Gathie Falk, whose own new works were about to open at Lizzie Nichols' Equinox Gallery.

Lukac's international reputation was given a big showbiz nod last January when Diane flew to L.A. to complete a 431,000 U.S. deal with Elton John for a must-have dyptych. By reception time a Zurich collector had already bought three of the current collection.

Bluesman Jim Byrnes joked that all this military stuff made him a mite nervous—he blew into Canada all those years ago because he felt a distinct draft coming his way. He seemed in his usual good humor by the time he reached Barbara Jo McIntosh's tony new little Cambie Street restaurant, called Barbara-Jo's, for the after party.

Adrienne Clarkson blessed the gathered with her pouty presence. She proceeded to interview Lukacs's parents for her TV show, which is humbly titled _Adrienne Clarkson Presents_, while they tried to enjoy Barbara-Jo's special sweet potato pecan pie and the party.

Among Lukacs's collectors are jewelry designer Martha Sturdy and Andre and Julie Molnar. Julie told me theirs is very big, has a rooster and a pig in it, and their four-year-old son just loves it.

And the catalyst for the evening's oh-so-successful opening? Farris herself. Although she would deny anything but luck in the success of her gallery, and the stable of up-and-comers and already-theres she now represents, more and more formerly fickle fine-art fingers are pointing straight at her.

Ta Ta Darling. Hedge against inflation. Buy art.

Valerie

THE YEAR 1991

THE SNOWY PEAKS OF A HOT PARTY SEASON
To ski and be seen, that's the whole idea at Whistler. Even Trudeau and sons showed up.

DRESS CODE: "SPLENDOUR AND ELEGANCE"
Opening nights and wallets with the Phantom.

ANSWERING THE CALL OF NATURE
Film big shots flooded North Shore Studios in support of a keen, green cause.

FASHION FIRMS UP CHARITY'S BOTTOM LINE
When three big fashion shows hit the city, not all the strutting is on the runways.

THE SNOWY PEAKS OF
A HOT PARTY SEASON

Barbie Darling,

Wended my way up to Whistler for a peek at that posh pinnacle of excess. It may not be Grenoble or Gstaad, but it's an acceptable cousin, and this was no motley array of recession-reticent moguls getting winterized. *Every*one was there, sporting everything from $800 sweaters to fake, fun or fine furs and designer labels that cost what their parents' first car did. Needless to say, the expected case of characters did yeoman duty shoring up the elaborate shenanigans. Highway 99 was drop-dead gridlock. Sleek Jaguars and Mercedes were one-upped by custom-colored Range Rovers and Jeeps, all aimed, like heat-seeking missiles, for high times in the current hottest ski spot in the country. The village's hotels, restaurants, bars and smart shops saw enough plastic action to go into overdrive. And the twin peaks of Blackcomb and Whistler, awash in high-voltage neon space suits, and clipped here and there by glacier-grazing helicopters, looked like a sci-fi artist's rendering of exactly what the resort's planners had *hoped* it would look like. Last year's million-plus skier visits made Whistler the top most popular ski resort in North America, and the mighty molehill's 25th anniversary this year will undoubtedly draw more.

Misha, Pierre, Sasha Trudeau

Trotted off to the Trattoria di Umberto (everything Whistler-wise is "di Umberto," darling), where any number of well-knowns were noshing. Mr. Jax's Louis Eisman seemed to have left his company cares back in the city as he tasted and toasted with friends. Television czar Stephen J. Cannell, blonde wife Marcia, and various *kinder* enjoyed the beanery's best, as did the large table of power-cum-powder hounds beside them. Big time developer Bob Annable and his rosy-cheeked and red-haired wife Jan were there, along with lawyer Dick Underhill and globe-trotting wife Lana, that laconic cutup Allan Fotheringham with a sleek and savvy Toronto model named Donna

DeMarco, UBC professor and Alcan Aluminium director Peter Pearse and his wife Penny, plus a smattering of others; all were enjoying a late-night, eight-course repast overseen by Umberto's right-hand man Mario Enero. It seemed Professor Pearse had snagged himself some first-class venison near his place on Sydney Island so the entree was deer to one and all in the Pearse party.

Umberto's Il Caminetto, the flagship of his Whistler eateries, was the scene of many a serious sighting. I swished in past spectacular his-and-her mink bomber jackets (so *arriere guarde*, no?) and spotted Intrawest's Joe Houssian and his wife Joanne. She, in a new short halo of curls, was fresh from her success with the North Shore Family Services ball (which she says she will happily co-chair next year), and he was fresh from negotiations for a new 250-room hotel on the benchlands at the base of Blackcomb Mountain.

Peter Brown on the slippery slopes

Meanwhile former Hawaii state senator Francis Wong and his Italian wife Paula snared a window seat with their close pals the Giulinis, who threw one of the best private parties (more later) of the season. Silver-haired architect Ron Howard and his successfully elected (to the West Vancouver school board) wife Barbara antipastoed with the best of them. Bluesman Jim Byrnes bared his considerable soul in the lounge, while Lynn and Kerry Dix visited with friends up from L.A. and basked in the parental glow of daughter Mya's delight. She and Trudeau's youngest son Misha (also 15, and also shy) had skied their little hearts out together and had hit it off quite well (Mya and Misha, could I make this up?).

Pierre himself, in finer fettle than any 71-year-old I know, had skied the Burnt Stew run with the Pearses, dined at the exquisite and much-touted Val d'Isere (and pronounced chef Roland Pfaff's fare "formidable") with his three sons and fellow lawyer Bill Ferguson, and enjoyed the apres-ski hearth of the inevitable Caminetto di Umberto. I can't tell you, Barbie, how many people thought he looked pretty good in retrospect, in light of the Mulroney morass. Ah, hindsight.

As you know dear heart, my idea of exercise is a good brisk sit, but one had to do a little schussing in the ozone snow-zone at the top of the mountain to catch up with the real rush-and-tumble crowd headed for the high-altitude restaurants, Christine's and the Rendezvous.

That scalawag Nelson Skalbania surfaced at Christine's (a truly haute cuisine pit stop, with its pink and gray table cloths and mile-high wine list), a mass of moxie except for his frost-laden beard and that hair mashed by his 100-year-old tuque. Perpetual-motion man Peter Brown moodily padded in, his 100-kilowatt charm somewhat dimmed, one supposes, by the pesky *second* Vancouver Stock Exchange fine.

Handsome Hughie Smythe, the president of Blackcomb Mountain Skiing Enterprises, and his darling wife Debbie were caught sampling the best of Christine's tray chic, while wealthy, politically-hopeful Woody McLaren opted for the more plebian Rendezvous restaurant along with his son Doug and beautiful blonde-like-her-mom daughter Nicole. Spotted ski champ Greg Athans chair-lifting it with the peg'o-his-heart Peggy Meyers,

Doug, Nicole & Woody McLaren

who is Dotty Kanke's sister (Dotty is Bud Kanke's wife). Peggy and Dotty are Dick and Gingie Meyers's daughters. The Meyers are great friends of Trudeau (Dick and Bud usually ski with him), but in fact they were friends of Margaret Sinclair's family first.

Back down in the valley there was a plethora of parties. Two of the best transposed from Vanland to Whistlerville the town-and-country smart set with only a quick change of clothes. Francesco and Deborah Giulini threw one of their sociable little soirees up in Snowridge Circle. Dinner-O for 30-or-so seems to be something that Francesco, who has elan with a flan and is an unparalleled pasta master, does with the greatest of ease.

John and Rebecca MacKay rallied forth perfectly prepped for the setting, he in a sweater Calvin Klein would have coveted, she perfectly pared after the arrival of bundle number three, in tobacco-suede pants and a white angora sweater that was belted not one notch bigger than before. Vivien Thom, svelte as a snow bunny in her size-six stirrup pants, brought at least one sister and brother from out of town, while her architect other half, David, was lucky to get himself there at all. He had insisted on taking his cellular phone with him while cross-country skiing in the woods, had taken a tumble and cracked a rib on the thing. A perilous era, I tell you.

Chuck and Julie Bentall flushed in from hot-tubbing with Allan

Fotheringham, while Julia (Molnar) Cowan, owner of Isola Bella, along with her husband Blake and sister Andrea - owner of the highly successful Bacci and Byblos clothing stores - just flushed in. Retail wise, darling, those two sisters are like good surfers, always on the right wave. A fan of the Molnar mogulettes revealed the duo's success formula: "It's the old bite off more than you can," he offered, "then proceed to chew it." A vowel-heavy bundle of talented Italians, town planners, designers, and architects, all confreres of Francesco's whose surnames I have no hope of reproducing without a roster, added just the right Zefferelli zest to _la dolce vita_, Whistler style. Three snowy nights later, the Feuermanns, Daniel and Ani, did their dazzlingest for their nearest and dearest, including an elegant array of relatives from Argentina. After dessert almost the entire clique ambled over for a nightcap at the upper crusty Chateau Whistler.

Ta ta Darling, beware of trends in high places.

Valerie.

DRESS CODE: "SPLENDOUR AND ELEGANCE"

Peg Meyers, Greg Athans & R. Kirby Cowan

Barbie Darling,

Flitted off to _The Phantom Of The Opera's_ opening night gala with 1,160 other pop-opera aficionados. Billed as "one of the most elaborate fund-raising events ever staged in Vancouver," and presented by Ballet B.C., the Dr. Sun Yat-Sen Gardens, and Vancouver Opera, the $500-a-couple blowout more than lived up to its brassy billing.

And so, my dear, did the production. A baroque take-off on the old backstage show-must-go-on musical, this "beauty and the beast" had some choice props, a few surprises, a swag of curtain and a whole caboodle of candles coming out of the floor on cue.

Monster mega-musical or not, it's your basic ghoul gets girl, ghoul loses girl. And if you ask me, Barbie, it was his own darn fault. Phantom-man Jeff ("Wow, I can't believe I'm doing this show") Hyslop plays the man downstairs who was dealt a bad face and is somewhat testy about it. His upstairs

245

neighbors in the - get this - Paris Opera House (bit of a location stretch if you ask me) are totally hysterical about his spooky sightings as they roar about trying to get the show on the road. Unless the Phantom's fancy (a wimp named Christine - cute, but schitzy) gets to play the lead, snafus like a Liberace-sized chandelier will continue to crash on any unsuspecting diva not of his choice. Petty, what? In any case, he plays most of his scenes in half a goalie's mask, in a slightly damp and definitely subterranean pad with some great Gothic furniture and its own in-house boat. My advice? Cut the sewer sojourn short, get a little sun. Bingo - no attitude problem. Andrew Lloyd Webber didn't ask, and I must say most of the 2,800 first-nighters sipping their champagne and eating truffles seemed satisfied with the showpiece spectacle just as it was. No accounting, is there Barbie?

Murray Pezim, Tammy Patrick

The post-premiere party was pretty spectacular itself under the sails of the Trade and Convention Center. The audacious undertaking, grand-scaled by hundreds of volunteers from the trio of charities splitting the estimated $125,000 benefactor's booty, was "let them have bread and circuses" to the max. Nine hundred and thirty guests had bought tickets, and were joined by 230 of the flushed we've-got-a-hit cast, crew and orchestra.

"Nothing will stay this lot from their appointed round of parties," I heard from the marinated-in-cologne tux behind me as we eased our way past a chain-link of limos. "Of course not," snorted his spouse mid-flounce, "there is more kiss kiss, click click hoopla here than we've seen in ages."

Frenzied *Phantom* pilgrims oohed and ahhed as they streamed into the party ballroom. A huge *Phantom* mask swayed from the ceiling, flowers and trees were shrouded in misty fog that swirled around the sweeping curtains and dramatic candlelit backdrops. Very stage-setty, darling, right down to the black lace tableclothes and theatrical lighting. The requested dress was "splendor and elegance," and there were more interpretations than that clattering chandelier (whose plunge I missed while rummaging in my purse for a mint) had lights. There was a real show of fashion force that rivaled *Phantom*land's ornate costumes, and less guilt about more gilt than I've seen since the Art Gallery opening. Stage door Johnnies were safe enough in their ties and tails.

"All those tuxes in a row at the buffet table look like an Andy Warhol silkscreen gone bad," I heard as I tucked into the wild smoked salmon and Indonesian suckling pig. (Of *course* they were separate dishes, dear heart). And the damsels of the opera? Exhibition dressing to beat all.

A dazzling array of corporate "Crystal" sponsors who gave a minimum of $10,000 each were marshaled, as diverse as the Royal Viking Like, Proctor & Gamble, Prime Equities and Plaza Escada.

Music hall of fame man Bruce Allen (who could write a mega rock memoir without half trying) hot-footed in it with his hot-pink-coated wife Jane. He was exchanging ruderies with affable money manager Steven Funk, who is always mentally changing lenses for the long shot as he chats up the room. Terry David Mulligan, as familiar as an old smile button, spouted pop-speak as he circled the very hip Alberta beef, while impresario Hugh Pickett, spiffed up to the seven-and-a-halves, dropped showbiz names.

Working aristos Countess Aline, in right royal-blue raiment, and Count Enrico Dobrzensky (who had done everything at least once) pronounced the production as good as Broadway and London. Art Phillips and Carole Taylor *pas de deuxed* posely not at all guarded from the paparazzi fire. And Gordon Campbell and wife Nancy proudly flashed that no-tan look from their second honeymoon in Palm Springs.

Norman Zagier, Garth Drabinsky

Phantom of the stock exchange Murray Pezim flaunted his Arizona tan, his ex-fiance, Tammy Patrick ("but I have a new girl," he said with his usual cuppa tease), his snap-open chequebook for charity, and, if I'm not mistaken a new, short, darker-than-silver hairdo. Vanity, thy name is *Murray?*

No-slave-to-conventional-fashion Nelson Skalbania wore a black shirt and a pale blue jacket in the face of black-tie conformity, while the elegant and ever-savvy Eleni in midnight blue and sequins lit up like a jukebox when she talked about flying to London for her proud daughter's grad the following week.

Jacqui Cohen sparkled in an electric-blue micro-mini theater suit from Neiman Marcus. It was a fashion first in Vancouver, but I spotted both *Designing Women's* Dixie Carter and *Entertainment Tonight's* Leeza Gibbons in it last month in L.A. What's a girl to do?

247

E.A. Lee's Barron Lee, sartorially splendid and looking like one of his own ads, was the perfect fashion foil for Diane Weiser in the evening's best "little black suit." Il Barino's Laura Markin in a fuchsia Christian Lacroix three-piece fantasy won "best opera coat" in a walk. And real estate wheeler Andrea Eng in charcoal and black satin banker's pinstripes looked totally focused as usual. Fairly smug, too. She had brought Proctor and Gamble to the heavy-hitters corporate table. Ah, that old warm-hearts-and-cold-cash combo.

The evening was divine. And positively label-defying. You had Long John Baldry, bluesman Jim Byrnes and rubber-faced actor Jackson Davies shooting the suave with the best of them. Canfor's Peter Bentley, Intrawest's Joe Houssian and biz whiz Caleb Chan letting their hair down and taking their masks off. Smoke and mirrors, Barbie, and a throwback to the great glory days of theater.

Nipped off to New York for a fast week in the fast lane. In seven days you can cram in half a dozen plays and an equal number of museums and art galleries. You can polish up your shine at the Big A by checking out the United Nations and the Empire State Building and catching a horse and buggy through Central Park. You can help Carnegie Hall (restored to its former white-and-gold splendor) celebrate its 100th birthday, or just poke around Sotheby's and Christie's. You can note that Bloomingdale's got a glitzy new boss, but it's still not the Bloomies it was in its glory days. And that the Fauvists, in all their splendid color, are at the Metropolitan Museum of Art. Or you can check out the real stuff, Barbie. Guess which I did?

Now I know there are people who know how to avoid crowds and exorbitant prices. I, however, am not one of them. Upper east side dining is still mind-blowingly expensive. But the people you run into!

Din din at the Russian Tea Room yielded a bonanza. Not halfway through the caviar and blinis, who walks in and sits at the very next table but Candice Bergen, her husband, director Louis Malle, *Saturday Night Live's* Lorne Michaels, his new wife, and a to-die-for young actor whose name I didn't catch. I had just missed Woody Allen (he had his usual blinis and sacher torte) who left to play his weekly Monday night clarinet gig at Michael's Pub. But back to Candy. She was on hiatus from *Murphy Brown* and was just heading off to their family home in France with five-year-old Chloe. She looks great for 45, has lost about 10 pounds since I saw her last year in Hollywood, still has that deadly cat-with-cream smile, that great cackle of a laugh, has very good table manners and walks there often when in New York because her apartment - which she has lovingly decorated over the past 20 years - is just around the corner on Central Park South. You're welcome.

Drinky-poos at the Algonquin were a bore. Since Dorothy Parker is gone and the Round Table has disbanded, the nearest to witty I overheard was what a blonde who dyes her hair brown has. Artificial intelligence.

Ta Ta Darling, and remember, sincerity is everything. Once you can fake that, you've got it made,

Valerie.

ANSWERING THE CALL OF NATURE

Barbie Darling,

Orbited off to what was billed as An Evening Out For The Earth, and with a sweeping come-on like that, who could refuse? It was ECO (Earth Communications Office) Canada's first big blowout for film biz environmentalists, and it flashed a high, wide and handsome assemblage of actors, writers, directors, producers and musicians.

Linda Gray

About 600 movie mogulites and celebrity cling-ons made the politically correct choice - it isn't easy being green, after all - to nip over the North Shore Studios and recycle about $30,000 big ones into saving the planet. The trouble is, an unearthly number of them arrived in carbon-coughing two-passenger gas-guzzlers or one-star-at-a-time stretch limos before lighting up their cigarettes and blowing self-congratulatory clouds of smoke. All this while trying to talk everyone else out of their earth-trashing techniques.

But before getting bogged down in deforestation and ozone depletion, do let's cut to the good stuff. It's a given, darling, that the smart money is on the environment as the *au courant* cause. And besides, these earnest show biz funders are always full of film fatales, cinematic cupcakes, and would-be screen queens with the IQ of a bundt pan.

"Oh, he's sooo cute," a black sequined bustier said to the barely there mini beside her. "I've loved him since his *My Three Sons* days," countered the chiffon chemise beside them as all three watched actor Ed Begley Jr. bicycle onto the studio lot. He had wheeled over the Lions Gate Bridge from Le Meridien before showering and changing for Hollywood-meets-Hollyburn.

"I never ride in limos," he told me as he stashed his backpack, grabbed a Koala Springs and, in his best *St. Elsewhere* voice, made his unusual lifestyle sound like the only way to go. He drives, he says, a "1970 electric car." (It's why he lost his last girlfriend, a Hollywood pal tells me - "too slow, and such a bore." The car, not him). He solar-energizes his Studio City, California home, uses a bus pass around L.A., writes his thank you's on recycled paper, is so pale of face and hair that he is practically alabaster, and has a 42-year-old parchment-dry wit that is obviously a holdover from his stand-up (he is six-foot-four) comedian days.

Dallas's Sue Ellen, Linda Gray, certainly aided the old environmental just

Pia Southam, Rob Turner & Becky Paris

by being there. She has breathtakingly beautiful eyes, almost translucent skin, newly bobbed short hair, overly capped pearly-whites and is, of late, a disastrous dresser. She once hit *McCall's* and *Trendsetters* best-dressed lists, but that night she looked like a 1960s throw-back in her flower child gauze, pale tights, mismatched cardigan, shoulder-duster earrings and flat shoes. Now 50, eyelashes still all aflutter, she tells you breathlessly that she is about to become a grandmother (daughter Kehly doing the honors). She is, she says, "thrilled." She was with an ECO executive named Gary Petersen who was actor-hand-some, two inches shorter than she, terribly attentive and, I am assured, they are an item.

Former soap opera star Marcy (love-em-and-leave-em) Walker of *Santa Barbara* was there looking all blonde in all black. "Migawd, she looks like she was born in a cafe," I heard as she sashayed past. She is "29" - sure - was in Vancouver shooting *Palace Guard*, a new prime time series, and has dumped hubby number whatever (father of baby number one) for James Contner, one of the show's directors. She and her ex are still "good friends." Oh, those soap stars: bubble, bubble, toil and trouble.

Michael Chiklis (John Belushi in *Wired*, now starring in the locally lensed Cannell TV series *The Commish*) bellied up to the buffet in the evening's best satin jacket as jokes were lobbed about waste-watch-ers being waist-watchers. The Man Of Steel himself, lantern-jawed *Superman* Christopher Reeve (whom I last spotted in Heathrow airport with his former live-in lady and his two kids) seemed sweet, subdued, in tip-top shape for a 38-year-old (save for his could-it-be-kryptonite thinning hair) and not embarrassed at all to have arrived sans cape by limo.

Local eco-friendly filmerati were greeted like salmon returning to the spawning grounds. Sandy Wilson (director of *My American Cousin* and *My American Boyfriend*), who "looks cuddly, thinks cobra" an admirer allowed, worked the industry insiders like the eye-on-the-ball pro she is. As did Deluxe Productions face-from-the-past Alan Clapp, who did the Vancouver/L.A. jaunt for years before settling back here. He is busy filming a documentary on artist Bill Reid's magnificent sculpture for the Canadian embassy in Washington, D.C. which, if the bureaucracy would just butt out, should be a gem.

Former local prime time TV newscaster Marsha Andrews, accompanied by husband Paul Ski, flounced in all crisp and flamboyant in a swish and shiny evening coat right on the talented heels of Pacific Motion Pictures' boy genius Matthew O'Connor and his flame-haired wife Diane Patrick-O'Connor. Madame O'C has just penned and published - it's ever-so-clever - *The Hip List*, an insider's guide for visiting film folk. Uptown, downtown, Gastown and Chinatown, it's all about where to stay, where to eat, what to wear and where to buy it.

Sandy Wilson

Pia Southam, Harvey's widow, slipped in for a while on her way back to Toronto. I spotted her on the beach at Qualicum the week before with her two youngest children, but boated past before we had a chance to talk. When we finally did catch up at ECO, she was candid, vulnerable, admirably intact and more beautiful than ever in a gold blazer suit. Subtly protected by friends in one of her first, very public forays out, she was straightforward, self-possessed and articulate. She said she will reconsider her Vancouver options at the end of the school year. The friends and family fold here would love her back.

Strand Development's blond and boyish Jamie Maw whistled in in his perfect custom loafers, bemused smile and observant eye intact. Wife Andrea's backless, lava red linen sheath did its share of global warming when she hit the dance floor to Jim Byrnes's bluesy beat. And when a pause was put on the pizzazz long enough to conduct a foundation-funding auction, the cause-conscious Andrea bought Jamie a birthday dinner for 10 at Il Barino for $1,400. Biodegradable, of course.

If you ever wonder how tightly intertwined things really are in this city, dear heart, let me do a quick whiz-through for you. Yaletown's Il Barino is one of the hottest eateries around. Everyone eventually shows up, and its owned by the exquisitely savvy and smoky-voiced Laura Markin, fast-moving charity circuiteer.

The blonde Signora Markin ECO'ed in wearing a high-octane Gianni Versace suit that she bought from Marie Leone, a long-established staple on the good-works go-around. One item in the auction that night was a painting by Ingrid Losch, whose works are prominent in Il Barino but were first exhibited at Arts Umbrella's Splash auction - an event organized by, among others, Andrea Maw, who is Ingrid's daughter. Also on Arts Umbrella's board, and at this Earth-y evening, were Countess Aline Dobrzensky and close chum Deborah Giulini, who convene with great regularity at Il Barino (Deborah's husband Francesco did the decor).

In fact, they met there mere days later to exchange photos of their How I Spent My Summer sojourns *en famille* on the Italian Riviera, and to decide whose beach was best (Punta Ala), and whose rented castle coziest (San Casiano). And finally, darling, Il Barino is tastefully touted at the drop of a bread-stick by Consensus Communications president Laura Vandriel (angelic-looking, devilishly smart), who just happened to put ECO's A-zone list for the ozone into orbit. Should you care about any of this, you are more than welcome.

Wiggled off to the Canadian Craft Museum's fall harvest wine party, though I usually loath these cork-popping blowouts. One sip, and a complete wine novice who doesn't know his Gewurztraminer from his Pinot Bianco will lapse into a John Houseman sniff about "disturbingly ambivalent little wines" with "quasi-officious bouquets, yet somewhat sheepish aftertastes." Nonetheless, the freeflowing fest proved remarkably free of jargon and airs, and it pulled in 550 feisty bacchanalians who gave the museum's new Cathedral Place setting a rousing rafter-ringing (and raised slightly more than $20,000, which is just what the spectacular Lutz Haufschild stained glass window happened to cost).

"Really, watching people marinate their livers, even in very good wine, has become such a bore," pronounced a large man in a pinstriped suit with a florid face and sweating brow. "At a real wine tasting, you are supposed to sniff, sip and spit. *These* people are swallowing it all!"

Since Bud Kanke is an enthusiastic and newish member of the museum's board and since Joe Fortes Seafood House is just one of his little endeavors, a cornucopia of Bud's fetish for the finest and freshest found its way from Joe's onto the tented tables ringing the inner courtyard.

The unrelenting Mr. Kanke was infamous at the party's start for having dropped the evening's headliner (a $3,000 bottle of 1878 Mouton-Rothschild). Wife Dottie, cheeky smile in place despite the four-star vintage breakage, lived up to her "the more outrageous, the better" motto in a black and silver romper so sprayed on you just knew there was nothing between her and her spandex. Julie Molnar, who had negotiated the museum's swish new space, surveyed the pricey wine stain and suggested we give that pearl gray rug a little wring-out and see what was salvageable.

That sybarite of girdled girth, James Barber, obviously decided he had to take a sedimental journey, arriving as Bacchus in full tunic and wreath, but with glasses, watch and Birkenstocks, much to the amusement of pretentious elder yuppies.

"Fleshy, exuberant, multi-dimensional, good backbone. Should age gracefully," I heard behind me. I looked around for the accompanying apparition to no avail, and realized they were talking about a mere wine. Put a cork in it, I thought as I headed out for a quick flit through the crush. Up bubbled Cynthia Levy in a gorgeous jonquil yellow sheath with matching suede shoes. Nearby, designer Robert Ledingham was checking out the garden bower-with-grapes decor, political ace Peter Hyndman was prognosticating, his wife, artist Joanna Staniszkis, was checking out crowd reaction to her Cloudscape, and newly bearded Lauch Farris (Diane's ex) was just checking out.

"Well, I've been wined, dined, declined and re-aligned," I heard from a young man in a white sports coat as I headed out of the corporate cathedral. You can lead a horse to culture, Barbie ...

Ta Ta Darling. Early to bed, early to rise, 'til you make enough to do otherwise,
Valerie.

FASHION FIRMS UP CHARITY'S BOTTOM LINE

Barbie Darling,
Galloped off to the gala on the waterfront, Holt Renfrew's *Collection Of Magnificence* fashion show at the spiffy new CP Waterfront Centre Hotel. A

suave, sophisticated and sold-out crowd of 400 paid $125 per well-coiffed head for smart cocktails, dinner, dancing and a blow-your-designer-socks off fashion show. The very collaborative effort - Holt's, the hotel's and Arts Umbrella's - was a perfect blendship of self-marketing genius at work. And if you thought the models were smouldering and strutting, dear heart, you should have checked out the *guests*.

Heather Belzberg

The Waterfront's general manager, Michael Kaile, practically popped his tuxedo shirt studs as he squired wife Diana, in black with a smattering of gold, around the coutured and cultured crowd. These folk knew their Calvin Kleins from their Christian Lacroix, their Armani from their Montana and, as they checked out the wall hangings in this in-est of the new inns, their Shadbolts from their Schmerholzs.

Reminding you once more how these things all manage to mesh together, darling, Trudy Pekarsky of Pekarsky Noble & Associates Inc., art consultants for the hotel, has been a major player in Arts Umbrella's efforts for the last several years. Each and every one of the 45 original paintings and sculptures was commissioned or specifically chosen just for the Waterfront, in an elegant "You scratch my worthy charity, I'll grace your hotel with my art acumen" arrangement.

Expo lands architect Rick Hulbert and his wife Tina checked out the be-seen scene, and rubbed shoulders with a number of other entrepreneurial tried-and-trendy architects of their own fate, among them the ever-adorable David Thom. David is busy bringing some of that artistic imagination for which he is known to the $750-million Vancouver-Richmond rapid transit line, while Flash Hulbert is busy unveiling a $7-million "mansion in the sky," as he calls one of his West end penthouse projects.

"He can call it anything he wants," grumbled a not-so-successful competitor. "It's the highest priced apartment per square foot in all of North America."

Manic-banterer and impressario of the deal Peter Thomas blew in with his longtime lady Rita Morrice (she in fuchsia and black polka dots), flushed from the launch of his new $27.95 *Never Fight With a Pig* missive. He still cracker barrels through conversations, often monopolizing them, and his unsuccessful bid to buy up PTL's assets after Jim and Tammy Bakker's fall from grace still gets tongues wriggling. "Imagine if he had actually gotten the assets - and the inherent publicity," murmured one bent-eared bigwig as he limped into dinner. "The PTL/Peter Thomas Legacy would be that he would never shut up!"

Spotted a Southam or two on the way in (Stephanie, in an exquisite black, teal and magenta dinner jacket), a Belzberg (Heather, in a bare, black and beautiful blast that would have stopped the show had she been on stage and not sipping and supping), and one Tolmie - Patsy - in Barbara-Bush-style black and pearls.

Marathon Realty veteran Gordon Campbell slipped in with white-clad wife Nancy for a checkup on his old employer (who had developed the hotel site). Former fashion industry exec and present Arts Umbrella board member Sandi Lee cast a practised eye on what she had wrought. And Le Meridien's wise and worldly PR person, Karen Hall, whose exotic clothes elicit jet-set envy in other not-so-worldly travelers, pronounced the sizzling

Rick & Tina Hulbert

extravaganza international class. Anyone looking for fashion flops, frumps or fiascoes here darling, was just out of luck. Models *or* oglers - everyone was first rate.

Laissez-faired off to Leone's splashy *Cinecitta* film retrospective cum flashy fashion show. Fellini would have loved the crush (800 strong) of socialites, models, fashion and beauty-biz players, press and paparazzi, movie and TV-types, fringe artists and would-be designers. With the tickets a mere $75-a-ducat, absolutely anyone could go; and so, it seemed, they did. The dressy do-gooders (giving their considerable all for a good cause, the Vancouver Museum) draped themselves decorously around the gray granite walls of the Sinclair Centre atrium and tried their best to look cool, continental and a shade world-weary.

"Well I see she managed to scrape enough velvet off her Elvis paintings to get a dress," I heard as I dodged the receiving line and headed into the fray. "But I'm pretty sure she has that dress on backwards," the knit-wit in the clingy little number continued.

"That dress needs accessories." a blonde, all nails and nasal whine, opined.

"I agree," the slip-shod satin beside her said. "What about a pitchfork? Those ruffles look like they could prick your hand."

"Forget it. The whole outfit looks like some sort of cult thing."

I was on my way to some much-needed bubbly when I bypassed Baroness Heidi von Pfetten and her exquisite daughter Stephanie. She was back from a sybaritic sojourn of several weeks through Europe, looking royally rested, and was in pfine pfettle.

Il Barino's Laura Markin swept in in one of her more extravagant fashion risks. I know it was Gianfranco Ferre, dear heart, but leopard-skin chiffon, amber boa and Shirley Temple curls? Call me unadventurous, if you must. Daughter Sylvia looked positively conservative in a cream coat dress. Interior designer Ginny Richards did a little exterior dude-ing up in a canteloupe orange suit, the VSO's Darlene Spevakow donned honeydew-melon green, and the museum's Lele Mathisen opted for eggplant purple. Fortunately at no color-clashing point did they try to meld.

"Do you have any idea how the average woman would look in that little beauty?" the pudgy pink power puff behind me asked. "Or in that size 4 Isaac Mizrahi sliver that Maria's daughter Patrizia has on?" she sighed as the evening's auction began.

Almost $24,000 was raised for the museum's coffers. The Leones bought themselves a "gone fishin" weekend at the Samson Lodge for $1,100, and one of artist Ingrid Losch's peaceful still lifes for $800. And Count Enrico Dobrzensky bought his beloved Countess Aline a 22-karat gold necklace by Haida artist Robert Davidson and a Raven great cape by Dorothy Grant. "Bellissimo," murmured one of Alberto Leon's fresh-from-Florence friends as he surveyed the glitzy *La Dolce Vita* scene. "Bloody meraviglioso," I thought as I hit the valet parking line. You couldn't make these evenings up even if you tried.

Pranced off to *Pandas, Prints and Prizes*, a benefit dinner organized by Mr. Jax for the Society of Intestinal Research, headlined by a spring 1992 fashion show. the $250 per place setting din din pulled in a whopping $67,000 for a needy goal and brought out some of the town's more moneyed majors, many of whom are more than picky about which of these philanthropic potlatches they deign to attend.

The Shon Group's Ron Shon and his wife Sharon slipped in. The quiet and classy Mr. S. is slightly more comfortable accepting congratulations on his hard-fought-for Cathedral Place as more and more skeptics sing its considerable praises. Sony's Joe Cohen, who gives at the office - and everywhere else he sets foot - sailed in with wife Fran, and Woodward's savvy president Hani Zayadi wended his way in with well-dressed (black and gold filigree) wife Diane.

Army and Navy's Marlene Cohen dazzled in hot pink, sapphire and jade green with her handsome and hearty husband, Harvey Wexler. They were guests of affable, ever-so-affluent Bud Herman (who was just off to Hong Kong) and his wife Cheryl. Charles and Isabelle Diamond were guests of designer-to-the-biggest-wigs Bill Switzer and his wife Frances. Maxine and Harry Gelfant brought friends and family (son Ben and his wife Barbara), and even corporate capos who couldn't make it bought tables and either turned them back or filled them up, including John Mackay (who is so underground lately he may be growing mushrooms), David Radler, Jack Diamond and Syd Belzberg. There in person: mustachioed stockster Ted Turton's wife Deanne (who is a soft touch for a good cause and lent some of her time and talent), Australian consul Bill Meehan and his wife Caroline (who shared their fine-wine stock), and Barbara Aisenstat (who tossed a $150 dinner at Hy's into the evening's very successful auction pot). Ex-attorney-general Alan Williams and his wife Marge caught up on the court chat with retired Chief Justice

Peter Thomas and Rita Morrice

Nathan Nemetz. Grace McCarthy bit her tongue and glowed grace-fully, and Speiser Furs's Jim and Wendy Laurenson faked it with a showtime display of some of the finest phony pelts to hit the environmentally fit list.

The evening really belonged to the Segal clan. Mr. Jax's feisty founder, Joe Segal, wife Rosalie and family flew full-force onto the scene. Sons Lorne and Gary and daughters Sandra Miller and Tracey Schonfeld (who had conceived and organized the whole successful shebang), pulled their wagons into a circled, tossed their hats into the ring, and relieved the townsfolk of their gold - all with nary a shot being fired.

Ta Ta Darling. That's enough clothes encounters for anyone. And remember: Be charitable ... before the price goes up.

Valerie.

THE YEAR 1992

MUSEUM PIECES
Colour at the Black and White Ball, and dinner with an Ambassador.

KITTY GLITTER
Fund-raising doesn't get much sassier than it did at Jacqui Cohen's Face The World bash.

WHOSE SOIREE NOW?
For those dreading pomp and protocol, the Midsummer's Eve bash came off as a delightful surprise.

FOTH, HYPE AND CHARITY
Allan Fotheringham celebrates a big one; and the oh-so-private Belzbergs go public with a cause.

THE FIRST ANNUAL VALERIE AWARDS
Here's to the good, the bad and the bubbly on Vancouver society.

MUSEUM PIECES

Barbie Darling,

Boogied off to the Vancouver Museum's third annual Black and White Ball, along with 700 splendidly embellished do-gooders doing well. There was no recession in this procession; it was a night long on beads, sequins and hem lines. The chic elite, dressed to the designer nines, paraded like the ebony and ivory show-stoppers in the Ascot scene from *My Fair Lady*. It was kiss-kiss, click-click all the way, as the fleet sailed in for pre-dindin drinky-poos and the

Frankie Anderson, Pamela Martin

inevitable eyeballing of who's wearing what—and whatever possessed them! It was an elaborate fandango, Barbie. One step forward, clutch hands, kiss cheeks—both of course—two steps back, check head to toe, nod and gust, and demand wherever did they go to A) get that tan, B) lose that weight, C) find that incredible outfit. Arthur got his in Venezuela—his tan, Barbie, and of course, I mean Arthur Erickson. "He may be $10 million in debt, you know, but he always looks like at least a million to me," gushed the redhead in the itsy-bitsy bit of flimsy-whimsy. "You're talking about Canada's greatest architect," her exasperated spouse glowered. "And everything isn't about money," he hissed as he fled to the bar. Whoops.

Anyway, darling, Arthur is always just back from somewhere you have always meant to go—African safari, noshing on the Nile, pagoda-hopping, dishing with the Dalai Lama, schmoozing in Venezuela—this time with our old friend Jean Ramos, the former Ottawa hostess with the mostest who dumped her far-too-stodgy spouse (The Venezuelan ambassador) and moved to Caracas to party heartier there. Arthur was with Lois Milsom (also no slough at hot-spot-hopping), who wore her black Givenchy again. "That dress has been trotted out more times than a derby winner," the fang-and-claw-Marks-ist behind her murmured. (Since Ms. Marks was wearing what looked like harem jammies, Ms. Milsom needn't be concerned.)

Cartier's Ani and Daniel Feuermann winged in from Joan Carlisle-Irving's home away from home on Mustique. They bought the sybaritic stay at last summer's Hot, Hot fundraiser at the museum, so they were both touting toasty tans in combo with his black (classic custom tux) and her white (sleek designer sheath).

Vencorp's venerable Moh Faris and his spirited spouse Yulanda, perennial heavy hitters on the charity circuit, fairly floated in with the news that they had just become first-time grandparents of a baby boy named Omar. Is this kid destined for greatness or what? Super promo-man Bruce Allen slid silently and semi-seriously onto the scene while wife Jane MacDougall gushed and goshed on in. Last seen traipsing down the red carpet at the Academy Awards in her hot pink coat dress (let me count the times), she actually stashed it for once and played hid-and-chic in basic black. Also noir-ing it that night was Bryan Adams's blonde, British architect Melanie Sainsbury, who left London to do some Adams projects here. One of them is a three-story Gastown warehouse our boy Bry owns and plans to turn into a recording studio. Unclear of the night's concept, Justice Minister Kim Campbell waltzed in wearing to-the-floor purple. Colourful enough normally never to get lost in a crowd, the possible future prime minister two-stepped in with soap-opera-handsome golf-course developer John McLean. Endeavour's former executive director Sue Lewis, flashing salmon-scale sequins (in a wild and crazy zebra print),

Sam Black and Cora Wills

pranced in proudly with Priority Projects cutie Richard Unger. Just back from Palm Springs, the duo seem delirious with each other and their future doings. He's got his Priority's straight, and she is going to swing her considerable clout into executively directing the Vancouver Museum. The ball's founding chairman Lele Mathisen, who fairy-tale-princessed about in a full-length silver cloud of silk organza by Gino Fratini, had also just Palm-Sprung it. She and old clubby hubby Chris will produce scion number four in September. And the last time I had seen Euro-Pacific's Phil Wilhelmsen (son of Whistler pioneer Franz Wilhelmsen) and his slim-as-your-wrist wife Marilyn was the previous week in Palm Springs.

GoGo girl Jacqui Cohen, up to her eyelashes in her Face the World Foundation fund-raising, flounced in with friends Kip and Cynie Woodward (these scions of retail fortunes have to stick together, darling), and close behind on teetering heels was lumber czar Herb Doman's dishy daughter Darcia. "Her life is one big ripping story, and she's wearing it," I heard from a black-beaded blockbuster behind me as we made our way into the certifiably glitzy ballroom for dinner. "Puccini could have scored her life there have been so many tragedies," the karats-and-schtickster beside her murmured. Three of us turned simultaneously to see just who was being skewered, though none of us are any the wiser.

The museum's amusing chairman, *Equity* magazine's equitable editor Michael Campbell (I swear he's possessed by a Disney character) had a small group in stitches as he joked his way to his table. His wasp-waisted wife Kathy, slim as a school girl again (after Campbell kid number three), did the latest Liz Clairborne white-and-sparkly sheath more than justice. Must be those laps at the Aquatic Centre.

Over the Thomas Hobbs calla lilies I spotted BCTV's tragically perky

Sam Belzberg, Stanley Kwok, Michael Phelps

Pamela Martin head-to-heading with semi-new squeeze Frankie Anderson. (Frankie can be caught almost any lunchtime at Il Giardino with other stock marketeers Peter Brown, Wally Dezura, Harry Moll—usually with a cellular phone coming out of his ear.) To their right was Il Barino's smoky-voiced Laura Markin, who told me that Robert De Niro had been in sampling her private label Batasiolo and that his Italian was "very good." Actor Robert Clouthier (who can't look formal even in a tux, with that "What's up, Doc?" gleam he has) got smothered by a rather mature fan whose bodice was a fallen souffle in need of boning up, and who just loved him as Relic in the late, lamented *Beachcombers*. Over the *carre d'agneau brosse aux herbes* (rack of lamb to you, Barbie) I watched lawyer Rodney Ward, the museums board's mustachioed mischief maker (snappy talker, pithy lines, the assurance of a casino blackjack dealer flipping cards), priming the pump for the next board meeting. Oh that Rodney, what a caution! "He always assumes his information is on the order of a sacred thunderclap," said a little busy-browed man with the thatch of man-made hair. And you thought these blowouts could blend into bland just because everybody knows everybody else, Barbie.

Sherry Taylor and her hardcore committee really know how to finesse a fundraising into the bigtime, and lest you think their yearlong work is a mondo coffee klatch, think again. "Building a bridge between private resources and public needs is essentially a grubby backroom business," a long-time society matron told me. Those young up-and-comers are basically carrying on what many of their mothers started—driving the art of cheque-collecting-for-a-good-cause to fine heights—with heaps of style. More and more, charity is becoming the place where all the elements come together. Money, fashion, publicity, product, people. It was all there, Barbie. In black and white.

Whooshed off to the Junior League's World Affairs Dinner. Who could resist? They had booked "the greatest living master of the English tongue"—former Israeli ambassador to the United Nations Abba Eban—to fill in any little pieces missing in the jigsaw that is Israel and the Middle East in the Peace Process and, in case you missed it, the collapse of communism. The small and exclusive reception before the dinner for 300 was held, appropriately, in the Hyatt's penthouse called Perspectives. Head table guests and afficionados of world-class diplo-speak, some of whom had bought tables of 10 for a tony $1,750, gathered for an up-close peek at a piece of modern history.

Fran Belzberg and Abba Eban

Mike and Beckie Harcourt hurried in, he from his preparations for the pesky western premiers' visit, she flushed and excited about the opening of her (and her sister's Gabriel Galley Two in Laguna Beach. Gordon and Nancy Campbell bustled in, he in his second-skin tux, she in a new short haircut and a white, backless, strap-full designer dress she would later see downstairs in black. Asked to pose with head tablers for a photo op, Madame Campbell joked that she was not sure she wanted to be part of this group. Sam and Fran Belzberg (she was the evening's _very_ smooth moderator) were just back from a Palm Springs break. The _Vancouver Sun's_ senior editor, Patricia Graham, the highest ranking female print journalist in B.C., was casting her laser-beam specs over the scene. And so was a very wary Michael Phelps, the canny CEO of Westcoast Energy, who was honourary chairman of the dinner. After all, Barbie, Mr. Eban is an original and idiosyncratic man and not everyone's cure-all for the Middle East's problems.

Over the _saumon farci a la mousse de flepan_ (a fish dish to you, Barbie), I checked out the nattily assembled dynamite duos, like Woody and Sherrill MacLaren—he's big in trust foundations and his private investment company, she's the author of _Invisible Power: The Women Who Run Canada_. They sat

263

with David Korbin who is the cashmere smooth mega-managing partner of Deloitte & Touche, and his wife Judy who is a top-notch labour relations negotiator with a Women of Distinction award under her Chanel belt. Charity maven Cynthia Levy was looking blonde and creamy and gorgeous in an off-white and curve-clutching skimmer. Busy-busy Carol Jackson of the Think AIDS programs flashed a thighs-the-limit black Moschino studded in pearls, and Ani Feuermann, who has miles of style, went for the gold in a black and gilt-y Escada (though not the one she spilled the nail polish remover on that ate through the fabric, Barbie).

But I suppose you want to hear about the very able Eban. He's large and rumpled, gray of hair, ashen of skin. He looks like one of the board of directors of an insolvent bank. He's disarming, but not self-deprecating. He is wheezy (allergic to non-intellectuals?) and you get the impression you are approaching an elaborately-wired security system. (Foolish questions and their perpetrators have, I am sure, been sunk without a trace.) He talks in 30-second sound bites from his past books and doesn't give anything away for free. If it's good, he has already used it, though the frequent speech-givers in the audience scribbled in the dark anyway. His bon mots bore Peter Ustinov intonations bordering on Richard Burton with a dash of Churchill. He has a propensity to cannibalize his diplomatic dogfights: "I remember my last conversation with the great stateman Anwar Sadat, who said, 'Democracy is a wonderful thing except for elections.'" He called Henry Kissinger an old friend and then zaps, "I don't know if Henry is a great writer, but if you got through his book, you have to be a great reader." I knew it was getting late when he said, "The hour is urgent, and the shadows are growing long," but the dinner left a great aftertaste.

Ta Ta Darling, and remember" Always tell the truth, but not all of it.
Valerie.

KITTY GLITTER

Barbie Darling,

Flitted off to the Face The World Foundation's "night of fund-raising magic," hosted by Army and Navy heiress Jacqui Cohen at her splendid seaside digs. It was a leafy, slate blue evening and the pale pink Point Grey palace was perfecto, full, as it was, of unrepentant capitalists, buttered with a lush slice of the city's most beautiful people.

It was a hip, young crowd if ever. Fledgling titans and almost-theres of society, politics, finance, media and fashion padded down the tiled and curving driveway past a car buff's bonanza of Porches, Ferraris, Mercedes and all, into a phalanx of lurking lenses playing snap-dragon. They would pause, pose for the paparazzi, camp it up and cuddle on cue, having mastered the finer points of social push and pull. (Like the tree falling in the forest, darling, if no one knows you were there, what's the point?)

"Ooooh. Shutterbugs doing glitterbugs," one streetwise snapper noted, sweeping past two private school products—or "heirs of the dogs that begat them," he muttered on into the fabulous, flower bedecked foyer. The airy, art-filled scene was glitzy enough to have been New York, Palm Beach or Monaco, but it reminded me most of all of that wonderful party we went to at that cliffside mansion in Puerto Vallarta with Peter O'Toole and Edna O'Brien. You just didn't know what to check out first, the high voltage decor or the high octane crowd. It was like an endless A-list dinner party.

"The barbarians aren't at the gate, my dear, they're already here," murmured an older Shaughnessy type in a white petit four of a dress. I turned to bump into that one-man revolt against conformity, Nelson Skalbania. Debt-encumbered, and possibly in the deepest doo-doo of his career (the trail comes up in November), the irrepressible developer-speculator answered his "How are you's?' with a best-face-forward—"As well as can be expected, and better than I deserve"—to which the loyal and lovely Eleni raised those seen-everything baby browns. Fast on their well-heeled heels were Lyn and Kerry Dix (he is the super-successful scion of business legend Wendy McDonald). Bubbly and big-eyed as usual, Lyn (whose hair-colour-du-jour is back from blonde to basic brown), was bursting with news of their Napa Valley swing through the Mondavi winery. "He's *sooo* handsome," she gushed. "The son?" I asked. "No, Robert Mondavi, the father." she announced. "He's a short little guy, but when he stands on his wallet, he's just the right height," she burbled as she spun off.

Cynthia Woodward, Jacqui Cohen, Carol Lee and Darcia Doman

Moving on into the spacious living room, I was hit by what seemed like a wave of wall-to-wall yuppies, most of them armed with business cards to spare, mingling, munching and mustering their contact attacks. From the horsey set to the Howe Street crowd, they were taking no chances with the glamour rap. Spotted were everything from a pair of gold beaded Ted Land pumps ($1,400 on Palm Springs' pricey El Paseo) to a $7,500 inky black little number by Oscar de la Renta.

"I like very dusky, musky perfumes," I heard as I headed off to the bar from a blonde in a life-spent-on-the-Nautilus-machine-body. "I like to smell like an old book. Why? To attract a rich literary man. Why do you think?" My dear, it's enough to make your writer's block reach critical mass.

Noted a number of lean, mean dream machines in the crowd as I headed out to the city-view patio. Since I had never seen any of them before, I asked a gorgeous young Narcissus with a crown of dark curls and ocean blue eyes who they were and was told, with what I definitely thought was disdain, that they were Canucks. When I looked blank (I was thinking we're *all* Canucks), he said slowly, as though I had a problem, "They are hockey players. There's Trevor Linden and Doug Lidster and Steve Tambellini and Glen Ringdal." Really, Barbie, if I cluttered my head with sports trivia, I'd never have room for the real stuff. I did know who Pat Quinn was, however, and his wife Sandra— but that's because he looks like Brian Mulroney, and she has great clothes.

It was with some relief that the very familiar Gordon Campbell hove into view. (Wife Nancy's backless sapphire sequined sheath was also familiar. Isn't that the spicy little sparkler His Honor picked up in Maui and slipped under the Christmas tree for Mrs. C.?) Wall Financial Corp.'s master magician Peter Wall stood nearby, as solid as his new three-building, multimillion-dollar Wall Centre, which is busily a-building on Burrard Street. And beside him schmoozed First Generation's ever-more-public (on the stock exchange and the charity circuit) Steven Funk, and to his right Prospero's prosperous, ever-affable Bob Lee. Lily Lee, subtle and understated even in shocking pink, was a jewel-toned contrast to her daughter Carol's aquamarine smasharoonie.

"She may be a gorgeous fluff-brain, but look at that body," said a broad-shouldered, beetle-browed little man to a rather ripe woman in a gold-toned sack. Those who overheard turned to check out body-building champ Carla Temple posing off to the side in a raven-black, double-deep-dish dress that exhibited more than a little northern exposure, if you catch my continental drift. I watched the icy-sleek Stephanie (Southam) Carlson, who sailed in fresh off the tennis court after a match with her teenage daughter, get cornered by a gabby Wally Dezura. She worked her way round a pillar and then was off and away. "Doesn't he look like a bad lounge act?" the mincing mannequin in the iridescent silver asked of the gulping young Howe Street buck who just happens to work with dear Wally.

I noticed that Orestes' very arresting Beverly Hauff had shed her white fox-tailed fur to expose not only her gloriously reshaped shape (those Palm Springs stays can be so re-defining, but the mother of all emeralds nestled just where it was supposed to—and it stayed there all night long.

As I headed out into the festive, scalloped white tents perched over the ocean and the covered swimming pool, I bumped into young fur magnate Constantine Pappas and his wife Sherry. We talked about Sly Stallone's great old ads for the company, and the very real infusion of seemingly unflagging Japanese money into the on-its-way-up-again fur industry.

Grazing at Umberto's sumptuous buffet, guests gathered and then chowed down on lobster claws, giant prawns and scallops, barbecued salmon and salads before feasting on chef Gianni Picchi's lamb and pasta dishes. Since Signore Menghi, freshly back from a sojourn to Seville, was under the weather, the ever-ready and oh-so-able Mario Enero saved everyone's bacon.

Tiny, doll-like Suzie Moll brought over famed South African heart surgeon Christiaan Barnard for a chat, though I really think, Barbie, that he was far more interested in getting his dinner. The man is 70-something, after all. He was in town to do a business deal with Harry Moll and seemed grateful that I shook his hand gently. (I remembered the medical problem with his hands and why he had to stop operating.) He currently has, I think, a 28-year-old wife and various small children, and that in the distant past he had an affair with Gina Lollobrigida. Anyway, he has the charm of a boulevardier (he told Suzie I looked like Elizabeth Taylor, though I'm not sure at what stage), is a loose-limbed fellow with a face as smooth and frozen as an arctic lake (and eyes as blue), and was certainly a gonzo side attraction to the party in my books.

Dr. Christiaan Barnard, Jack Cohen

Peter Thomas's Face The World auction antics started up just as soon as everyone sampled the sinful array of desserts. "He obviously has a firm hand on Dale Carnegie's five great rules of selling," I heard over my shoulder as Thomas blitzkrieged through 11 pricey items in little under 30 minutes. Harald and Sharlene Ludwig, who are as "cute as two bees on a blossom," (as Grandmama would say) snaffled the private Jet Ranger helicopter picnic-for-four for a tasty $5,000. Wonder if they'll take new baby Alexander? Kip Woodward snapped up the Derek Murray photo session for a tony $2,500, and Yorkton Securities' Mike Rogers plunked down $7,000 for two weeks in Maui at the Plantation Inn, scuba diving, dinner at Gerards' (so *delicieux*, remember?) and the use of a BMW convertible. Investment wizard Assa Manhas, lumber luminary Darcy Johal and John Tognetti, who is on the "In Your Faceboard" (as the overly-imbibed wag to my left kept calling it), will three-couple-it to Las Vegas for three nights at the Sands in Peter Thomas's dear little Hawker jet.

And the street-smart young founder and president of the Face The World Foundation herself, Jacqui Cohen? Out on a limb, she hyped this second annual event to the Nth and actually delivered the goods (in good old retail-trade fashion). The nervy and curvy ring-mistress of this three-ring circus of the stars did some nifty networking with her cohorts Darcia Doman and Cynthia Woodward and an ever-growing pack of philanthropists-in-embryo. "the Me Shall Inherit the Earth" generation actually seems to be breaking out of its mold. They are aggressive, don't care if you gave at the office, and pull in "I'll sponsor yours if you sponsor mine" markers as serous as any casino caper.

No doubt these events are status-reinforcing. They raise both the profile of the patrons and the philanthropic pot of the beneficiary. But in the end, connections are forged, images are polished and kitties are filled. This little blowout, with its tickets-at-the-wicket a pricey $500 a duo, raised a hot $135,000 for Canuck Place Children's Hospice, teens in crisis and various other groups in its own innovative, nonprofit, nonpartisan, nonconformist way. It pulled in a bumper-car pile up of biggies (280 of them)—everyone from the head McCheese at McDonald's, George Cohon, to rocker Long John Baldry, with an impressive smattering of hip and cutting edge revellers-with-a-cause in between. And from the sheer numbers still jamming the dance floor in the wee smalls, or chatting each other up in every corner well past the usual "we can go now" hours, this was exactly where they wanted to be.

Ta Ta Darling, and remember: the best combination is to be born fabulously rich and not be afraid to use your money, honey.

Valerie.

WHOSE SOIREE NOW?

Barbie Darling,

Meandered off to A Midsummer's Eve, the consul general of the United States David Johnson and his wife Scarlett Swan's swank garden party for the Canadian Cancer Society. The velvet evening mixed tony veterans of tens of these silken soirees with the tried and true financial foot soldiers who are the backbone of the city's high-profile good-deed-do's. That a smattering of fast-rising doughboys chose to infiltrate, some for the first time, what has become a don't-miss annual event didn't hurt the posh picnic one bit.

Nestled on a tree-lined street in Shaughnessy, the grand old house has been the scene of many backyard bash, with its rolling green lawn and cool, shady walled-in privacy, and on this night shielded from the stars by a lofty red and white tent held up by chiffon-draped poles of twinkling lights. Inside, white linen tableclothes were dotted with gargantuan sprays of flowers. And just as the derby at Epsom Downs signals the opening of the British summer social season, so too does the U.S. consul's grassy chowdown-on-the-back-40 kick off what passes for ours. (These people have cottages, islands and boats they could be in and on, Barbie, and the fact that 160 of them showed up for this little luau is impressive.)

Resigned to the pomp and protocol I had experienced at endless Ottawa embassy parties an eon or two ago, I was trudging up the driveway to this one when I overheard ahead of me two portly pandas in their pinstripes who were finishing off Lord knows who with a zingy "He has no enemies, you know, but he is intensely disliked by his friends." I took heart, Barbie, that the evening might be a shade less straight laced than the diplomatic corps sometimes deems necessary.

Chris and Lele Mathisen

The receiving line took a proper two minutes per guest—hosts Johnson and Swan, the Cancer Society's B.C. and Yukon division president Sheila McDougall, executive director Phyllis Hood ("Pleasure, pleasure" and Philip Armer (he's just retired from the Bank of Nova Scotia) who spearheaded the corporate campaign, and then it was through the elegant living room (not a gold State Department seal in sight) and on out to join the rest of the in-crowd that had spilled out onto the patio and gardens.

I ran smack into sawmill king Bill Sauder and his definitely not run-of-the-mill wife Marjorie-Anne, who flashed a smashing rhododendron red quilted suit and matching headband around her blonde curls and walked away with the night's Most Glamorous Grandmother award. They were off to a summer sojourn with their various kinder on Bowen Island. Just behind them were supersalesman Malcolm Hasman (Bell Realty—he's part-owner and partner— sold more homes in West Van than any other firm in the last 15 years) and his new altared-state wife Cathy. The earnest Hasman (35), who moves into super-charge with the desperation of a frisky puppy, commented that he just loved the green in my outfit. "Of course you do," I chided him. "It's the color of money." Hasman just happens to have sold $150 million worth of real estate since he turned 30. I had passed Concord Pacific's direct and senior vice-president Stanley Kwok on the Lion's Gate Bridge earlier that evening (a large Mercedes sedan, I think), but I was also checking out the glamorous passenger's shoulder-duster earrings. (Shallow is my life, Barbie.) As they swept onto the patio, I had a chance to check out the rest of the impressively-credentialed Eva Kwok's smashing flower-laden silk. No shrinking violet, the new Mrs. Kwok had all the right mauves—and reds.

Bill Vander Zalm's swift-as-a-kick lawyer Peter Butler ambled in with his should-be-sainted wife, the darling Lucia. ("Five kids and Peter, too," I heard from the Judy-with-a-punch at my elbow, "and she looks so calm.") The brazenly individualistic Butler, who plays befuddled country bumpkin with great effort but is nonetheless operating in overdrive mentally, always looks slightly unhinged. He is given to stammers and long, reflective pauses (disguising what would otherwise be a ruling-class, lockjaw accent). And he has a funky, but intelligible style of telling a story that always gets an enthusiastic reception.

"His voice booms and fades in the courtroom like a randomly programmed organ," the Butler-stung banker's suit beside me offered. "He has a sly look when he's got your contempt," he continued. "And that's just before he zaps you."

"He's like Columbo," said lawyer Steve Sobolewski, and obvious admirer of the highly successful Queen's counsel who seemed genuinely knocked out by the bold and successful Peter Principal in the Vander Zalm case. As usual, Butler the baron of barter, stole all the attention in his corner in a delicious act of petty larceny.

"Why is it that by the time some men have money to burn, the pilot light has gone out," muttered the beautiful young blonde trader by day, party girl by night in the vanilla sheath and the Manolo Blahnik shoes ($650 should you care, Barbie). She is obviously fairly focused on her future, because I had seen her on the sea wall the previous week with a T-shirt heralding "A fool and his money are fun."

Spotted Il Barino's feisty owner, the irrepressible Laura Markin, in her usual cloud of Winston smoke. She was wearing poison green ("Boboli," she said in her heavy Italian accent. "Not expensive."), one of her gold Karl Stittgen boffo bijoux, and her vigorously maintained mahogany tan, which she pursues, she says, in the sunny nook behind her Yaletown success story. She had donated, in her expansive way, the exquisite cuisine—from the salmon tartare through the roast strip loin of beef down to the last olive, which certainly helped the Cancer Society coffers. Now if she and her gorgeous blonde bambino Sylvia would just curb that secondary smoke screen they are always engulfed in, we would all breathe a little easier.

As corks popped and conversation bubbled, and happy campers lit into their poached pears and coffee, I got a change to check out some of the somebodies I had missed earlier. Mike and Beckie Harcourt had swished in— he in fine fettle, constitutionally, she in pink linen, sartorially—on the NDP heels of jocular MLA Bernie Simpson. But the only remotely political chat I heard was one wag's reason for going into politics: "So you won't have to waste money looking up your family tree—your opponents will do it for you." Barbie, why do people tell me these things? This is the same yawn-spawner who, when I mentioned how many lawyers were there—John Norton and Art Smolensky, Dwight Harbottle (who is with Peter Butler) and his lawyer-wife Sandra, and on and on—said, "If you add insult to injury, my lawyer will love it." As I say, Barbie, why me?

Now if this had been Ottawa, dear heart, one would have expected the men to disappear for cigars and brandy after dinner, but as Jean Chretien might have said, and in fact did, "We had work to do." The live auction zipped by like a slick bird with the always-there and always-good Barry Scott at the controls. He had already given those magic pipes of his a good workout at the Celebrity Waiters Luncheon for leukemia research (raising a good day's $100,000) and was thrilled, he said, that this night's mike worked. The items offered were an alphabet soup mix of must-haves, and since bidders are very much on show for the cause, every glinty eye under the big tent watches with great interest who buys what for how much. And just as every self-respecting Junior Leaguer knows her silver patterns cold, every auction item acquisitor knows exactly what he or his significant equal bids on is worth in actual value or in public goodwill.

Hard-core player Steven Funk (a hefty bidster at the celebrity luncheon that noon) shifted into second gear to snaffle an extremely rare nine-litre bottle—hand-etched and sandblown—of Signorello "Founders Reserve' Napa Valley Chardonnay 1989 for a healthy $1,400. Raymond Signorello, the handsome padrone of Signorello's hillside vineyard on the Silverado Trail, beamed from the sidelines. (Since he had produced only 200 cases of Founders Reserve Chardonay that year, if each of them went for that much a bottle, let's just see, that would be...)

The shy, soft-spoken and outrageously talented artist Clarence Mills—he's a member of the Eagle Clan at Skidegate—watched his 18 carat Haida raven design gold bracelet go for $5,500 to Intrawest's Joe Houssian's wife Joanne. The Four Seasons Hotel's Ruy Paes-Braga's fabulous Maui get-away went for a bargain $9,000 to the president of ASM Capitol Corporation's Assa Manhas (who's been the boy-with-the-most-toys at the last four auctions I've been at). And the two three-day, reserved-gold grandstand seats at the Molson Indy Vancouver, a night at the Royal Suite at the Waterfront Hotel and dinner at Hy's went to Chris Mathisen, the VP of Arpeg Holdings for a mere $1,500.

As the boisterous bidding picked up and the auction wound down revved-up revellers took to the dance floor, cutting a wild would-be rug to the music of the aptly-named Zaniacs.

"Migawd, it looks like an elegant daycare center for obstreperous children," the two old-family, old-money bags besides me offered, as they watched the cut-ups.

Definitely not Ottawa, and definitely not protocol-bogged I thought as I thanked consul general (charity begins at home) Johnson and his gracious wife Scarlett for their good ol' American hospitality, and sailed out into the midsummer's eve.

Ta Ta Darling, and remember those dancers: pull your own weight until you're high enough to throw it around.

Valerie.

FOTH, HYPE AND CHARITY

Barbie Darling,

Fairly fa-la-la-ed off to Allan Fotheringham's big six-oh birthday party. The cheery invitation, sent out to 60 of the gnomic know-it-all's closest-and-mostest, featured, somewhat incongruously, a dancing bear in pink ballet slippers and a frilly purple tutu. It promised that the Annual Fotheringham Birthday Bash would be particularly momentous this year, because the demon columnist had managed to put away six full decades under his finest-of-leather Gucci belts.

An eclectic mixture of luminary and literary lights descended upon the charming, old and gray mansion (so apropos) belonging to long-time acquaintances who nonetheless insisted upon anonymity. Have you seen the sputtering, spewing letters to the editor this man gets, darling? His surefire-satire, thumb-in-your-eye digs really stir up the loonies out there.

Sifted through the crush of household names jamming the front hall to find the mass murmurer of metaphors himself holding court near a kitchen cabinet—delusions of political grandeur beating ever in his tiny heart. I arrived mere seconds behind killer-watt cartoonist Roy Peterson and his wife Margaret, whose gift to the now certifiable sexagenarian (many have suspected he was one for years) was 60 new tennis balls and by far the evening's most original birthday card. A hearty Happy Birthday, Murray! was lettered on the front (Allan was born Murray Allan Scott), and on the inside was one of those exquisite caricatures of Foth that only Peterson can do, in full tennis regalia, with a headband that read "Bobby Riggs Lives," reminding him that six-love sounds so much better than six-oh. And if you thought Peterson had captured Fotheringham, Mulroney and now Harcourt to a whisker, you should see his fat and freckled Fergie. As one who was this close to the dowdy duchess and her soon-to-be-passe royal wedding. I can tell you, dear heart, it's dead-on.

Bumped champagne flutes, and black-and-white silken shoulder, with the smart, shrewd and hard-scribbling Helena Zukowski, ex-editor of the very-so-slick and glossy Palm Springs Life magazine. As if she wasn't privy to the stuff of mini-series and maxi-settlements among the celebrated desert-dwellers she formerly dealt with, she criss-crossed the country a year or so ago as a member of Keith Spicer's alienate-the-nation commission. Under that shiny helmet of Theda Bara hair, those nut brown peepers have seen it all. (Now if only she'd stop believing discretion is the better part of Valerie.)

Francesa, Allan, Kip Fotheringham

That prickly thespian Bruno Gerussi grand-entranced in grand style, wearing an indigo blue bomber jacket and pants so perfectly tailored to him the combo could have been one of Wayne Newton's jumpsuits. Beachcombing no more, except in syndication somewhere in the Maldives, he's back to his roots, Shakespearean and shallower, on stage in the east, and loving it. His constant party-of-the-first-part, ex-judge Nancy Morrison, who is happily back in private practice and who has a distinct inability to spout cliches, was as flippantly incantatory and gorgeously slapdash as ever on her way to a giggle, and she always beats you to it.

"He's a rich, balding, wife-discarding scum bag, now that you ask," I heard about heaven-knows-whom as I crossed to the bar. "Yes, well, she's careless with her husbands," the reply trailed off. "More than two of them that I know of have been misplaced."

273

I bumped into former NDP cabinet minister Gary Lauk dome-to-dome-ing with that gregarious and convivial bon vivant Paul Manning. I knew them both when they had hair, darling. Manning is one of those professional news junkies who knows the good, behind-the-scenes stuff on everything, and lawyer Lauk is a politico who never serves up pre-cooked answers. (When I first met Gary, he had married Rosemary Nash, making his son a certifiable Lauk-Nash monster.) We were joined by Jake Kerr, the jet-haired jet-set CEO of Lignum who is the chief lobbyist for the B.C. forest industry in Washington, D.C. When I asked where the gorgeous Madame K. was, he told me she was fulfilling a lifetime dream in Graceland, doing her Elvis Presley thing, and that the rooms in the Grand Ol' Opry Hotel were really "quite reasonable." (And people think I make this stuff up.)

Spotted the benign, bespectacled ex-deputy attorney general Dick Vogel and his doctor-wife Patty as we were being herded in to dinner, along with U.TV's executive producer George Froehlich and his wife Linda. George had

the job's requisite three-day beard and bloodshot eyes, and since we had no time to chat, I can only surmise he is pleased that U.TV has been supplanted in the staff-revolving-door decathlon by BCTV. Smoked salmon, caught and smoked in the Maritimes by fisher king and fisheries wizard Dr. Peter Pearse, was tucked into (as were platters of rare roast beef) before, bombarded by wacky and irreverent jibes disguised as semi-compliments, we raised a glass to the man of the lengthening hour

Fran Belzberg and Marion Reid

himself.

First to tuck his ego into a holster—the room grew so quiet you could hear the flattery drop—was the Oatmeal Savage (a Fotheringham coinage), Jack Webster. The great grouch's stories, usually full of self-aggrandizing tidbits, were as gracious as the old veteran of the warring airwaves could manage without a cigarette (he had run out). Fast on the heels of his ever-polished brogues was Senator Pat Carney, in menopausal lavender and her ever-present Martha Strudy jewelry.

Shoes off, the machete-tongued upper chamber maid, who is as neutral as Switzerland on absolutely nothing, was in her pussycat mode as she unrolled her I-knew-him-when yarns. Allan's son Kip, whose exotic travels his father sometimes works into his columns (their father/son meeting at the equator in Africa was hilarious), read a just-for Foth birthday poem penned by novelist

Margaret Atwood, which I found a little name-droppy—don't you think? And then it was the birthday boy's turn to speechify.

With as little coyness interruptus as he could manage, Dr. Foth faced a sea of glasses raised expectantly by everyone from his much-loved mother Edna to as many relatives as could be mustered. And clinking, too, were an old soccer buddy; a world yachtsman and geologist I had met aboard his boat in London harbour; a correspondent to the _London Daily Telegraph_; _New Yorker_ writer Edith Iglauer (_Fishing With John, The Strangers Next Door_); _The Plastic Orgasm's_ lively Laverne Barnes (now tamely with Tourism B.C.); multimillion man Jimmy Pattison (who blew a Garbriel-like happy birthday blast on his golden coronet); and a gaggle of gorgeous _Beverly Hills, 90210_ Muffy-Buffy-Jody-Biff clones (who turned out to be friends of Kip, and Allan's delicious daughter Francesca.)

The pop troll, all fopped up in navy cashmere,was at peak pitch, though his earlier private dish on everything from the Barbara Amiel/Conrad Black merger to the unflinchingly hot galleys of Marjorie Nichols explosive new tome was hard to top. His stints on _Funny Page Challenge_, as he calls it, his columns—for _Maclean's_ and _The Financial Pest_ (more Foth)—his 12 or so speeches per year, his blabbermouth books (publisher Anna Porter locks him in a room for a month or so and throws food to him through the transom) and his much-envied travel (his assignment this year was to visit the 10

Isabelle Diamond and Ani Feuermann

most exotic resorts in the world) have honed his flinty schtick to the nth. He mentally log-rolled his way from his birth during a total eclipse in a mud slide in Hearn, Saskatchewan (where the townspeople, we are assured, are called Hernias)—and he went on at warp speed from there. For someone who scans the bar code of new pop culturisms for all they're worth, and who pricks the pompous egos of established icons and sends them home in a cigar box, it was a surprisingly sweet little speech. But then the prairie boy (whose childhood pals were gophers and who studied in a one-room schoolhouse) has always been, deep down (he does so have a deep down) a marshmallow in the tullyweeds.

Slipped off a mere afternoon or so later to Sam and Fran Belzberg's spectacular new Shaughnessy home for a little tea and enlightenment. It was a gathering of 20 or so high-profile inquiring minds, committee members and friends of the Dystonia Medical Research Foundation that the Belzbergs helped set up and have been funding privately since their darling daughter Cheri was first diagnosed with the neurological disease. I remember sitting beside Sam at a dinner party at Senator Jack Austin's one night years ago, and Sam telling me about it. I remember thinking that this vital, silver-haired czar of a far-flung business empire seemed strangely vulnerable for someone who was supposed to "have it all". His frustration over a disease that was not only incurable, but largely unknown, even in the medical profession, was apparent. And now the Belzbergs were hosting a one-night performance by dystonia patient Neil Marcus, who wrote and was to star in the play *Storm Reading* later that week. It was a fundraiser that Fran calls their "first foray into the public to raise as much awareness as possible for a disease that has a larger patient list than muscular dystrophy or Huntington's, but that hardly anyone has heard of."

"Most people think dystonia is a Balkan state," volunteered the bright and beautiful Laura Vandriel, Consensus Communications' plugged-in-president, as Dr. Donald Calne, head of the division of neurology at UBC's University Hospital, answered a variety of curious questions. He and his sharp and sassy wife Susan, an RN who works with him in the field, have worked with Oliver Sacks, the doctor Robin Williams played in *Awakenings*, and they had the best insider stories on everything from the movie's opening night parties to the work Dr. Sacks is doing now.

The stellar stalwarts of many of the city's charities were there that afternoon, and several—like Isabelle Diamond, Ani Feurermann, Maxine Gelfant and Carol Jackson—had joined Fran's committee and worked on the theater evening. Beckie Harcourt and NPA candidate Lynne Kennedy took a break from the rigors of political life to lend a hand and an ear, and there was a smattering of detail divas and guardian angels who raise profiles and profits like there is no tomorrow.

It was a frustrating afternoon, Barbie. The house was the stuff of *Architectural Digest*, kind of Mediterranean-elegant, nothing overdone. In spite of the number of wheels-of-fortune from some of the city's finer zip codes parked outside, the heavy hitters inside were subtly, suitably understated. Sam and Fran, who were focused and gracious and informed, left everyone feeling upbeat about, as Sam says, "some sort of a cure coming out of all the work being done." And, well, basically, Barbie I couldn't find anything to criticize. Nobody said a quotable zing about anyone, and we all left feeling uplifted.

Ta Ta Darling, and remember: If you can't say anything nice, sit next to me.

Valerie.

THE FIRST ANNUAL VALERIE AWARDS

Barbie Darling,

Well, I have been firing off these missives to you for a good 10 years now—the good, the bad and the bubbly. Together we've done London, Paris, Geneva and Rome, Guatemala, Fiji, Cancun, Hong Kong and Bangkok. We've shopped Rodeo Drive, slogged through the jungles in Tikal, climbed pyramids, done fat farms, danced at Annabel's, shaken hands with kings (Juan Carlos and Carl Gustaf) and queens (Elizabeth and Sofia) and boogied with rock stars Elton John and Eric Clapton. We've eaten off gold at Government House and off our laps in the San Blas Islands, had canapes with Kissinger, escargots with Iacocca and tea with Thatcher. We sailed through the Panama Canal and up the Eiffel Tower, into private clubs in England and into exclusive Hollywood hangouts. Do a gilt-edged whiz through the last decade with me, dear, and here's a champagne toast, Cristal Brut, of course, to the next 10!

Andrea Maw, Tracy Rand and Sharlene Ludwig

Shooting Stars: Where The Celebs Hang Out

Other than the very obvious Academy Awards every year, the odd royal wedding that crops up once in a great while, and some flushed and famous jet-set wateringholes, serendipity plays a major role in spotting celebrity faces. Restaurateur Barbara-jo McIntosh spent Christmas in Aspen a few years go and just *happened* to witness a small scene between Marla Maples, a tearful Ivana and the undauntable Donald Trump in a slope-side bistro, and knew there was trouble in Trumpland *weeks* before the *New York Times* reported on it. (And that Fergie and Steve Wyatt were "very good friends.") Liz Taylor found out that Malcolm Forbes was a gayer blade than even she suspected much later than a friend of mine who frequented the same after-hours jazz joint in New York as Mr. Forbes, who appeared dressed in black leather and chains, driving his Harley-Davidson and accompanied by two equally-bedecked-beefcakes—a beautiful muscley blond in helmet-to-heel blue leather, and a brunette hunk all in red.

At the Oscars (or in Westminster Abbey) you can expect the famed and frisky to be hanging from the ceiling. You don't expect, when you are in Trader Vic's for your favorite Bongo Bongo soup, that all 300 pounds of Raymond Burr at the next table will order enough for a family of four while dining alone. Or that actor Christopher Plummer will be in Gerard at Le Meridien one day and on the same small plane beside you the next, flying to the Gulf Islands (and that sure isn't Mrs. P with him). Or that Peter Ustinov will tell you as you stare tongue-tied at his feet in a Hotel Vancouver elevator that his shoes are "12...triple E." I've run into Buckminster Fuller looking for a washroom at a Habitat forum, Timothy Leary buying ice cream in West Vancouver, and the Dalai Lama having dinner in the old Grosvenor Hotel. I spotted Andy Griffiths

Jackie Houston

in a Gastown cafe, Ella Fitzgerald and Harry Belafonte (on different occasions) in the Four Seasons lobby, Barbara Stanwyck in a sporting goods store, Mae West in a hotel restaurant, David Niven on beach in Waikiki, James Garner in an art gallery on 41st Avenue, a Saudi Arabian prince at Arthur Erickson's, and Donald Sutherland in the Denman Inn. So, there's no where special to spot'em. They're *everywhere*.

Have Tux, Will Travel: The All-time Best Escort

Best all-time favorite escort has to be Paul Manning before he married, and again now that he's divorcing. His network spans all factions—his working network, I mean. He was close to Bill Bennett and W.A.C. before him, and he worked with Trudeau. Ron Basford urged him to leave his VP job at B.C. Place to run for Vancouver Center, and Pat Kinsella is a buddy, as are Edgar Kaiser and John Turner. Jack Poole and Peter Brown raised funds for his early-'80s Ottawa bid. He's so charming, you can't stay mad even after he passes your secrets on to the right ears. He is seen at all the right parties, and no matter what is happening in his career, he lands on his good-natured feet. He is seen as a safe escort for wives of absent husbands (he and I did an evening with Prince Charles in our old Ottawa days), and he's trusted by both sides. Significant other out of commish? Need an elbow with tux? Manning's your man.

My Kind Of Town: Vancouver's Best All-time Bash

Really hard to choose, but probably the Inaugural Ball at the courtly new Art Gallery in the fall of 1983. It was $500 a pop per duo—big money in those days—and probably the most elegant evening the city had seen in years. People winged in from everywhere to attend, and then stayed well past the witching hour, not wanting it all to end.

The evening was a Darwinian struggle—survival of the flashiest. The picky paparazzi would not snap just *any* Cinderella scurrying up the grand staircase past those foreboding lions. She had to slip out of a long limo, and she had to provoke a hum of awe. It was a couturier tournament: Givenchy, Dior, Saint Laurent. More than half the women bought something special for the night, and referred to it later as their "gallery opening dress." It was vintage Vancouver; even the old guard who grace such gatherings less and less sensed a once-in-a-lifetimer. They left their cozy dens of antiquity, glanced tolerantly at what posed for blue-blood those days, and sighed contentedly at being part of the previous generation. Old money seems duty-bound to put something back into society, and this understated little zinger made it easy. It was so *grand*. Ex-governor general Roland Michener popped in wearing tails and a flowing white scarf, looking *very* Barrymore. Fran Belzberg wore Mary McFadden, and gallery director Luke Rombout's gorgeous blonde wife Maxine wore Saint Laurent. The evening's chairperson, Maxine Gelfant, wore Oscar de la Renta, Lois Milsom

Mike and Beckie Harcourt

wore a backless Bill Blass, and Natalie Austin reverted to the white frosted number that she wore on the *Britannia* for dinner with the Queen.

There were a smattering of senators, artists the ilk of Toni Onley (with a quarter-million dollars worth of prints upstairs in the gallery), then-mayor Mike Harcourt, star guitarist Liona Boyd, who had flown in from Greece, and then-Canadian ambassador to the U.S., Allan Gotlieb and his very obstreperous ("deliciously offbeat"—too much bubbly as I recall) wife Sondra. There was even what became known as "The Pappas Fur pack" there that night—a fuzzy trio of silly bunnies who wandered round all evening long, steaming toward celebrity in $30,000 worth of mink, lynx and lamb, which they didn't remove even to eat. Peter "The Rabbit" Brown was there (in the days when he still went to these things). He and Ted Turton had donated the Emily Carr Gallery, so his stock could hardly have been higher that night.

As the evening wound down, I remember thinking that the stellar gala with its world-class setting and truly beautiful people could have been Rio or Rome, and that we had finally arrived.

A Moveable Feast: The Best Out-Of-Town Bash

No contest. Puerto Vallarta, off-season, 1982. They jetted in from London, Paris and Rome, from Houston, Dallas and Sante Fe with absolutely no regard at all for the calendar. Birds as exotic and primitive as this slice of Eden itself. They seemed to surprise each other and certainly the townsfolk by showing up out of sync. This "sleepy little fishing village" (the local know-it-alls call it "PV") earned its spot on the *mapa internacional* in the early '60s when Liz and Dick and Ava were headline stealers (as much for their steamy off-scene scenes) and the locals became absolute experts at spilling the beans—refried, no doubt—about who was doing what to whom, senor.

But back to the party. An incredible hillside villa (used off and on by Liz). The sunset performed on cue—pink-and-blue marbled sky, blue sea swallowing orange sun—and so, most assuredly, did the guests. There was Michael Childers, world-famous celebrity shutterbug, just in from a visit with Franco Zeffirelli in Positano, Sylvie Vartan, the French chanteuse formerly married to the Gallic Elvis, Johnny Halliday. And writer Edna O'Brien, floated about in something mis-matched and filmy, like a deranged Blanche Dubois, asking everyone "Do you know me, dear?" only to evaporate before an answer. "Her luggage was stolen" someone offered, as though this would explain both the outfit and poor Edna.

I had my first real encounter with Peter O'Toole that night (I saw him years later in London). He was clearly the star of a very crowded show. He knew how to make an entrance and hold center stage. He was fashionably flaky in a '30s ice cream suit a la Gatsby. He was pasty-faced and his limpid see-through eyes were red-rimmed. His long blond hair was graying and slicked back, his gaunt, bone-rack six-foot-four frame looked older than its 50 years, he smoked continuously, spilling a lot of ash around, and he talked—literately, resonatingly, beautifully—through a great yellow toothed grin. He was one of the most fascinating conversationalist I ever encountered, and the evening was unforgettable.

Midnights At The Oasis: Best Palm Springs Party

"The Springs" as most desert dwellers call it, is a sumptuous little sandbox that over the years has been the winter escape of an incredible roster of B.C. biggies: the Peter Bentleys, the Clarke Bentalls, Bob Bonner, Ron Cliff, Ralph Cunningham, Victor McLean, Ed Phillips, Bill Saunder, Bob Wyman and their families. Sleek Challenger jets—Sam Belzberg's, Jimmy Pattison's—are often parked on nearby runways as you land. The most banal stuff falls into your lap down there. Every manicurist, hairdresser, maitre d' and golf pro has a celebrity story they can't wait to tell, and if you share a housekeeper (should you not have your own live-in) or a masseuse, you know everything. The best PS party I've been to? It would narrow down to two—one a chichi but riotous luncheon that could have been a scene from a Judith Krantz novel, and the other a twilight bash as cool and sophisticated as it gets.

Jim and Jackie Houston's Palm Springs pad in the Las Palmas area is a grand and gated getaway arranged around a central pool and gardens. The Kirk Douglases are neighbours. You would never know from the street what a little Eden lurks behind its garden walls. The happening was Jackie's seasonal ladies luncheon, wherein she gathers a spicy mix of Vancouverites, tossed liberally with a tasty sprinkling of Palm Spring-chickens, and comes up laughing. Jackie herself, a former Miss Washington State who worked with designer Edith Head and auditioned for films with Fernando Lamas, is an epic traveller who is always just back from the pyramids, safari in Africa, the Amazon or Carnival in Rio. "She's like a Harlequin romance heroine," one of her flossie function-eers told me, "but hipper, with more punchlines." A master of spin control, she can tap dance off the top of her head on almost any subject, and she assured me that every woman at that luncheon had an interesting life story.

Paul Manning, Stephanie Southam

Vancouverites Cheryl Herman (who was a McFarlane, then was married to architect Gerald Hamilton and is now married to Buddy Herman) swished in in a beige and gold St. John knit and was long-lost greeted by a cream-suited Diane Forsythe, a former model who was last married to Jim Forsythe, who is skater Dorothy Hamill's father-in-law. From a retired Orange County society writer to one of the stars of _Kismet_ on Broadway, to fabulous flights of fancy named "Pigeon," "Joni" and "Schnitzel," the impossible-to-invent cast of characters just kept popping up all afternoon. And Jackie was dead right about the "interesting life stories." My eyebrows shot up like broken window shades for three hours, and I felt smothered in soap opera bubbles as I careened out the gate that day.

The best cocktail shaker was tossed by Sony's Joe Cohen and his wife Fran at their architecturally perfect _pied_ in The Springs section of Rancho Mirage. There was a jaw-dangling combination of assets there. Army and Navy's

Marlene Cohen with newish hubby Harvey Wexler, investor Gerry Gale, Gordon and Mary Christopher, big-time broker Ted Turton and his wife Deanna, ex-hotelier Mel Zajac, and a lotta $1,000 silk jackets and Italian-tailored suits among the short formals and couturier south-western Indian designs. The exquisite food, flown in for the evening, was no more indignous to the desert than the picture perfect guests. It was a *Palm Springs Life* magazine cover.

Hooray For Hollywood: The Best Oscar Party

The very first Oscars I ever went to, in 1988, just happened to be the big 60th Annual Academy Awards, so it was special for me, but a big deal, too, to the 6,000 other attendees, some of whom hadn't put in an appearance for some time.

"It's our track meet," Katharine Hepburn told me later, "however artificial." Limos aligned, red carpet unfurled, helicopters whirring away, flash-bulbs popping, fans screaming and the dress code—wear everything, and what you can't, carry.

That night it was Charlton Heston (with surely the world's worst toupee); Audrey Hepburn, splendid and sweet; Liza Minnelli as Batman's wife in a splendid red cape, Omar Sharif (I hadn't seen him since London at a party with Trudeau); Candice Bergen, whom I would see months later in the Russian Tea Room in New York; Daryl Hannah with her platinum teeth and hair; Mel Gibson, Patrick Swayze, Tom Selleck and Michael Douglas, all there for the gasping, up close and personal. Kevin Costner didn't have a patch on Sean Connery, who actually buckled my knees that night with those blackbird-bright brown eyes. Faye Dunaway, Glenn Close and even Olivia De Havilland didn't touch the sheer powerful presence of Cher. In subsequent years, the night would spill forth Jack Nicholson, Dustin Hoffman, Michael Caine, Geena Davis, Jane Fonda, Jody Foster and Jacqueline Bisset for my star-struck scrapbook. And Michael Jackson and Madonna, Julia Roberts and Tom Cruise. But in all my Oscar nights they paled in comparison to Gregory Peck and Sophia Loren (who were *everything* I expected) and my all-time fandom treat Sean Connery. Shallow *is* my life.

Ante Up: Charity Events You Don't Dare Miss

Not so long ago, big-buck charities had the black-tie beat all to themselves. Now, scratch any local hospital or a struggling arts group, and you'll find gala-eventing wanna-be. The showier benefactor-bonding events tend to be more cultural than cause-oriented. (It's hard to deal with the homeless or the hungry while scoffing caviar and smoked salmon in your Christian Lacroix) Charity may begin at home, but it still prefers to be seen to be done rather publicly. I guess Endeavor (which calls itself Canada's largest, most successful one-night dinner auction) is the local grandaddy of them all. _Very_ Establishment, it used to cost $100 a couple; it's $225 per head this year. For sheer showiness and good will (it does benefit 14 charities), it's a must-do marathon that lasts a full seven hours.

The next biggie, and a pure elegant extravaganza it is, is the Children's Hospital Foundation's Crystal Ball. It's $500 per crystalline couple, and it pulls in a tony 380 sparkle-and-shiners. The inaugural ball raised over $400,000 five years ago, and financial heavy-hitters like Sam Belzberg and Joe Segal ante-ed up big time for a heart-tugging cause. It brings out the kind of selective crowd that doesn't just go to everything.

The same goes for Arts Umbrella's Splash, which pulls in a happening young crowd; it's backed up by a group of smart and savvy women who really know how to merchandise their cause.

Top Of The Heap: The Best Whistler Party

Certainly one of the most show-offy smashes I've been to at that St. Moritz-for-the-locals was one of the first of Whistler's Celebrity Ski Invitationals, which pulled in at last 30 Hollywood types with their tips up. Half of Vancouver and all of Whistler seemed beside themselves to be beside the likes of Cliff Robertson, Barbara Eden, Susan Blakely, David Foster and all. Alan Thicke seemed miffed that the squealy teeny-boppers were only interested in Kirk Cameron and not him. Robert Redford and Paul Newman had skied the previous day (Redford was the better skier), and I have never seen the village so buzzed. Abby Dalton was better dressed at the razzle-dazzle Blitzkrieg black-tie blow-out, but Barbara Eden's full-length lynx was impressive. (She wouldn't _dare_ nowadays.) Linda Thompson Jenner was totally tacko, Cliff Robertson had the most class, and Kevin Dobson was the most regular guy. Actor Richard Roundtree pronounced Whistler "as good as Aspen only not so snooty." Speaker of the House (in those days) John Reynolds chatted up Long John Baldry; Herb Capozzi trotted out his tired one-liners; and Terry David Mulligan tried to show Hollywood how hip we were. My tablemates included Cassandra Peterson ("Elvira, Mistress of the Night"), and even without her black vampire wig she was pretty scary, but a font of Hollywood info.

The Royal Wedding: Memories of Andy and Fergie

In the summer of '86, I headed off to Blighty along with half the civilized world to attend the wedding of Fergie and Andrew. I had a very good friend in Buck House who got me an incredible seat within mere yards of the timely twosome. By the appointed hour, 1,800 of the bride and groom's nearest and dearest had edged their way into Westminster Abbey.

It was here a Mrs. Peregrine Chadwick-Healey, there a Lieutenant-Colonel

Seymour Gilbert-Denham. Over there the Duchess of Abercorn and beyond her that pesky Nancy Reagan. Old Etonians and peers peered as eagerly as the rest of us. Various viscounts, earls, lords and ladies were sprinkled about, plus a whole passel of dukes and duchesses. And, of course, *all* the royal family. As you will remember, Wills was a little devil, Di smiled and Charles frowned. The wedding went off without a hitch. Bells pealed, bugles fanned their fare, and privileged participants sought out their chauffeurs. I had promised CBC TV that I would chat a bit for Canadians back home to bring some local color to the day. Little did I know this would be shot from a scaffolding 20 feet up so that the Abbey would be the backdrop, or that in mid-prattle about who-where-what, the bells would start pealing, my sound man wold tear off his earphones in pain, and I would be forced several decibels up to a near-scream, looking like a demented Italian sailor (in what I thought had been my smart hat). Truly one of life's low moments. Barbie.

Dinner For Eight: The Ultimate Guest List—Pierre Trudeau

Regardless of what you think of his politics he has one of the most fascinating minds I've ever run into. Get him talking about that year he spent going around the world checking out the occult, or what he thinks is Kurasawa's best film and why.

Peter Ustinov The best storyteller ever, and he will tell you them in dialect. A true ambassador of the world, a leading expert on Russia, and one of the funniest men ever.

Barbra Streisand Sensitive, bright, opinionated, but she can back it up. Is into everything from color psychology to where to buy great antique clothes.

Shirley Maclaine Right off the wall in her approach to things; gives the term "open-minded" new meaning. Curious about everything, and feisty. She means what she says.

Baroness Philippine Rothschild As jumpy as a java junkie, she's a dotty and dear whirling dervish, an ex-actress who after years of faux-pas-ing her way through life, doesn't give a damn anymore. She's been there, done that, so you can relax and not try to impress her.

Arthur Erickson Knows absolutely everyone, has been everywhere from the hot spots to the spiritual, and can talk about both so you all share it.

Sean Connery No reason...this is my dinner party, remember?

Ta Ta Darling, And Remember

As grandmama always said, "Be alert, Try to please. Marry money."

You can't have everything—where would you put it?

Money is not the key to happiness, but if you have enough, you can get one made.

See no evil, hear no evil, speak no evil—and you are no friend of mine.

Stay out of hot water—unless it's an 18-jet Jacuzzi on Mustique.

Don't eat health foods. We need all the preservatives we can get.

All the world's a stage, but some of us have trouble learning our parts.

Sincerity is everything. Once you can fake that, you've got it made.

Always tell the truth—but not all of it.

If you can't say anything nice, sit next to me.

Valerie.

THE YEAR 1993

THE WAY OF ALL FLASH
A tell-all Florida update, from the old-money power plays of Palm Beach to the low-key loafers of Key West.

THE SOUND OF MONEY
The third annual Lover's Ball opened up the treasure chests for the VSO's benefit.

WINNER'S DINNER
On the road to 24 Sussex Drive, our Kim stirs a Campbell soup of Vancouver bankers, barristers, and brass hats.

MOGULS ON THE MOUNTAIN
The VSO rolls into Whistler for a hot flamenco fund-raiser.

THE VALERIES AND THE GLORY
The Valeries. A review of months past. Parties, people, clothes, parties. The important stuff.

THE WAY OF ALL FLASH

Barbie Darling,

Frittered off to Florida for a fabled fix, those mid-winter melancholies being what they are. And lest you think the Sunshine State is all blue hair and blue herons, dear heart, it's also underrated treasures and overrated pleasures, and more salacious slices of scandal and hits of hyper-luxury than even I anticipated.

Let me start with Palm Beach—a place with a palpable past if ever. That gilded ghetto had Kennedys, Kimberlys and Cushings, Phippses (we have our own Vancouver branch, of course), Fords and DuPonts, Auchinclosses, Wentworths and Vanderbilts. And tripping over a Trump or two (they are *so* nouveau), or spotting a Pierpont in the bougainvillea, a Weyerhaeuser in the frangipani, or a Bronfman in a banyan tree was as easy as finding out that the smart little lunch you just had at Club Colette cost as much as your return airfare. (I should have twigged when I asked for water, and they replied, "What year?") I thought I had heard it all. You know: "In Palm Beach, they distribute care baskets to people with only one tennis court" and "The only fast food is Kentucky fried pheasant" and "The daily papers are delivered by polo pony." My dear, how close they were.

Several old families here are tied into "generational" money passed down for several hundred years. And 10-figure inheritances are no more out of line than $10 million mansions fit for monarchs. Old money, old names, big houses and blue blood may live ruddy cheek by flabby jowl next to retired captains of industry, statesmen, professionals and financiers but, by George, they don't have to like it. Trust me, darling: born-with-a-bundle is still best.

"Those ever-popular triplets Privilege, Wealth and Power crop up everywhere," one old Guardette told me. (You can hardly beat a Vanderbilt married to a Whitney.) The more you look into it, it's a cosmetics fortune or publishing scion here, a chemical empire married to department store megabucks there. And there are even brand names behind the grand names. James Kimberly's millions came from the Kimberly-Clark conglomerate. The next time you use a Kleenex, you are helping indulge the playboy-sportsman's love of fine wine, gourmet food and motor racing. He's divorced and lives alone, but forget it darling—he's 83, and his last divorce blew (Kleenex, of course) Palm Beach society's mind. Colgate-Palmolive's Stanley Rumbough was married to Dina Merrill (Post Grape Nuts and E.F. Hutton). Budweiser beer heiress Diana Holt-Busch has the dearest little Palm Beach pad, but she is usually on safari in Africa or playing bridge around the world. In 1882, Sue

Whitmore's great grandfather invented Listerine, which has made billions for the fresh-breathed heiress. Zuita Askton's first husband invented Q-tips, and while you stuck _that_ in your ear, the company made hundreds of millions. Robert Fisher's "Body by Fisher" frames for General Motors lifestyled him right into an exotic $7 million Spanish-tiled mansion with exotic gardens full of jasmine, ivy, sandalwood and wild orchids. Now, he's not to be confused with the other Fisher—Max Martin Fisher, a charity bigwig worth the nice round $330 million he made in oil.

"You can be born with it, earn it or marry it," I was told, "and some have turned that into a career." The ex-Mrs. Charles Revson (Revlon Cosmetics), now Mrs. Anky Johnson, ex-ed four others and managed to "house-keep" rather well every time, if you catch my drift. Estee Lauder's lair (she earned it herself, rare but true) gives the neighbors a real run for their real estate. It's one of the better abodes, backing onto the vast property of the famous Breakers Hotel, and she uses it to entertain visiting royalty, being a cosmetics queen herself, I guess.

But it's casino and real estate magnate Donald Trump who owns Mar-a-lago, the most prestigious, most expensive piece of Palm Beach. He only pops down in high season, and he's trying to get the 17-acre, $25-million estate subdivided for sale (he bought it for a fifth of that). The divine Ivana gets it one month per year—it's in her divorce settlement—and she holds an annual "girls only" house party. They pack up their furry mules, totter aboard the private jet and fly on down. Then it gets hectic: aerobics, massage, pedicure, lip gloss, dinner—just one thing after another. Only the likes of Lynn Wyatt, Barbara Walters, Anne Bass and Georgette Mosbacher get to go. "I must say the food wasn't as good as last time," one sniffed. "She had these wonderful lobsters, and everyone was waiting for them."

"Still," gloated one non-invited grande dame, "she got half the fortune and all of the credit, so she gave other soon-to-be-exes hope."

The Kennedy house, on the other hand, was _not_ looking great. The helicopter pad built for JFK is somewhat potholed, the house needs paint, the carpets are thread-bare, it sports sea-air faded furniture, and the 50-foot pool is full of pond scum. (No Barbie, I am not talking about the guests.) The kindest thing to say—and one unusually tolerant neighbor said it— is that "like true patricians, they display disinterest in conspicuous consumption." Besides, it is supposedly being fixed up and sold soon.

Now, as befits a resort created by the very rich for the very rich, Palm Beach studiously ignores trends that sweep the outside world. Strolling through the Bath and Tennis Club (PB's most exclusive private club) is like watching an old movie colorized by Ted Turner. One finds old Palm Beach plutocrats in immaculately cut blazers ($3,000 from Trillion on Worth Avenue), cream linen shirts, Turnbull and Asser silk ties or ascots, knife-edged worsted pants and Gucci loafers sans socks. (These men lunch at the White House, appear in *Time* and *Newsweek*, and they're always "on.") Ladies wear large hats and three strands of clam-sized pearls at the beach, and they change into diamonds and little silk dresses for bridge.

Evenings, it's full-length ball gowns (the average socialite has 24) and tiaras— everyone has a tiara. Really. Things seem to be jaw-clenchingly proper, "there is no such thing as Too Much," and "outsiders never seem to get it quite right." Although there are nautical clothes everywhere, nobody actually sails, and those gleaming white ocean-going yachts stay docked except for sunset cocktails. Polo is still a reigning sport; Prince Charles arrives periodically for a chukker or two, and at times the town is swarming with titled Europeans ("Euro-trash" muttered one local), Argentines and South Africans. PBers who own polo ponies, but have never been near one, sport jodhpurs and silk shirts for the duration.

What else can I tell you, Barbie? Peter Duchin still plays his Steinway for the smarter Palm Beach parties; an "average" Palm Beach wedding costs $90,000; a debutante's coming out, $26,000; and 38 percent of PBers over 40 have had plastic surgery. No one is called what they were really named: the women are Bunny, Deedee, Muffy, Loulie, Chessy, Tolly, LaLa, Bus—or worse. Household staff (if the house has 20 or more rooms) cost an average $34,000 per month in salaries, and charity galas, the favored Palm Beach "strut," raised $25 million last year. (I sat beside the Kenan family at dinner one night at The Breakers—they own the hotel and half of Miami and have given, I heard, over $40 million to their favorite causes.) A ton of Canadians own here: Charles Bronfman, Paul Desmarais, Robert Campeau and Conrad Black. Brian and Mila pop down whenever they can.

Au Bar, the scene of the Kennedy kerfuffle is no big deal. It's a large, members-only club ($300 per year) in a shopping center open from 10 p.m. till 4 in the morning (big mistake), and it was in danger of closing before *la scandale* Kennedy. Now biz is booming, and they even sell Teddy/Willy T-shirts.

I stayed at the intimate, elegant Brazilian Court Hotel, scene of many a great star-struck bash (and a fave of my hero, Dominick Dunne). The multimillion-dollar Kravis Center for the Performing Arts opened the last day of my stay, and the after-party was at the Brazilian Court. It was all paper-white faces (no face-lift in its right mind tans, darling) and $18,000 Bob Mackie beaded dresses from Sara Fredrick's on Worth Avenue. Everyone danced for the cameras and showed up the next day in the "shiny sheet," as

Palm Beach's society paper is called (many are posed, but few are chosen). "There are so many dances here" one PBer declared, "because flirting on the dance floor is permissible, and it's a great time for a little judicious social climbing," said a TK. Says it all for me. Barbie. It looked like the only game in town.

Skedaddled off to Key West for some downtime before heading home. _Nothing_ happens there, dear. (Well, it _may_, but not during my stay.) It's funky, faded and fey. Everything smells not-quite-dry, which is what it is, and one takes leisurely tours of things—who can move in this heat? I now know more about Harry Truman and his "Little White House," Tennessee Williams and his depressing writing travails, and Hemingway, his house and his many-toed cats than even I, on a slow news day, care to. The sunsets, flaming inferno-colored, were world-class, but unless you're into bar-hopping, loud music and people you hope to never run into again, skip this Key, darling. It's so perfectly awful, it's like stuffing a capon with larks: if you aren't careful, you can spoil the rich effect.

Off to Orlando and the mind-blowing, five-diamond Hyatt Regency Grand Cypress Resort. This $110 million baby has 45 holes of Jack Nicklaus-designed golf, a 21-acre lake with sailboats, canoes and paddleboats, 12 tennis courts, an equestrian center, a 45-acre Audubon preserve, a helipad and one of the world's largest swimming pools. The sky-soaring, 20-story atrium lobby is flooded with lush tropical forest, a multimillion-dollar art collection, paintings and bronze sculptures, life-sized carved deer studded with semiprecious stones, and gargantuan flower sprays bursting out everywhere. (And filled on a good day with a Mel Gibson, a Joan Rivers, Bob Hope, Diane Sawyer, Billy Joel with Christie Brinkley, or a Michael Jackson, who is Captain Eo at the stones-throw-away Epcot Center.) My room overlooked the whole gorgeous layout—with eight black swans-a-swimming below, miles of deep green tree tops and the sound of waterfalls. There were fruit and flowers and the fluffiest towels, orchids in the bathroom, face cloths folded as fans, and chockies on the pillow alongside a single rose. I had the best time. The place was pure fantasy. Now if only I hadn't worn my white safari pantsuit, I wouldn't have looked like a valet parker when I left.

Ta Ta Darling, and remember: No matter what happens, there is always someone who knew it would.

Valerie.

THE SOUND OF MONEY

Barbie Darling,

Dusted off my dancing shoes and twinkle-toed over to the third annual VSO's Lover's Ball, held in the Hotel Vancouver's Pacific Ballroom. It was a sterling silver society sortie, dear heart, with a definite upper-crust thrust. And filled to the ornate rafters it was, with gilt-edged corporate sponsors, gala helmspersons and the very charity spark plugs who make these glitter-dusted affairs rich pickings for the city's cultural treasure chests.

"Some enchanted evening," I heard from the Prince Charming (not mine) behind me as we swept up the royal-purple, gold and flower-swagged marble staircase past the Vancouver Academy of Music's pint-sized Paganinis, who were lining the steps, playing their little hearts out on their tiny violins. "This is pure froth for hard-core romantics," he went on while a small group of us melted into the champagne reception, crossing a mist-encircled drawbridge, past knights in shining armor, and through an enchanted forest into Sleeping Beauty's castle. The giant center-of-the-room ice sculpture (a fiery dragon), the golden harpist (who played like an angel) and Sleeping Beauty and her prince (a picture-book-perfect live tableau at one end of the chandeliered anteroom) worked like Merlin's magic on the crowd.

"I guess a little of the old glitz, glamor, smoke and mirrors can really boost a needy budget," noted one corporate capo to another as they sipped and surveyed the packed and happy room. "And I daresay it's a good way to dip into a little luxury without feeling guilty," responded the other, "but even with the tax write-off, my wife tallied up what we would have spent last year if we had accepted all the 'should-do's' we should have, and do you know, we could have dropped $55,000!"

Bumped headfirst into arch-architect Arthur Erickson as I was social-circling the room. Tanned to the teeth, he had just winged in from Bombay, Singapore, Malaysia or all of the above (you can't expect me to keep his pit stops straight, Barbie). But best of all, he had been to Banta, where Fergie and the girls went to hide out with Johnny Bryan, after she was spotted at the oh-so-secluded Amanpuri resort by, among others, Vancouver's own Dick and Lana Underhill, who were grabbing a few days alone away from a lawyers' convention. I tell you, Babs, that royal red-head can't do anything without somebody tripping over her. I now know—I didn't ask—that in spite of being Her Royal Dumpiness, she has no cellulite, freckles absolutely *everywhere*, and her darling daughters just adore ner.

Arthur far-flung in with longtime co-hort Lois Milsom, who, like him, has been almost everywhere, and knows almost everyone. She was looking very ex-Conover model, which she is, dressed in, you guessed it, the same old Givenchy (soon to join her treasured Bill Reid bracelet, which she donated to the Smithsonian or the Museum of Civilization or whatever) and a great new upswept hair-do. "She does manage to make recherche *so* nouveau again," noted one of those women who manage to wield cheekbones and zingers at the same time. Spotted society's favorite decorator William Switzer and his wife Frances chatting with symphony supporters Moreno and Dagmar Gabay (haven't seen them since that charity ciao-down I went to last fall at Umberto's in Whistler).

"Just looking at that outfit gives you glitter goose-bumps," I heard as I turned to check out Leslie Diamond's little silver-and-black shimmerer. She was eyelash-deep in conversation with Hildegard Cavelti, whose husband's laudable baubles were gracing any number of the room's swanlike necks, ears and wrists. Yes, I know swans don't have wrists and ears, Barbie—bear with me, alright?

Followed Bernard Ledun through the mirrored ballroom doors as we were called in to dinner. If you were casting the soap-opera role of a handsome consul general from France, you couldn't do better than this silver-tongued (in French *and* English) charmer under whose consular privilege the evening's champagne, wines, and liqueurs were imported. (*Tres importante* to evenings like this, *ma chere.*)

Amin Lalji, Hank Stackhouse, Bill Dalton and Ernest Hui, Nazmeen Lalji, Cindy Stackhouse, Starr Dalton and Barbara Hui

Spied the Baronesses von Pfetten One and Two through my table's giant vine-entwined candelabra. The gorgeous Stephanie was wearing a white lace and fuchsia silk Catherine Regehr, topped with the dearest little $30,000 necklace-and-earring set of tube sapphires, diamonds and 18-karat gold to be auctioned off later. And Heidi, no schlepping beauty herself, was top-to-toe in a jewel-belted, champagne-colored Mary McFadden. She was off to Joan Carlisle-Irving's little hideaway in Mustique for a week. "Joanie must have her hands full, now that K.C. Irving has died," noted the woman behind me. "Five billion dollars is *such* a lot to divide, even when you're divorced out of the family. I mean, those gorgeous children deserve *something* to remember their

293

grandpa by." She did go on, Barbie, but all I heard was "18th-richest family in the world...."

It was a great chance to check out the exquisite and exquisitely peopled ballroom, although flickering candlelight, huge sprays of flowers and hot-and-cold-running waiters (black-tied, white-gloved) made things a bit dodgy. The corporate tables ($5,000 per well-rounded circle of 10) were closest to the dance floor, and to maestro Sergiu Comissiona's concert performance of Tchaikovsky's *Sleeping Beauty* ballet waltz.

In just one swing-through, I spied the Hong Kong Bank of Canada's bright and ever-so-everywhere Bill Dalton and his wife Starr; Polygon's powerhouse Michael Audain; Richardson Greenshields' Bob Fairweather and his wife Kazue; Bentall Corp.'s vice president Graydon Hayward and his wife Shirley; and financier Robert Grey and his wife Glenda. Sighted as well: oil and gas-man Richard Bowes (with the smashing Tatiana Rose), Ruth and Robin Garvin from the VSO board of directors, realtors Heather and Bill Notman, the Vancouver International Airport Authority's non-flighty David Emerson, barrister-publisher Ron Stern and his fund-rousing wife Janet, and The Lazy Gourmet's Susan Mendelson who didn't exactly turn up her nose at *la belle au bois* dormant dessert (which is, of course, Sleeping You-Know-Who in French).

The most flamboyant couple on the dance floor was the blonde and beauteous Ewa Taubenfligel and her husband George (of Mercedes-Benz Canada); they looked like a Harlequin romance cover come to life. The most romantic line I heard was when the maestro's wife Robinne kissed her husband Sergiu for the cameras, and turned and said, "I really mean that, too." The best dance-floor line? Middle age is "when anything new in life is likely to be a symptom." And the best powder room frothball (a lot of half-time odometers got turned back there) was after an unsuspecting soul had departed and a gruesome twosome turned back to the mirror with a chatty-catty: "Let's just say she shops with more enthusiasm than savvy, shall we?"

The quick and classy Nazi Khosrowshahi won the Chantilly race in lace—jet-black. The De Silva family (jewelry-designer Shelton, who had donated the pricey auction pieces, his wife Lanka and daughter Patra) flashed a gemdom's ransom in supernova-sized sparklers (kind of gives a new meaning to "home shopping network," doesn't it?). And the evenings chairman, Paula Startup (as pale as a Victorian grande dame in her long ivory silk), did more than bring friends to the Lover's Ball. She brought her whole family: husband David, daughters Cathy and Susan, and son-in-law Lyall Knott (who is *very* Tory now with his new government appointment).

Small things considered, Barbie (and they were), the evening was detail-perfect. Bloomin' loverly. Who but the VSO knows better how to say it with music? That night they just tried a little ardor.

Ta Ta Darling, and remember, people don't live on bread alone. They need to be buttered up every now and then.

Valerie.

WINNER'S DINNER

Barbie Darling,

Shimmied off to Kimmie's din din, where 2,100 friends, fans and foes plunked down $150 each to break bread and clink glasses with the very honorable Kim Campbell at the largest political benefit ever held in B.C. The Little Bunfest That Grew (it started off as 500 of her closest and mostest) pinballed into the big time when it became clear that what folks had here was a whole lot of precedent-setting goin' on. Would she be the youngest/first woman prime minister ever—and from our very own Vancouver? My dear, there was more intrigue bubbling in the Trade and Convention Centre that night than a boatload of Borgias could cook up.

Lele Mathisen, Kim Campbell and Diane Norton

To deft observers of the scene, the national manhunt for a good woman led to one of the most pyrotechnic pre-dinner receptions they had witnessed. To say that the enthusiastically assembled were a mixed bag was like saying we had a shower or two in April. An extraordinary cast of characters threw themselves into scene-checking little factions, from a cheerleading cross section of dyed-in-their-blue-wool pinstripes Conservatives to brand new bandwagoneers. The site was littered with latent and longstanding Liberals, lobbyists, lawyers and looky-loos, up close and cozy with corporate, politically motivated, marketing-wise strategizers right in there with hard-core grass-rooters. Hesitant or curious or gung-ho committed, they were there to check out this feisty phenomenon. Canada's first-ever female defence minister, attorney-general, justice minister and now prime minister was recent memory's most anticipated guest-who's-coming-to-dinner.

"Migawd, I could have a collective hack-and-flack attack just looking

295

around here," noted one Tory party hot-shot to the faceless dullard beside him. "There are enough PR and media people here to launch a coup d'etat."

"And enough big business and bank clout to finance it," nodded the know- it-all beside them. "In my little swing-through from the bar," he continued, "I spotted heavies from Cominco and Canfor, Air Canada and Fletcher Challenge, from Teck and Price Waterhouse, from Bull Housser Tupper and Burson-Marsteller to Hill & Knowlton and National Trust, with B.C. Gas, Tel, Sugar and Central Unions in between."

It was true, Barbie. The check-out-Campbell curiosity actually had beak-and-claw legal eagles in somewhat civil conversation. Davis & Co. was speaking to Ladner Downs, Farris Vaughan was head-to-heading with Stikeman Elliott, and Campney & Murphy was huddled with Clark Wilson. Big business of all stripes certainly bought into the evening. But so did Coopers & Lybrand, Peat Marwick, Burns Fry, Park Georgia, the Imperial Bank, and Colliers, Macaulay Nicolls. What was billed as the dearest little love-in for our baby-booming "local girl does good" quickly took on nationalistic proportions. As soon as the Lotus Land orchid with the stem of steel poll-vaulted into favored front-runner status, why, best buddesses who had been (the pre-Kim) Avril Phaedra's friends since toddlerhood had their soft silk shoulder pads elbowed aside by the big boys in suits, who flex instinctively from old habit at the mere whiff of political clout.

"She's cuddly Auntie Kim," I heard as Campbell was bagpiped in. "She could be your sweetheart, your sister, your best friend," the pundit behind me burbled on as we applauded the poster child for PM while she bear-hugged and cheek-pecked her way into the enormous room. "That's if your best friend has a three-digit IQ, plays the cello, is multilingual and has a fetish for facts," he droned on as the room raised its collective lorgnette and peered at the dinner's tirelessly table-hopping diva.

It was a most movable feast, Barbie. Between courses, everyone tumbled out of their seats and pit-stopped shamelessly. Between the baby Lolla Rossa salad and the perfect poached salmon, Madam Popeye ("I yam what I yam") worked the room and slowly coaxed the crowd open like a time-lapse rose. Playing "I spy" for the rest of us was socially forgivable this once, and certainly politically correct. Politicos Mary Collins (who in her patterned suit looked like an ambulatory urn of exotic flowers), Russ Fraser ("Mr. Socred-Liberal Coalition"), Stumpin' Tom Siddon, and a buoyant and brightly beaded Rita Johnston all shook hands and slapped backs at full-tilt election pitch. Old-time Vancouver Establishmentarians the Victor McLeans and the John Spencers shared airs with Victoria Cross-holder Cecil Merritt, John Pearkes (son of a former lieutenant-governor), and the indubitable Davie Fulton, PC, OC, QC.

Artsy-crafters like Joe (anything-but) Average (who painted the most favored Campbell portrait so far), Martha Sturdy, who designed the now-famous Kim pin, and artist Sam Carter, who flooded the tables with spring color, happily mixed and mingled. And a hard core of hard-ball players mealed and dealed in pulsing pockets throughout the night, "gauging whether to cast their cash upon the coffers," one wag suggested.

As to whether the keynoter hit all the hot buttons in her speech to the committed, converted and convertible, let's just say she successfully dodged a hail of plaudits. There was much socio-political pondering in the lengthy hallways after. "Too soft," I heard on one side. "I didn't expect flowcharts and graphs, but I wanted her to address the deficit and not defend the budget."

"It was wonderful," I heard in my other ear, "like one of her old poly-sci classes." And in-between, "Behind all that camouflage of all that manufactured heat, you have the feeling that there is definitely something simmering at its vortex. She's got the flair and chutzpah to carry it off. I hope she gets there."

As I headed off into the heady night, I looked back to watch her lay a witching hour hands-on goodnight and thank-you to the last of over 2,000 people. Come hype, hoopla or high water, Barbie, she was firmly at the helm of her one-of-a- kind Kim-ship. Whether she could sail it home to 24 Sussex Drive remained to be seen.

Blasted off to the Vancouver Museum's fourth Black and White Ball at the Hotel Vancouver. A now-annual wham-glam affair, it seems to inspire scores of city slickers—this year a ballroom-busting 720 fashion-flaunters to give the night their best uncolor-coded shot.

"It looks like a high-gloss fashion shoot," noted one klieg-light couple as they flashed teeth (his) and diamonds (hers) up the staircase and into the flashy fray. "Some of these tuxes get trotted out for 'walkies' more often than their doggies do," the multi-carated one continued as they swept in. And more than a few have obviously taken a vow of opulence, I thought, as I scanned a spun sugar sea of cost-be-damned couture.

"They ought to clean it you know," I was told with finger-wagging force while trying to sip and survey. "The museum," added the portly-courtly Gerald Hamilton. "I built it 25 years ago, and they have never done a thing to it." I turned to note a red tapestry vest under the tux. No surprise, Barbie, since I always see him in a silk dressing gown no matter _what_ he wears. And mere feet away, fellow architect and _homme du monde_ Arthur Erickson, just back from receiving an award in Mexico, was in the midst of a full-fleshed tale, miming all the parts. "Boy, the last thing he will ever remind you of is anyone else you've ever met," I heard from a rail-thin, absurdly-angled woman, "but I hate that good-sport grin of his. He's been so underappreciated."

Did a swift eyeballing around the room, Barbie, and spotted a stunning display of vamp and camp. A number of the whiz-bang wives who work on these cultural committees are ex-models who know more than a thing or two about sizzle, among them Tracy Rand and Rebecca Mackay. Joan Carlisle-Irving had just jetted in from the mysterious east, B.C. Gas's Bob and Bobbie Kadlec were just heading off to trek Nepal, Howard Phipps III and his wife Terry are still revelling in their newish son and heir, and power mortgage-broker Dee Dee Sung's Armani tux gave any ball gown there a marathon run for its considerable money.

Smoke machines were churning out their swirling vapors as we all swept in for a little roast rack of lamb and an even rarer evening. Shakers come prepared to party for this gilt-edged get out. It's a less-uptight crush than most. Nobody stays put, everybody gets out dancing, and they jump headfirst into the auction

Starr and Bill Dalton

action with the hope of snaffling anything from a Sam Black painting (the ball's chair Cora Wills' proud and prolific papa) to a $5,000 shopping spree for trendy trinkets at Cartier. And midnight still finds the jammed and jamming dance floor a picture-perfect braid of black-and-white focus pocus. All the right moves, but don't let *me* color your thinking.

Ta Ta Darling, and remember, I'm trying not to repeat gossip lately. If someone doesn't get it the first time, that's just too bad.

Valerie.

MOGULS ON THE MOUNTAIN

Barbie Darling,

Roared off to the Vancouver Symphony Orchestra's Country Splendour gala in Whistler at Mario Enero's La Rua Restaurante. Billed as an evening of "fine food and flamenco," the Spanish flair was *everywhere*, right down to the *grande coinola* dropped and raised for a good cause. It was a brilliant recreation of out-of-town theater, and it looked like half of Vancouver's tony players had brought their swell selves to the mountains. More than a hundred "chichi culturati," as that snobby friend of yours calls anyone who patronizes the arts, dressed down and partied up for the flashy fiesta.

"You'd think they hadn't seen each other in years," noted a very Zsa Zsa Gaborian woman to a small pointy-headed man in a blazer. "Surely these people run into each other in town all the time," she continued, as I eased my way past small knots of air-kissers who were greeting each other like long lost _compadres_.

The crush of compassionate _fashionistas_ crowding the entryway bar of Mario's little Blackcomb bistro was in full bubbling flight by the time I arrived, waving across the crowd to each other like touring heads of state in open-air Rolls-Royces.

"Getting everybody all together is like trying to herd cats," I heard a silver-haired smoothie chuckle as I worked my way across the room, "but they have such a great time once they get here," he concluded as I reached Ted Nebbeling, Whistler's blond and boyish mayor and one of the evening's patrons. He was head-to-heading with Board of Trade boss David McLean and the blonde and bubbly Brenda, who is vice chair of the McLean Group. Mayor Ted was up to his baby blues that week with "Shirazic Park," as the locals are calling the huge hole behind the Keg restaurant in Whistler Village that

Dave and Pamela Richardson

had been well and truly dug by Larco Investments' Shiraz Lalji before work stopped over the dearest little multi-million-dollar technicality. Everyone _that_ night was on their best-behavior tippy-toes about voicing their opinions. Still, I did hear one of the cheekier waiters suggest that the crater would make a great toboggan run for the winter. Or a holding tank for all those Larco shopping centers and hotels.

Big-time taxmaster Ian Scobell filed in with his wife, Joan, who was a sparkly symphonette in silver and white. "Ian must have gotten his nights mixed," offered a mustachioed mountain mogul as he checked out the mellow Mr. Scobell's checkered-flag shirt, which would have been so apropos back in town during the Indy race. Very Conservative lawyer Lyall Knott appeared positively _sportif_ in a greenish glen plaid suit and, of course, a matching tie. (Barbie, have you forgotten _how_ conservative?) One of the Knotty one's prestigious clients, the Hongkong Bank of Canada's president, Bill Dalton, and his wife, Starr, who are big symphony supporters, were hosting a lively table of eight, including the Knotts and the Laljis.

Whistler Mountain Ski Corporation's tall timber Maury Young and his wife, Mary, passed on Mario's tempting tapas—among them shrimp the size of hand puppets—but everyone else dug in while flamenco dancer Rosario Ancer stamped her little feet to husband Victor's steamy strings. The Latin rhythm really eased everyone into a great mood and people were being more theatrically dramatic than usual, even for this crowd. Cartier's Ani and Daniel Feuermann swept in to dinner, Ani in a rose cashmere Mondi serape, which she flung off at one point only to discover that she was wearing the same fabulous Donna Karan frill-of-it-all blouse as Lois Milson. Thank the gods of haute couture that Donna dear designed it in more than one fabric. Madame Milson, who has been nearly as many places as her fabled luggage, was busily brushing

Lyall and Susan Knott

up her Italian in weekly classes along with David and Pam Richardson and Hiroko Ainsworth, who were all planning a *leetle sojorno* to Italy this fall. Too late for Umberto's wedding in Tuscany, but I'm sure they remember that Vancouver's own Deborah and Francesco Guilini are still Milano-ing it big time. (Deborah is apparently photographer to the Milanese smart set and Francesco is managing his famous conductor-father's career.)

Spotted Vancouver Symphony board-woman Darlene Spevakow wearing just what the pharmacist ordered—that's husband Bob, who is a Shoppers Drug Mart franchisee. Her tunic sweater was plastered with the names and poster faces of great operas (a *Carmen* here, a *Puccini* there), and her slim black pants were studded with silver button-coins down the side like a bullfighter's. "I hope those aren't Hermes mariachi suede calf pants," noted one nearby green-eyed prima donna, "because they were $6,375 when I looked at them in Paris last month, and *that* was U.S.!" (These evenings have such a divine energy to them, darling. I love them all.)

The symphony's new general manager, Graeme Page, swept into his place at the dinner table in shades of black and blue, a sure sign the formerly troubled, structurally reassembled VSO is slowly being bench-pressed out of the red and into shape. Page himself is sort of salt and peppery, with a wind-sheered jaw and dimples deep enough to store spent cartridges in. He seems much liked by both the board and the band.

Over Mario's *apertivos*, Mediterranean pasta and *cordera castila*—let me dispel you of your suburban ennui, dear heart; that's rack of lamb to you—I had a leisurely chance to check out the evening's high-altitude troupers. The very successful Herbert Menten and his gracious wife, Maria, were happily chatting over the Chardonnay (Vina Santa Carolina, if you must) with Carlo and Erica Rista. The Mentens had generously offered a picnic cruise for four on their 42-foot yacht, *Mr. Sandman*, in the silent auction. Nazi Khosrowshahi, who's the whirlwind fun-and-fund-raising chairman of the board, was cool and classy in this season's evening pants and an ice blue crocheted sweater draped with ropes of crystals. Her husband, Hassen, who created the Future Shop empire and has a business brain as smooth and precise as a Rolex Oyster watch, always looks bemused at these evenings, like there has been some cosmic clerical error and he is really due somewhere else.

Bentall Corporation executive VP Grayden Hayward looked to be having a great time at his raucous table, and so he should have been: side by simpatico side with him were the mayor, Howard Jang (since moved to Ballet B.C.), the symphony's finely tuned maestro, Sergiu Comissiona, his wonderful wife, Robinne, that flexible repertory-rich mezzo Judith Forst, her handsome husband, Graham, her sweet-as-a-sonata mother, Evna, and smashing 17-year-old daughter, Paula. Sorry about all that temporary sweetness

Bill Dalton and Nazmeen Lalji

and light, Barbie; must have been the Marie Brizard Charleston Follies Exotic French Fruit Liqueur.

Nothing lasts forever, as I soon overheard. "She's as shallow as a child's wading pool, and he's wearing a Hotel du Cap T-shirt under that jacket, as if there is anyone left who doesn't know where they summer." This from a whey-faced sun-shy sweetie in a really bad floral-patterned dress.

I chatted with John and Marietta Hurst, who looked like a tiny matador in her black leather pants, gold chain belt, Seville-ian shirt and black and gold studded jacket. And with Harry and Maxine Gelfant, who was wearing the ultimate softwear, chiffon.

This little *noche* revved up the VSO's revenues by a high-note $24,000, and everyone was giving Hiroko Ainsworth all the applause. Gracious chair of the evening that she was, she kept saying it was an ensemble act and her entire committee deserved the ovation. Mountain elevation or not, it was a peak performance that really scaled the heights.

A number of the event's high-flyers had just sauntered down from their mountain mansionettes for the evening. But a virtual chorus was checking out of the palatial Chateau Whistler at the crack of noon the next day. Lois Milson was wearing that so amusing Hope diamond copy she bought at the Smithsonian. We all agreed our rooms had been fab and lunch in Wildflowers *sooo charmant*—and one never knows just *who* one might run into in the lobby. A few months ago, it was the rosy-cheeked, balding Prince Edward. And I had already told you, Barbie, about Priscilla Presley, Jane Seymour and that naughty Kenny Rogers. Of *course* not together. But also Chateauing it have been Robert De Niro, Jasmine Guy and The Supremes, The Temptations and Motley Crue. What is it about singers and that high-octane air?

Ta Ta Darling, and remember: people who aren't afraid to face the music might someday lead the band.

Valerie.

Daniel Feuermann, Ani Feuermann, Jason McLean

THE VALERIES AND THE GLORY

Barbie Darling,

Well, another year has skittered by. As usual, we flung ourselves as far out of town as often as we dared while still keeping our multi-carated pinkies on the pulse around Vanland. In the time it took the earth to do a three-sixty around the sun, we managed to get the skinny on a smattering of stars, flesh out the fine points of a film festival or two, do Disney World and Epcot Center, sample the sand from Palm Beach to Palm Springs, from Key West to Kihei, and still have time to pamper ourselves through some of the most sinful new spas to hit the destination resort route in many a moneyed moon. We hit the highlights of the year's gushiest galas and billowiest balls, skied the continent's longest vertical drop, and slummed at the Oscars with Liza and Liz. We lost some favored friends, made a few new ones and plowed through more than enough fundraisers to last a light year. So free up some fizzy, fill a crystal flute or two, and let's tut tut away.

Best Celebrity-Ogling Ops, Next To The Oscars. Basically, you get out of town. Stars fall into your lap in airports, elevators, lobbies. To drop just a sprinkling in an oozing-out-of-the-woodwork year, let's start with Robert Redford, spied in the lobby of the Four Seasons in Toronto. He's got really red hair, runs a silver rinse through it to make it blonder when he's shooting, has three prominent warts on his right cheek, has Sundanced way too much (that face is weathered) and loves talking about his three grandkids. As I left the lobby and got in the elevator, there was Jeremy Irons, riveting, but sinisterly smooth and oily; then, on my way to lunch, I bumped into *Picket Fences'* craggy-faced Tom Skerritt and his wife, Sue, who live in Seattle when he's not playing Hollywood hunk.

In Hawaii, that coochie coochie girl Charo lived in the same Honolulu highrise I was staying in, and she's as full of beans in tennis and workout clothes as in those outrageous costumes and five-inch platforms she wears on stage. The beach at the Grand Hyatt Wailea Resort and Spa coughed up Suzanne Somers and the dishy Patrick Duffy, John DeLorean's ex, Christina Ferrare, and the most decadent week of pampering imaginable.

From a few Hollywood parties (one at the Canadian consul general's), I now know way more than enough about "Scud Stud" Arthur Kent (all from him) and the ever-everywhere Alan Thicke, and not nearly enough yet about the much-admired Norman Jewison.

The posh and pricey Peninsula Hotel in Beverly Hills—"Dionysian digs" a friend calls the in-est inn—afforded up-

Rue Paes-Braga, Valerie Gibson

close-and-personal peeks at Sir Anthony Hopkins, Barbara Walters, Glenn Close, Tom and Roseanne Arnold (they are all over like a bad flu), Michael Bolton and Julie Andrews, who was recovering from the dearest little lift done by Victoria Principal's plastic surgeon husband, Dr. Harry Glassman. The hotel's breathtaking rooftop view and Rolls-Royce service were almost as good as a lobby nod at Catherine Deneuve. Why, even Vancouver stocksters Harry Moll and sidekick Frankie Anderson stay there.

Of course you can bump into notables anywhere. Florence Henderson from *The Brady Bunch* was powdering her nose in a washroom in the Mirage Hotel in Las Vegas, and I now know she was the youngest of an Indiana sharecropper's 10 children, who grew up in a house with no water or electricity. Diet guru Richard Simmons, that sultan of svelte, was eating at a little False Creek cafe and bubbling about a letter he had just received from

Barbra Streisand and how his shrine to her in his never-say-diet digs is growing daily. I file some of these encounters under "things I didn't ask about that are none of my business and that I'd like to forget."

Gone, Not Forgotten: Famous Faces Faded. We lost two more greats from our global family this past year. The first was the incredible Audrey Hepburn. Her last film role may have been as an angel in Speilberg's *Always*, but to most of us she will always be Holly Golightly, her face forever frozen in time as the ultimate gamine. I first met her five years ago at The Gift of Music concert she was in town to host for UNICEF, and twice more when she was glammed up in Givenchy at the Academy Awards. During our drink here (she had a small whiskey), I had a long, slow time to etch her forever in my mind's eye. Her face was deeply lined, like finely crumpled tissue paper. "I've been living on planes, and am just back from Ethiopia and the sun," she sighed. "I've never spoken in public in my life until UNICEF, and it scares the wits out of me." No nail polish, no wedding ring, a small-stoned pinky ring on her left hand, truly great eyebrows, a velvet voice (though she smoked like a peat bog fire) and Eliza Doolittle enunciation that made words like "totally" (and the occasional ladylike "hell" and "damn") sound like a long, slow river rafting "doe-da-lee." Five-foot-six and 92 pounds, she had the tiniest waist, flat-test stomach and the firmest barely-there upper arms. Her trademark chignon, dyed chestnut, set off that sculptured jawline. The neck was swan-like and strained and her ears long and pointed, giving, with those sparkly brown doe-eyes, the timid fawn-like look that was her. Her teeth were just wonderful and her smile was sweet, distant, as though remembering snow on the Alps; she seemed painfully exposed, in need of sheltering. She pressed her own clothes, did her own hair and makeup, and was always on time. She called herself "a very skinny, very lucky broad. "I love people who make me laugh. I honestly think it's the thing I like to do most, to laugh. It cures a multitude of ills." Not all, sadly. She died last January at age 62.

Darlene & Robert Spekakow

The second late-great was that bad boy of the barre, Rudolph Nureyev. In 1989 the Tartar star was 51 and in town to dance at the Queen Elizabeth Theatre. At an age when most primo ballerinos had hung up their tights and tippy-toed into the wings, he was definitely a little long in the tutu to be *rivoltading*, high *cabrioling* and *grande pirouetting* across the boards, but he did put his best foot forward, even if his landings were a little shaky. From the first time I saw him in London at the Royal Ballet to that night at the Queen E, he took the greatest bows. He always spoke of himself in the third person—"Nureyev does not wait for taxi, he is most famous dancer in world"—and swept into the after-party at Las Tapas like a cossack in a cape, cap and scarf. He had a retinue in tow (itsy bitsy bite-sized ballerinas and all) but you noticed only him and those sheet-lightning eyes. He drank his Corona beer from the bottle, spooned his *sopa deldia* like a borscht-slurping peasant and dived into his *ensaladilla rusa* as though they might run out. He seemed utterly impervious to criticism and said he would only stop dancing when the public stopped coming to leer. I watched him limo away into the silver night and thought that when Pushkin comes to shove, Nureyev will still be there, because as I marveled at the time, "Rudolph the Red knows reign, dear." Last year that reign ended.

Top 10 Overheard Lines (And you know that what we overhear is more interesting than what we hear). "They say the older you get, the less sleep you need. A couple more birthdays, and I won't need any at all." (At Joe and Fran Cohen's glitzy little dinner for 120 in Palm Springs.)

"By the time I could afford designer clothes, I couldn't fit into any of them." (At Holt Renfrew's Fashion Gala for Arts Umbrella.)

Jamie and Andrea Maw

"Enough is what most of us would be glad to have if we didn't see others with more." (At the Leone dinner with fading social trend seer Faith Popcorn.)

"As I struggle up the corporate ladder, I keep wishing I had taken the elevator." (At the Gordon Campbell Dinner at the Vancouver Trade and Convention Centre.)

"Let's say I do alterations on birthday suits." (A Beverly Hills plastic surgeon at an oscars after-party, upon being asked what he did in the movie industry.) And locally, "Plastic surgery? They won't bury her when she dies, she'll be recycled." (At the Vancouver International Film Festival.)

"He's a genius. He can open the door of your car with one hand, help you in with the other, and still have one left for the tip." (A fellow guest about the door-man at the Grand Cypress, Orlando, as we waited for our cars.)

The true sign of riches is having laundry marks on your socks." (Michael

Caine at Spago, Beverly Hills.) And same night, different dropper, "If a man can't see why a girl wears a strapless gown, she shouldn't."

"As any politician will tell you, you can fool all of the people some of the time, and some of the people all of the time—and usually that's enough." (At the Vancouver launch of Pierre Trudeau's new book.)

"Confidence is what we have before we understand the problem, and tolerance is what we have towards matters that don't directly affect us." (At Kim Campbell's fundraising kick-off in Vancouver.)

"No one really listens to anyone else, and if you listen for a while, you'll see why." (At the chichi opening of Markus Wieland's new Yaletown restaurant, Alabaster.)

Ian Thomas, Starr Dalton, Nazmeen Lalji, Felicity Thomas, Bill Dalton, Amin Lalji and Nezhat Khosroshahi

Worst Party Of The Year. The year's Gibson Golden Guillotine Award has to fall upon a little Palm Beach blowout at the Brazilian Court Hotel. Palm Beach, as I told you last fall, is full of Kennedys, Kimberleys and Cushings, Pierponts, Wentworths and even a tacky Trump or two. It's where millionaires go to play house by the ocean, buy tiny, tony, treats on pricey Worth Avenue, and swap good causes from time to time, to spread the wealth a little and make themselves feel better. Once in a while they stop shopping for themselves and get civic-minded, club together and buy the city a big present, like another hospital for its aging population or a little culture. This year it was the new Raymond J. Kravis Center for the Performing Arts. Marble floors, sheet glass walls, tumbling blue fountains, twinkling star ceilings, $55 million big ones. The $1,000 a-ticket party cost a breath-catching $1 million, and ended fairly early (these people get up at the crack of a Florida dawn to see if they made the society pages from the night before). In spite of that, some were determined to get their money's worth out of their shiny new duds and ended up at my hotel for a late-night party. It was a humid 96 degrees, and many of the beaded and jewel-encrusted gowns tipped the scales at a spine-snapping 15 pounds. The women (who have been nipped and tucked within an inch of their frail 100-pound lives) all look like they're out with their grandfathers. They avoid the sun so avidly that they are a stretched-face, thin-skinned, chalk white. In that heat, watching them with those weighty wigs and weightier gowns, trying to dance and smile while avoiding a very public cardiac arrest, I truly felt I was trapped in a really bad Fellini film. That, or *Night of The Living Dead*.

The Dinner To Die For. It was ghoul-of-my-dreams time at the Vancouver opera's Night of 1,000 Dinners dinner. Twelve very picky people got right into the theme, which revolved around Anne Rice's vampire characters. Ruy Paes-Braga, the oh-so-suave manager of the Four Seasons Hotel and the evening's host, played the sophisticated Lestat and made a great vampire in his blond wig, black cape and fanged teeth. I played Akasha, Queen of the Damned (no typecasting here), the Egyptian queen who was the first female vampire. Among the deadly diners were business and charity biggies Moh and Yulanda Faris who, after Ruy climbed out of a vapor-swirling, satin-lined coffin, shared a chilly glass of champagne with the Gothic groupies and led us to an unforgettable, dangerously delicious dinner in Chartwell. Bitter greens, garlic soup, bitten halibut cheeks in beet-root blood, an organic beef filet, staked and severed on an edible black cape with sunlight sauce, and a dessert that came as a chocolate coffin filled with a moonlight-pale mousse. You get the picture. And the red wine flowed like what else? To *die* for, darling.

Peter Thomas, Jacqui Cohen

The Golden Tux Award: The Year's Best Balls. The Lover's Ball at the Hotel Vancouver was the most romantic, set as it was in Sleeping Beauty's castle: draw-bridges, knights, enchanted forests, clouds, candelabra and champagne and enough hard-core corporate heads flooding the symphony coffers with currency to bring a song to many a board member's heart. All waltz, a little schmaltz.

The Black And White Ball, which traditionally gives Vancouver's more colorful young hotshots—720 this year—a chance to flash their best in *blanc* and *noir*, was a stunning display of vamp and camp, as the city's yup-and-coming young charit-eers bolstered the Vancouver Museum's burgeoning bank.

Taking a bow as the classiest ball of the year was the Crystal Ball at the Four Seasons Hotel, where a sold-out crowd of tony titans painted the town rouge in their best bibs. A real jewel in a seasonal blaze of glittery gathering. The deluxe tuxes and silken foxes that slip into this little do-gooder are as selective with their fund-worthy dollars as they are dedicated to the Children's Hospital, and it shows.

Most Over-Rated Party Of The Year. The Oscars. Despite the hype, just not the glamor glut it used to be. Maybe it's the new breed of 5 o'clock-shadowed and limp-haired brat-packers, or maybe the low-key, self-effacing mugging of Clint Eastwood and Al Pacino. Even Liz Taylor and Sophia Loren seemed a little faded.

Best Brunch. Bob and Jan Annable's brekkie at the top of Blackcomb Mountain, New Year's morning. Champagne and eggs Benny *and* a near-fossilized Allan Fotheringham with his never-right New Year's predictions. And, too, there's something about a dozen or so of you skiing down and out that makes the rest of the year take wing.

Best Political Dinner. Gordon Campbell's billfold-fattening banquet for 2,100 bolstered his campaign chest, rallied the masses and cut a cross-section swath that's still being talked about while Kim Campbell's gathering of the clans set a nice months-earlier precedent.

Glam Bam, Thank You Ma'am. The most glamorous house party of the year, and the one that revved up revenues for local charities in the most breathtaking way, was Jacqui Cohen's Face The World wingding. Also up for the More Peek, Less Boo Award. There were more racy lacy young things there bathed in the odd hot-buttered sequin or playing the immaterial girl in what looked like gauzy black underwear than a Victoria's Secret catalogue. Rio or Monte Carlo had nothing on us that night. Most uplifting.

Leftover Hors D'oeuvres. The Dalai Lama, and his most famous disciple Richard Gere. Robin Leach. Prince Edward. Bill Clinton. Katharine Hepburn. These and a multitudinous mob of other name-worthy ones all hit our shores last year, dear heart, and I'd really like to sort the wheat from the chaff in this bumper crop, but I think it's time to take the lampshades off our heads, rub our tired feet and get a grip before we give it a go all over again.`

Ta Ta Darling, and remember: To know where you're going, you've got to know where you've been.

Valerie.

THE ULTIMATE CONFESSIONS OF
A GOSSIP COLUMNIST

*S*ome of the best and worst whatevers that surfaced over the years; **The Shouldn't Have Been Caught Dead In Award:** A daring draw, bare-your-buffed bod, tush-toned tie, between body builder (she certainly did) Carla Temple and restaurateur-maven Dottie Kanke, for any number of barely-there outfits both have worn over the decade. Which led to:

The Best Putdown From a Contemporary Award for, "Those two don't fish for compliments, they gillnet". Which in turn earned the: "**Tut Tut Tootsie Award**" for the prepetrator.

The all-time worst wearable whatsis I ever saw was at the Academy Awards three or four years ago. Exhibitionist Edy Williams, who can never quite seem to actually get a ticket inside the show, always manages to do a slow strut past the sidewalk-lining, panting papparazzi outside the threatre. This particular year she wore a skirt, and I use that term loosely, of yellow and white fluttering ribbons, and a slingshot bra, such as it was, stuffed with two totally confused, nervous and squirming, tiny white poodles.

The Honk if You Were Once Married To Me Award: for four trips, trying for five, to the altar, our favourite TV News Anchor (does the word mean nothing to the man?) Tony Parsons, with a nudge from the nuptial flavour of the month man Edgar Kaiser.

The Best Excesses I Have Shown and Loved Award: would have to go to our very own, whether we want him or not, Peter Brown. Skip the fantasy resorts with their gondolas and monorails to take you to your room, the luxury suits at the Mirage with the TV that comes out of the floor at the touch of a button, the $1,000-dinner at the Peninsula Hotel in Hong Kong, the Grand Ball at the Grand Hotel in Rome. Peter B. drops borrowed watches into champagne glasses at lunch, only to replace them with limo-delivered, upgraded models that DO keep ticking and ticking, uses a golf cart graced with a Rolls Royce grill to convey him to tennis on Bowen, and throws other people's video cameras into the ocean when he catches them shooting him when he does not wish them too. All tame tidbits. So many excesses, so little time.

The Enough To Make Your Head Spin Revolving Door Award: As he careered from Canfor to the Commonwealth Games, from Hedy Fry's campaign to poobah at the Port, who else but now-you-see-me-now-you-don't, the ever-reincarnated Ron Longstaffe.

Best Dog and Pony Act: No, not Murray Pezim and Harry Moll. (Murray's up for the Always Have a Gimmick Award—Remember Pezapples, Pez-everything?—and Harry's up for the "Small World After All" for trying to conduct business from the Grand Caymans.) I'd have to go with Allan Fotheringham and Jack Webster. Past their prime Front page Challenge curmudgeons both, they pretend to be pals while barely besting each others tired part-fact and and part-act one-liners.

The Don't You Dare Nod Off Award: Best gossips about almost anything from off-broadway to off the wall, deft and daffy writer Edna O'Brien and the one of a kind and exhausting at that, Peter O'Toole. And similar vein, different plane, the **Socrates Sits Down To Talk with Plato Award.** That aristocratic, diplomatic Abba Eban and the absolutely incomparable Peter Ustinov. I met them separately, but would have loved them to dish a deux, with maybe Kissinger moderating and Margaret Thatcher forced to just sit and listen.

The As Much Fun As a Tax Refund Award: to Jackie Houston, the Perle Mesta of the West always goes all out for her theme parties. Short of one's owning the back lot at Universal, they'd be impossible to out-prop.

The Very Little Fit to Print, So Much To Tell Award: To the forgotten but not gone, J. Bob Carter, the only cigar smoker I have ever seen stub his stogie in the Ceasar salad.

The "It's Gold Watch Award Time Bucko": for Herb Capozzi, the carved in stone perennial M.C. He's changed his nose, his Hamlet hairline (best reincarnation of a 60-something), now he must really get some new jokes or hang up that silver mike.

The Chutzpah Challenge Cup Award Winner: Nelson Skalbania. Our very own little high diver who swims with the sharks takes his knocks (usually self-inflicted) and bobs up battling. Damon Runyonesque and seemingly undefeatable. And the hands-down **Grace Under Pressure Award** to the always gracious, always gorgeous head-above-above-it-all, Eleni Skalbania.

Best Couple Who Have Come To Resemble Each Other: Arthur Erickson and longtime best bud Lois Milsom. Arthur was actually up for **The Perpectual Tan Award** too, almost nudged out by Jackie Longstaffe, and Lois herself was right up there for the **"My Luggage Has Been More Places Than I Have,"** travel award.

Worst "Breath to Knock Over A Water Buffalo": All-time champion, bar-none, no competition, Sir Richard Attenborough. Too long with the Ghandi man? A kamakazi close second was designer Romeo Gigli.

Best Connected, Most-Plugged-In, Most Gracious, Countess Aline Dobrzensky: titled, travelled, from Monaco to Mustique, she knows all the players. She'll use everything from flattery to fanfare to her own deep pockets to put a fundraiser over the top. If only she weren't so discreet and diplomatic—most of the great stuff she knows can never be repeated.

Speaking of which, **The Best European Party** I was ever at with apologies to dear friends in London and Paris was in Geneva the night Sophia Loren's first baby Carlo was born. She had been trying for years, sequestered for months, and the party was at the home of friends of hers who were overjoyed for her, and who proceeded to reminisce, thankfully in English, dropping the most fastinating international dish I have ever been served on a plate.

In the Kudo, Catcall and Characters I-Have Met category, ever so quickly: The Smoothest was designer Oscar de la Renta, the Sleaziest was Robin Leach—he actually oozes. The Zaniest, giggly diet guru Richard Simmons—the energy is exhausting. The Surliest, Rod Steiger—I had no idea he was manic depressive, and in a second encounter, was much improved. The Best Bon Vivant was tobacco connoisseur Zino Davidoff who advised tycoons, statesmen and lesser mortals how to choose both a good cigar and a good woman. The Suavest was Roger Moore—he really is 007.

The Biggest Ego was Scud Stud Arthur Kent, the Flakiest, Phillis Diller. The Best Eyes, Brown, were Omar Sharif, Best Blue, Sean Connery. The Most Bizarre Mock-up: Self-made legend Mae West—you just couldn't tell what, of the strangely-constructed look was actually real. The Funniest was Sir Peter Ustinov, the Blandest, Clint Eastwood (and a surprise that was). The Coolest Under Pressure: still Trudeau. The Most Evocative Audry Hepburn—you just wanted to hug her. The Shyest was Ella Fitzgerald. The Weirdest, Michael Jackson—right up there with Andy Warhol, and Mae West. Most Compelling, the incredibly riveting Rudolph Nureyev. The Feistiest: Margaret Mead—she was fairly elderly, and just <u>nothing</u> was okay with the world. The Happily Trashiest was Cher. Most unassuming: for their brilliance, Buckminster Fuller, and economist Milton Friedman. Most Intellectual, unintelligible-to-me: "Name of the Rose" Novelist Umberto Eco. Most Prickly: Shirley MacLaine—whine, whine, whine. Most Thrilled To Meet: Eleanor Roosevelt

And from me: Eternal Gratitude-They made it all so easy.